chosen

—

How Opening My Home Healed My Heart

—

Sandra E. Smith

Simon & Schuster

New York Amsterdam/Antwerp London
Toronto Sydney/Melbourne New Delhi

Simon & Schuster
1230 Avenue of the Americas
New York, NY 10020

Some names have been changed.

First Simon & Schuster hardcover edition August 2026

Interior design by Lewelin Polanco

Manufactured in the United States of America

1 3 5 7 9 10 8 6 4 2

Library of Congress Control Number has been applied for.

ISBN 978-1-9821-9825-1
ISBN 978-1-9821-9827-5 (ebook)

chosen

HOME DEPOT

prologue

"Do you think we are making a mistake?" Elijah, all six feet four and 230 pounds of him, was staring straight ahead as he sat in the passenger seat of my car.

We were waiting in the parking lot outside of a sprawling Home Depot, located off a busy arterial road in suburban Maryland, between a gas station and a self-storage complex. It was late summer and hot, not in a thick and humid and slightly languid way like June, but in a dry, exhausted, vaguely dusty way, with the feel of an overbaked season that had already stayed on a bit too long. Outside of the car, the air was only a notch or two below suffocating. For years, this weather was, to me, synonymous with the start of football season and always accompanied by the clop of cleats, the thud of shoulder pads, and the slap of the leather ball between two hands.

"I don't know," I answered. "Maybe we are."

Cool air from the dashboard vents washed over us. The parking lot occupied two levels, and we were in the lower one, so it was oddly dark even though the sun was blazing above. When I pulled in, I had thought about shutting off the car, but that would have compelled us to exit, and neither Elijah nor I was ready.

"What if he doesn't want to see us?" Elijah asked what I was already wondering.

I took a breath and used my most matter-of-fact voice. "Then we will say, 'Okay, Ryan. We are here anytime if you want or need us. Just know that we miss you and we love you.'" Elijah nodded and continued to look straight ahead. But neither of us made a move for the door handle, and I didn't reach up to push the button to silence the motor.

"Maybe we need a plan," he said.

Elijah was the last of my football sons. I started with one—Justin, my biological son, in ninth grade—and ended up with three more, for a total of four by high school graduation, all living in my home, a raucous band of laughter, stray socks, and voracious appetites. Ryan came into our lives as my second son.

Elijah and I tried to strategize. We decided that we would ask for the Home Depot floor manager, and then ask if Ryan was in. We already knew that he was inside, but asking would be slightly face-saving on both ends. It would feel less intrusive somehow if we requested permission to see him. Then we started wondering about Ryan's work hours and if he was possibly on break or not working on the floor. We agreed that we would both start off relaxed and noncommittal, saying something like "Hi, Ryan" and "Great to see you. How's it going?"

The idea to come here was both Elijah's and mine. It had been more than a year since we last saw Ryan, since any of us had seen him or heard from him. We learned from his mom that he was working at Home Depot.

Elijah and I stayed in the car until it was almost embarrassing to be waiting so long. I could hear the air-conditioning kick into a higher gear. As the minutes passed, I was grateful for the slight tint on the windows. There were a few glances from passersby pushing their carts and balancing their plastic bags, but in the dark and with the tint, we were largely shadows existing behind reflections. Finally, I reached over and shut off the motor. Elijah and I got out. I heard the familiar hydraulic sound as the car doors simultaneously locked. There was no going back, only in. We started toward the entrance. Someone had already put out an anticipatory display of rakes, leaf bags, and sacks of dark brown mulch stacked on a pallet, the way reels of Christmas lights and inflatable Santas and reindeer appear en masse right after Halloween. In a few weeks, or maybe even a few days, there would probably be bins for spring bulbs and little trowels and canvas gloves, subliminally urging weekend gardeners to think about spring. The pneumatic doors glided open, and the bright orange wall of scaffolding beckoned.

Two other people might have reached out to squeeze hands for a moment of reassurance as they stepped inside, but that is not Elijah and me. We are not physical in that way. We are too self-contained and, truth be told, too burdened by our own complicated histories. Ryan, however, is a hugger and sometimes, in private, a crier, too. He is big and demonstrative, and when he wants, he can light up a room. Quietly, I said, "It's going to be okay." Elijah just nodded. The store was busy enough with contractors, do-it-yourselfers, retirees, and a smattering of slightly frantic, single-minded homeowners who awoke to a busted washing machine, or fridge, or hot-water heater and needed to find a replacement as quickly as possible, hopefully on sale or with a rebate.

The good thing about a Home Depot during that hour on a weekday is that most people have come with a list and a mission. They aren't browsing. They aren't particularly interested in their fellow shoppers, so they won't spend long looking at the externally obvious: Elijah, who used to play the offensive line and is Black, and me, a middle-aged white woman with straight blond hair, as we got our bearings and walked together toward the customer service section.

Later, when I replay this day in my mind, I will see the faint symmetries of the story's ending and its beginning: both featuring a covered parking garage, time waiting in a car, and the heat. But mostly, what I will see is Ryan's face as I remember him.

The parking garage at the Sidwell Friends School, perhaps the most elite of all the private schools in Washington, DC, is designed to showcase one of two virtues: mothers (and occasionally fathers or grandparents) with the privilege of time, for whom waiting for their students is a higher calling, or families who hire nannies, housekeepers, professional drivers, or call an Uber to perform the chore of picking up their children. The garage is partially underground and dark; cell phone reception is patchy to nonexistent, and depending on the season, the air outside ranges between brutally hot and icy cold. Everyone is required to sit with the car engine off and wait—this was before high-end electric vehicles became ubiquitous. I learned the rules by observation; this particular afternoon was my first foray into the pickup line.

I remember it was about 6:30 or 7 p.m., and I was watching the last of the late-day heat shimmer up in tiny waves from the asphalt, tinged with the slight residue of exhaust fumes as, one by one, car engines were switched on. Suddenly, Justin, drenched in sweat, swimming in his football jersey, holding his pads and helmet in his hands, appeared at my window, saying, "Mom, Ryan needs a ride to the bus stop." I looked past my son to see a tall, handsome young man with a bright smile that lit up his face. He had a huge Afro with golden-red highlights.

He called me "ma'am," to which I replied, "Now, if you call me that, I'm going to feel old, because only old ladies get referred to as 'ma'am'!" He laughed and promised not to do it again, and he thanked me for agreeing to give him a ride.

Justin and Ryan were both in ninth grade, new to the football team, and new to Sidwell. Founded as a Quaker school—initially, for years, it was known simply as the Friends School—Sidwell prides itself on promoting Quaker principles and values of equality, justice, and community, as well as global and environmental stewardship. Quakers were the original conscientious objectors and longtime peace activists. Today Sidwell ranks among the most prestigious private schools in the nation—it was the choice of the Clinton and Obama families for their daughters, for the Bidens for their grandchildren, and for numerous high-profile diplomats and other powerful political families. Our family fit none of those descriptions. Tom and I were California transplants. My last major professional stint was as an in-house lawyer representing Apple in complex litigation, but by the time we arrived in Washington, my role was as a full-time practicing mom. Tom's high-powered legal job was why we had moved our family east, but we were outsiders and certainly not political or household names.

I had assumed when I said yes to Justin and Ryan that the bus stop was close by. It was only when everyone was buckled and I was inching my way out of the garage that Justin casually told me to head north, explaining that Ryan needed to be dropped off three and a half miles away in Bethesda, Maryland. At that time of night, three miles felt like thirty and took about as long to drive. The traffic was fierce; it was a sea of taillights snaking along Wisconsin Avenue, from the leafy segments of North Cleveland Park, with its sprawling, renovated Victorian houses, to the long blocks of retail strips and office buildings, behind which radiated side streets of brick center-hall colonial suburban-style homes. Even the tiny ones carried price tags of at least $1 million. After that first football practice, driving Ryan to his bus stop became my new routine.

Initially, I only took Ryan as far as the public Metro bus stop on Montgomery Avenue in downtown Bethesda. But it was dusk by the time we arrived, and I felt guilty dropping him off alone with all his gear at a plexiglass shelter across from a dark, concrete parking garage and next to a largely empty office building.

So, after a few more trips, I tried to find his home.

That's when I realized how brutal his school commute was. It was not simply north, but east, over the aptly named East-West Highway, heading away from the comfortable houses at the edge of quiet, leafy Chevy Chase, one of the nation's first planned suburbs. As we drove to his apartment, we passed collections of tiny postwar ramblers and dated apartment buildings that rose along the edge of the more densely populated Montgomery County, Maryland, city of Silver Spring. We had to travel deep into a warren of side streets to find the Section 8 apartment buildings (now they are known by an acronym, MPDU), the county's designated "affordable rental housing" for families hovering near the poverty line. This was where Ryan lived. Ryan's building had a massive brick facade. The apartment units were packed together, and even though it was late, children had gathered outside on thin strips of grass and concrete walkways. The thick smell of food cooking wafted out of the open windows and made my stomach rumble. There wasn't a clear building entrance when Ryan directed me to stop the car. There may have been one on the other side of the building, but Ryan just told me to stop near a nondescript door, and he bolted from the car and ducked inside. This was where Ryan lived with his mom, his older brother, and, episodically, as I would learn, his dad.

Ryan was attending Sidwell on a scholarship. There were no official sports scholarships, but the football coach and a sports parent who was very active at the school had seen Ryan play in middle school football leagues. They convinced Sidwell to admit Ryan, and they convinced Ryan (and his mom) to attend. I can only imagine the promises and opportunities they dangled before Ryan and his family, including the dream of a college scholarship, the shiny pledge of a Sidwell education as a golden ticket to upward mobility, and even the opportunity to rub elbows with the Obama daughters in the school hallways. To entice Sidwell's admissions office and administration, the coach and the parent had no doubt concocted a separate virtuous elixir of generosity seasoned with modern-day noblesse oblige.

In a different manner, football had also been Justin's path to entry to Sidwell. Lacrosse, soccer, and even tennis were viewed by many families as more prestigious sports than the injury-prone gridiron. Thus, interested football players with basic talent got at least a favorable look. Justin couldn't compete at the level of Ryan, but the football coach had conducted his admissions interview.

I'm not quite sure how Justin and Ryan found each other for the first time on that crowded practice field—was it because they were both in the same grade, or both new to the school, outsiders on a team where many of the other players had known each other since kindergarten? Justin was a solid lineman, feet planted along the scrimmage axis, a formerly husky kid whom we had pushed into sports, while Ryan was a more fluid linebacker, a mixture of speed and strength, ready to run, seeking out the opponents' weaknesses and trying to exploit them. But the two boys connected on a different level because they are so much alike as people, both deep thinkers with huge hearts. Neither was remotely fluent in the East Coast prep school code, all the small signals, the unwritten dress codes, the labels, the shoes, the vocabulary choices, special inflections, and the subtle ways of doing the most basic things that are ingrained even more deeply perhaps than reading, writing, math, and history. It made them natural allies, on the field and off.

Football practice was every day, and to start, the boys had a lot of time in my car.

Each evening throughout August, as I threaded my way north, windows open to dilute the smell of sweat, the boys would keep up their banter and razz each other in the back seat. I'd listen to their voices, cracking occasionally, still trying to find their way into that lower register for men. They joked about being freshmen on the team and how to handle the not-always-good-natured hazing they endured at the hands of the older players. They joked about the coaches' quirks, told me how hungry they were, and pleaded, Would I please bring snacks the next time? When I promised I would, they spontaneously whooped and cheered.

SANDI

one

Perhaps the first thing to know about me is that for three decades, I vehemently did not want children. Being a lawyer by training, I tend to see the world in terms of objective facts and subjective opinions. And if I were rising to give a summation of my life, I'd have to begin with a pair of unimpeachable facts: my parents are two people who should never have had children and, particularly, should never have had children with each other.

I can't remember a time in my childhood when they were not at each other's throats. It didn't matter where we lived: sunny California, where I was born in 1961 in the Los Angeles suburb of Downey, or humid New Orleans, snowy Utah, or the flat lands of Idaho, where our first home was a shack without plumbing on a pinto bean farm. Later, we moved into a motel, where I scrubbed toilets, changed beds, bused tables, and worked in the small restaurant kitchen in a barter-style exchange for our room while my mother sat sunning herself by the pool. It didn't matter whether we had a nicer house or lived in a trailer or whether our front yard had slightly respectable grass or was overflowing with the carcasses of rusting vehicles until it looked like a rattletrap junkyard. The script was always the same, full of sound and fury.

Before I could say my name, I knew I was a bad child. As a toddler, I apparently had systematically unraveled the playpen mesh until I was able to escape through the freshly created gap in the side. My mother, furious at my disavowal of her rules, reacted by throwing the closest thing she had, a cup of scalding coffee, at me. One of the few photos of me as a baby shows me holding on to the sides of my crib. More accurately, it is a photo of my back, wrapped in some kind of makeshift cloth bandage with an angry red burn peeking through from where the hot coffee had singed my skin and scarred my neck. I don't remember that exact cup of coffee—many others went flying in my direction over the years. But I remember what came next: the closet.

We—my parents, Eugene and Janice Smith, my younger brother, Kevin, and I—had moved to New Orleans, a city so hot and humid that the air itself seemed to hang half-solid with geological layers of moisture. Inside this urban jungle of steam and unruly vegetation, there were the sounds of noisy buses and a large pickup truck with a little merry-go-round strapped to the truck bed that drove by every afternoon, playing jingly music. I would try to pry open the stuck window in our walk-up apartment furnished with gold crushed velvet chairs so that I could listen to the music. Once, either my mother or father took my brother and me for a ride on the circular contraption.

I can still picture the curling flecks of peeling paint on the doorframes and windowsills of our apartment. Some days, I imagined they were colorful bits of candy, and I would pull them off and eat them when no one was looking. Most days, no one was.

I was enrolled in a Catholic school where the nuns did not like the students. They walked around holding rulers in their hands and immediately rapped the students' knuckles if we did anything wrong. To quiet everyone on the playground, the nuns had a special routine. One of them would blow a whistle, and the children were expected to instantaneously freeze; every limb, every finger, everything had to freeze. One time, I froze so hard, locking my knees and holding my breath, that I fell over. No one realized that I had passed out; instead, they were furious with me for not following the directions.

At home, my primary obligation, aside from being obedient, was to take care of my younger brother. My mother instructed us to sit quietly on the gold upholstered chairs, and sometimes I would fall asleep, which was a punishable offense. Many things were punishable offenses, even saying the wrong thing, and my main punishment was to be locked inside a tiny clothes closet for a very long time. The locking up was for my "own good," my mother would scream. I needed to go into the closet.

Each turn of the knob and click of the lock was terrifying. The dark was very dark after the bright sunshine. It was impossible to move or turn around; the clothing hanging inside made it feel as if the walls were closing in. I could only fit if I sank to the floor. I remember making myself small, sitting on my butt, drawing my knees up against my chest, inhaling the stale smell of clothing that I could not see, and being absolutely terrified of the darkness enveloping me. As the minutes ticked by, my chest tightened, and I felt as if I couldn't breathe, as if I were going to die. I remember my brother would crawl or, later, pad over on his two wobbly feet and sit outside so I wouldn't be alone. We would talk back and forth until someone appeared to unlock the door. Kevin was two and a half years old, while I was five. To this day, unlike me, he remembers nothing about living in New Orleans. I spent years being pushed into closets until I eventually grew bold enough and tall enough to force the door open.

Whatever dream or scheme that my father was chasing in New

Orleans must have gone bust, and we returned to California, carting the gold furniture along with us. I cannot recall if we had our own house for part of the time or if we only lived with my grandparents—I do know that by the end, we were living with my grandparents in their home. I spent my days in school, where I loved playing with my friends and hated nap time. Even then, I never felt as if I fit in when I visited my friends at their houses. Their parents were so different; one mom was always giving me food that I liked, something I didn't have with my mother or even my grandmother. This family had a pool in their backyard, and my friend's older brother liked to play tricks on us, including making us think that he had drowned, which terrified me. But even though I left these playdates with my heart pounding, I felt empty when I returned home.

At home, my brother was my playmate, but it was not the same. Our mother was very protective of him and mad at me if I kept a toy too long or didn't "share" enough. "Sharing" in her definition seemed to mean that I would just watch Kevin play with all the toys and never touch them. One of our favorite games that we used to play involved the hose and sprinkler attachment. We were mesmerized by how the water looked when it caught the sunlight and, for a few seconds, appeared to be transformed into little diamonds that flickered and then suddenly disappeared with a splat when the stream hit the ground. Sometimes, I felt like one of those drops—flickering with shiny, colorful love for a moment, and then, splat, it all went dark. Then there came a day when things did go dark, and that darkness cast a shadow for a very long time.

◀▶

It was sunny out, because in Southern California the days were almost always sunny, and I was looking at rows of boxes because we were moving. We were leaving Downey for somewhere new, Salt Lake City,

Utah. I was almost six. To me, "going" was still an abstract word that lacked any more significant meaning. We were standing outside my grandparents' house and a rental truck was parked in the driveway. My grandmother was outside with me.

My grandmother's nickname for me was "Butch." For some inexplicable reason, on that sunny day, she walked me around the side of the truck and showed me the control panel with the buttons that operated the liftgate at the back. She placed a stepladder beside the rental truck so I could reach the two big red buttons, one for up and the other for down. I couldn't see the back of the truck from my perch on the ladder—only the buttons and the truck's side. My grandmother told me that I could operate the lift with those two buttons. I felt so grown-up standing there. I was being trusted to do something important; I had been deemed "responsible." I planted my feet on the top step of the ladder, raised my arm, and my grandmother told me, "Okay, Butch, go ahead and push the top button." With great pride and a huge smile, I did exactly as I was told.

I heard the lift engage, shuddering into motion and making a clanking noise as it started to rise. And then I heard the screaming. Lots of screaming. By that point in my life, screaming didn't really unsettle me. My mother screamed all the time—at me, at my father, at her mother—and everyone screamed back at her. So I tuned it out and kept staring at the bright red buttons. Above the din, somehow, I heard my grandmother quietly but urgently say to me—"Butch, press the bottom button, *now*. On to off." Once again, I did as I was told. This time, I turned to see my mother flying forward, shrieking at my grandmother and me.

At first, I didn't understand what she was saying, but I could tell that something terrible had happened. I climbed down from the ladder as my mother ran to the back of the truck. I dashed behind her. As I turned the corner, I saw my brother, who was also screaming. His face was covered in blood, and his ear had been ripped from his head; it was dangling from the side of his face, held on by a thin thread of skin. Now, as I looked, I began to scream. I was afraid Kevin was going to die, that he would be gone from our lives forever.

It took some time for me to piece together what had happened. The lift had been loaded with boxes. While I was sent around to push the button, my father had decided to allow Kevin to stand on the lift and "ride" up with the boxes. But Kevin had slipped, and his head became trapped between the lift and the truck. It was slowly being crushed as the lift rose.

As I ran toward Kevin, my mother grabbed me and yanked me backward. Then she slapped my face. Hard. This time, I understood her perfectly. She was screaming, "You did this. This is your fault. You tried to kill him!" There was pure hatred in her eyes. I couldn't speak. I couldn't even breathe. My father had already scooped up Kevin, and with my mother following, he ran to the car to rush him to the hospital. I sprinted after them and tried to climb into the back seat, but my mother reached around and locked the door. I pulled on the handle frantically. "Get away from him," my mother screamed. Those were the last words I heard as they sped off without me.

I came to the hospital to pick up Kevin on his discharge day. He had more than eighty-five stitches running across his head, and his skull was wrapped in white bandages. I was worried that, even though the doctors promised that his ear had been saved, he would not be able to hear. At first, Kevin seemed so fragile that I was afraid to touch him or even talk to him. I didn't want to do anything else to hurt him. I believed this was my fault, and day after day, I cried in bed alone.

We couldn't move to Utah until Kevin had recovered. While we waited for that day to come, he and I slowly returned to playing in the backyard. This time, when we played our water game, he always held the hose and sprayed the water. I never asked to do it once. Instead,

I would stand beside him and watch the water drops glisten in the sun before they disappeared into the ground. I wanted to disappear, too. After that terrible day, my mother frequently and openly blamed me for trying to kill my brother and accused me of wanting to do it again. For years, even my brother believed his accident was my fault and often said so. My entire life became consumed with the epic task of earning back my parents' and my brother's trust and love.

Now that I was no longer fit to watch Kevin, my new job, according to my mother, was to protect her from my father, from Grandma, and from everyone else in the world who was out to get her. She would tell me over and over how her father had abused her as a child while her mother defended him and how she had married my father to escape her home, only to discover that he was worse. She told me her children were her life—when she wasn't saying that she wished I were a boy—and that she would do anything to save us from "this terrible man." Her words were like an odorless, colorless, tasteless contaminant that seeps into groundwater. With every sip I took, I was drinking in the toxin. I believed her, and I believed I was responsible.

My mother grew up an only child. Her mother was from a Syrian family who had immigrated to the US. My grandmother Edna was a strikingly beautiful woman with dark eyes and dark hair who could cook an incredible range of Middle Eastern dishes and was regarded by almost everyone who knew her as a wonderful person. The exception was her daughter, my mother, who hated her with a passion. Jan Carlson, my grandfather and Edna's husband, was a musician and a heavy drinker who, by the time I knew him, used to bury his liquor bottles in the garden of his small Culver City home so that no one would know—or at least could measure—how much alcohol he was consuming. Jan could play almost every instrument and had been a bandleader for the pop music crooner Perry Como back in the day; he trained his daughter on the piano, including rapping her hands with a wooden ruler whenever she missed a note. My mother became a concert-level pianist, talented enough to play on the radio and in concert halls until she refused to perform anymore. Her parents' response was to send her to secretarial school; women, she was told, did not go to college, no matter how much she might have pleaded otherwise.

My grandfather was not a nice guy. I can remember reaching for him once when I was very young, and in response, he grabbed my hand, squeezed hard, and twisted it. It hurt. A lot. The excuse made for his behavior was that he had false teeth in his pocket and was embarrassed by them, and my hand got too close. Being hurt was thus my fault; if I had not reached out to him, he wouldn't have needed to grab my hand. I tried to stay away from him after that. Whenever he was around, my mother often rolled her eyes as if to say, see, it was just as she had reported: her mother did nothing but support her father. But I still adored my grandmother.

In my mother's world, however, the dichotomy was simple: loving my grandmother meant that I was conspiring against my mother. Inside of me, there was always an internal tug-of-war, a nagging question of which side I would join. Loving my grandmother made me feel as if I were betraying my mom. The smallest display of affection toward my grandmother was proof to my mother that I was a secret participant in a violent plot to do something horrible to her. The plots changed on a whim, but the victim never did: it was always my mother.

After we left California for Utah, my grandparents came to visit maybe four or five times. I have a few faded snapshots from these trips, but there was almost always conflict, or at least my mother would constantly complain about her parents behind their backs. At some point, I recall that my grandmother accompanied my father to look at something to purchase, possibly a piece of property, perhaps even to assist them financially. My mother's response was to accuse the two of them of having an affair. She spent days proclaiming that her mother was sleeping with her husband, and every time she said the words, they became more convincing.

Like so many things, though, there was a grain of truth mixed in. My father did have other women. Even perhaps during those months in California when he lived in his in-laws' home. The image of at least one of these women is boxed up along with our family photos. A snapshot shows a lady with a big, blond, beehive hairdo, looking awfully chummy alongside my father. Much later, when I was older, my mother sent me into my father's closet on the pretext of looking for something. What I found instead were photos of him naked with other women. In many of the pictures, he is holding his gun. I was eleven years old then, and the glossy prints were horrible and disgusting. But I could never forget seeing them. Only when I was grown did I realize that my mother had probably sent me into that closet with the express purpose of finding them.

After a few months, my brother was well enough for us to complete our move to Utah. My mother was glad to be getting away from the other women. I don't recall seeing the small moving truck a second time, only a collection of cardboard boxes and green trash bags to carry our things. We piled these stray items into the back and set off in one of my father's retrofitted contraptions, a big, blue jeep-like vehicle with hard benches for back seats. The route to Salt Lake was, I would come to know, a straight shot northeast on I-15. My father gunned the engine, and we were off, Kevin and me bouncing around on our benches. In five years, I would be the one up front behind the wheel, boosted on a pillow, underage and illegal, navigating the ascents and descents and straightaway flats of I-15 myself for as many hours as whatever north–south trip we were making took.

two

MY PARENTS WOULD NOT HAVE met without automobiles. Literally. My mother was riding with a bunch of girls in a car on Sepulveda Boulevard in Los Angeles when their car broke down. My father happened to be in the car of young navy enlistees who stopped to help them, and Janice and Eugene started flirting. A different road, a different time, even a five-minute gap in either direction, and none of this would have happened.

One of the youngest among eleven siblings, my father was raised in the Arkansas Ozarks and possessed nothing beyond an eighth-grade education. He grew up in the woods, in a small house, and liked to refer to himself as a "hick." His father was a preacher, all fire and brimstone, with hardly any money to support his family. My father inherited his silver tongue and a similar disdain for mundane paid work. As far as I know, after I was born, my father never held a regular, predictable job of any kind. He was either around or he was gone.

Eugene Smith wasn't the least bit handsome; he was short, stocky, stoop-shouldered, and almost completely bald. He mostly wore short-sleeved blue coveralls, dressing the part of an inventor. He couldn't see without his glasses; he wore a Clark Kent style with black frames. But somehow, none of that mattered once he started speaking. He always tried to charm money from people, and for years, he was able to talk enough people out of almost anything. He claimed to be an inventor and bragged that he had designed and built a concrete pump that could be used for high-rise construction.

He did not pick a small project as the showcase for his invention; he told us—and anyone else who would listen—that he had poured the concrete used to build the partially complete Landmark Hotel in Las Vegas, which had been designed to look like Seattle's iconic Space Needle. When my parents, Kevin, and I finally made our way to Utah, we even drove through Las Vegas and stopped to see the Landmark Hotel, rising just short of its planned thirty-one floors. I was awestruck and remember telling my father that it was beautiful, and I was so proud of him. Perhaps he had worked as a laborer on the construction site, or perhaps he had designed a concrete-pouring process for some lesser building, but there was no way that he could have been in charge—building records state that the concrete work was performed by Consolidated Construction Company. Yet, in part, because the story was so fantastic and he told it with such conviction, it took on the aura of truth. Who would be audacious enough to make up a lie that big and complex? My father successfully bragged about building the Landmark for years. And I continued to believe his words even long after he was gone. Almost proving the truth of it, my mother maintained that the project pushed him into bankruptcy because "your father didn't know how to manage money."

There were so many variations of stories involving fantastic inventions that over time, they blended into each other. Some of my earliest memories are of me sitting beside my father on the sofa as he talked about his invention ideas; I was mesmerized and thought it was "cool" to have an inventor as a father. He was convinced that he could perfect almost any machine to have it do something else. The flip side of that meant he seemed incapable of using "normal" objects for their intended purpose.

For a while, he tried to sell his concrete pump invention or supervise it at construction sites, or at least that's what I was told. It's also possible that his only successful inventions were the elaborate lies that he constructed. Mostly, he was gone from our house, chasing his schemes or escaping the chaos, while my mother was stuck at home, living off whatever bit of money he doled out for household expenses.

My parents fought all the time, usually about money or other women, but money mattered more to Kevin and me. My father controlled the cash; back then, there was no such thing as a credit card for a woman in her own name. He would hand my mother a $20 bill and say, "This is for food for the week," and then leave. She didn't know if the money would have to last one week or two. As a consequence, Kevin and I wore terrible clothes and had choppy, kitchen-bowl haircuts. Most of what we ate came from a makeshift, chaotic garden in the backyard and a chicken coop—these two objects seemed to materialize almost no matter what house, shack, or trailer we were living in. My brother and I would be sent out with little baskets to pick tomatoes and dig up carrots and onions. There were several winters when we lived off a couple sides of venison in our freezer from a deer or two that my father had shot when he was out with other neighborhood men. Almost everyone in the area had a bit of deer meat in their freezer. The difference was that those families didn't eat it as their main food source. We did. When there was no more venison, we ate squirrel, rabbit, or even the occasional decapitated rattlesnake that my father dragged home.

I sensed we were different from other families early on, but I also didn't spend enough time around other kids in their homes to fully distinguish how or why; I was too busy trying to navigate my own surroundings. My mother would often erupt without warning or pattern. The rules seemed to change minute to minute and even second to second; something that she previously thought was funny or cute would suddenly become unacceptable. There was no way to predict and, consequently, no way to prepare or fix anything once her rages began. We lived in a constant vortex of her deep instability until upheaval, anger, lashing out, and outright violence became acceptable. They were our norm.

Both my parents were the hitting types. If you did something wrong, or what they defined as wrong, often their first instinct was to smack you. Especially my father. At home, he would spank me over the slightest provocation; I simply had to be "bad." As soon as the spanking stopped, I would run to the bathroom and grab a Band-Aid so I could be "healed." On the road, if I goofed around in the back seat, got too loud, annoyed my brother, or made the wrong joke, my father thought nothing of reaching one of his long arms back to strike at my head and shoulders while he was driving. If I squirmed away, he would simply pull the car over and rotate around to unleash his full fury and rage with both hands.

◆

I can't say if my father loved my mother then or ever, but he loved cars, all sorts of machines, and anything else mechanical. In addition to that ancient blue Jeep that we took to Salt Lake City, where he was sure he would strike it rich with his concrete pump invention, he built his own wheeled contraptions. He called them "flivvers." They were cobbled together from spare parts and abandoned junkyard wrecks, especially sturdy, wide Packard sedans and Ford pickup trucks from the 1940s and '50s. By the time we moved to our third house, assorted flivvers and their odd components resided in bits and pieces parked across our front yard. Most of his flivvers lacked doors and roofs and seat belts. One had a blue bench seat ripped from an old truck and suspended over a chassis. But the flivvers' engines always ran. They looked like a somewhat demonic version of the car in the 1968 kids' movie *Chitty Chitty Bang Bang*, except no musical fantasy awaited us.

The kindest thing to say was that my father was a thrill seeker. The more dangerous, the more it energized him. He insisted on pushing these flivvers to the literal ends of the earth. My father drove them along dirt roads or off the roads entirely, racing them downhill and getting us stuck in huge mud fields, where the car would sink as if it were quicksand. Other times, he drove them up hillsides and foothills, over huge boulders the size of houses, and to the edges of high cliffs, terrifying my brother and especially me by running the wheels right up to the sheer drop and slightly beyond. I would close my eyes, grip my hands around whatever I could find, and scream. My father would respond by offering a faintly sinister smile. My mother would look around and laugh uproariously.

The overwhelming memory I have of riding in those flivvers was of screaming—more than at any other point in my life.

Utah was a perfect place for flivvers. LA was car country, a big, crowded, sprawling place where it was easy to spend an hour in the car, much of it in traffic. Utah, even Salt Lake City, was much more remote; there were fewer people and fewer vehicles. Here, a flivver was more of a curiosity and less an immediate, outright danger. But I tried to avoid them just the same.

For the first time, in Salt Lake, I could use my feet and go outside. I could walk to a local store, run around, and see neighborhood kids out on the sidewalks or in their yards. Behind us, the snowcapped mountains rose toward the sky, and very quickly I learned I could race away from our house and into the foothills in my bare feet, where I was free to dash through the wild, rough spaces, stepping on stickers and grasses and God knows what else.

At one point, running around in my bare feet, I stepped on a large glass shard. Blood spewed everywhere. I ran home to try to fix it, but my brother had chicken pox, so I wasn't allowed inside. I stood at the sliding glass door, and my brother's pockmarked face looked panicked as he watched me bleed. I don't know how long we stared at each other through that glass partition and cried—we did the same thing many nights in our adjoining rooms. My mother didn't return until hours later. That night, she whipped me with a homemade switch for interrupting her day and forcing her to take me to the emergency room for stitches.

Our first house in Utah was a small, ranch-style design that sat on the upward slope of a suburban subdivision hill, with a view of the mountains and the city. There were three bedrooms and one bathroom, which was painted a strange blue and was always cold. Kevin and I had small, adjoining rooms, and we would keep each other company at night by talking through the thin walls, much as we had done with the closet in New Orleans. As we grew, we tried to teach ourselves Morse code so we could tap messages to each other because our mother would scream obscenities at us if she heard us talking. Inside the house's garage was a freezer where we kept the meat that my father had hunted for food. He would field dress the freshly killed animals on the concrete floor and then pour water on the bloodstains, but they never fully washed away, so there were always a few dried blood trails and an overall pinkish hue.

The living room inside the house had a low, white sofa pushed up under the wide picture window. During the winter, huge snowstorms would roll in, along with ice. To pass the time, Kevin and I would sit backward on the couch, stare out the window, and wait for the passing cars to slide on the icy road. We'd watch them spin one by one, pirouetting in slow circles down the hill. In Salt Lake, the weather wasn't regarded as an impediment for anyone. I walked to school in the storms. Once, I was hit by a driver backing a car out of her driveway. It wasn't serious, I was only knocked over, but the driver was hysterical, thinking I was hurt, and she wouldn't let me leave until I could prove to her that I was okay. As a result, I was late for school, and the teacher yelled at me. She was certain that I had made up the story. No matter where I was, I could not, it seemed, do anything right.

It wasn't only the physical environment that was so different in Salt Lake, it was my parents as well. Suddenly, we were going to a new church, and we had to be excited about the prospect of becoming members. I quickly understood that everyone around us belonged to this church, the Church of Latter-Day Saints, better known to the rest of the world as Mormons. The change in my parents was stunning. I could never remember seeing them with friends or other people in either New Orleans or California. Now they were cultivating relationships with everyone in our larger neighborhood. But there was something deeply uncomfortable about this change. At home, while my brother and I tried to play on the dull gray indoor-outdoor carpet, or while we sat at our white Formica kitchen table amid the counter clutter and the slightly drunken-seeming kitchen cabinets, whose doors had warped and never quite properly closed, my mother would complain about how antisocial my father really was. It was all, she said, about getting money out of "these people," which I eventually figured out meant getting them to invest in his business schemes.

My parents made me get baptized in the Mormon Church because they thought it would be a way for our family to fit in and for my dad to find more people who might be convinced to partner with him. No one else in our family was baptized into the church, just me. Being a Mormon meant that I had to attend the church's after-school program as well. By the time I was in third grade, I refused to call myself a Mormon. When adults told me to be a "good Mormon girl," I would respond that I was *not* a Mormon, adding that I would just be a "good girl," without the Mormon part. They, in turn, would reply that I was not "a good girl" and my family was "dishonest."

I pieced together that my father had borrowed money from too many of our neighbors, money that had vanished without any return. The adults in the neighborhood grew to hate my parents, and soon, their kids hated me by association. I remember being invited to a sleepover and feeling so excited and happy. I brought my clothes to change into and my cheap sleeping bag and snuggled up inside when the lights went out. I woke to the sensation of hands around me and being trapped in the bag's fabric. Then I realized that there was something wet, sticky, and foul-smelling soaking my pajamas. The girls had opened one corner of my sleeping bag and dumped rotten tomatoes inside. As they were poured into the bag, the tomatoes burst, spraying their putrid, rotten seeds, flesh, and juice all over me. The next thing I knew, I was being shoved, half of me still inside the sleeping bag, out a first-floor window. I landed on the hard ground below. As I struggled to free myself from the bag, a dirty hamster cage (sans hamster) came flying through the same window. The girls had stuffed my clothes inside. I picked myself up and walked home, barefoot, in my filthy, stinking pajamas, carrying the hamster cage. My mother only said that it served me right, that I should keep away from those girls, "that trash," as she put it, and stay home.

three

For a while, I didn't know what I dreaded more, being out in the car with my mother or being at home with her, just my brother and me, alone. My mother constructed what I now know was a very elaborate system of delusions. It was not simply that my father was sleeping with her mother and numerous other women; it was that strangers or even our neighbors were out to get us. They were trying to break into our house, she said. She also told Kevin and me that our father wanted to kill us, that our father's family was intent on destroying her financially or on having her murdered, and that the banks and the grocery stores were somehow enemies as well, trying to make us suffer. She insisted that Kevin and I join her in this fantasy world.

Even as a fairly young child, I could see that some of her claims were flawed and not based in reality. But if I questioned, contradicted, or refused to go along with her, she would retaliate, often with anger—throwing hot coffee or anything else that happened to be nearby, threatening to call my teachers and tell them what an awful, ungrateful, stupid child I was, or unleashing her fury via the switches that she insisted my father make out of long branches dotted with thorns. I bit the inside of my mouth and felt my eyes well with tears as the switch hissed in the air and then stung my bare skin. But my mother also used another tactic that left no outward marks: fear.

If we were in the car and I disagreed with her or simply had what she considered an objectionable look on my face, she would kick me out of the car (sometimes while it was still moving) and leave me by the side of the road as she screamed at me to find my own way home. It did not matter to her how far away we were from the house or how long it might take me. Fortunately, I had memorized our address, and I quickly learned to walk up to houses that seemed nice and safe, knock on the door, politely explain that I was lost, and ask for directions. It was an odd practice for things to come. Later, my mother would drive my brother and me to other strange homes and send me to knock on their front doors. Invariably, a pretty woman would answer. I had to lie and say that I was lost, while my mother stared out the car window and studied the face in the doorway. This, I was always told, was the latest woman with whom my father was having an affair.

But there were plenty of times when our home was anything but safe.

Most often, the drama unfolded as the sky grew dark. Outside, through the window, my mother said she had spied a man walking near the dirt path that led to our house. The light was dusky, with only a tiny bit of skylight amplified by the streetlights and a few intermittent porch lights. He was coming, she informed us, to break into the house. He might even kill us. We had to be quiet, she said. We had to arm ourselves. She raced around, turning off the lamps and overheads, and as our eyes adjusted to the darkness, she rushed to the closet and returned with a slew of vacuum cleaner parts, mostly solid metal nozzles and tubes. Kevin picked up one, and I held another, a long nozzle attachment. Our mother gripped a hammer.

"Now we have to patrol," she told us. We followed her, marching from room to room, checking the doors, brandishing our cleaning implements, ready to strike and repel the invaders, who, according to her, were only seconds away from smashing through a door or a window. Each creak of our footsteps on the floor was terrifying, at risk of giving us away. After we had made several circles through the rooms, she hissed at us to lie down on the floor so "the bad guys outside" could not see us. When my legs had started to hurt from being so still, she pulled us up to march again. All night, the three of us spent hours either marching from room to room, Kevin and me clutching our vacuum cleaner parts, or pressed against the sofa for cover, or stomach-crawling as if we were infantry soldiers advancing through fields or under a lattice of barbed wire, dragging ourselves by our elbows until our skin burned as we maneuvered across the deep burgundy shag carpet. All the while, we had to keep our breath shallow and try to become invisible so as not to give ourselves away.

The threatened invasion did not happen that night (or ever), but the ephemeral threat appeared again and again. Occasionally, our mother had us arm ourselves and hide in the daytime, but mostly it was at night, in the dark. We spent countless hours with our "weapons," scurrying across the floor in the dark, avoiding the windows and doors so that no one from outside could peer in and see us. The "bad guys" who were just on the other side of the glass or the keyhole gradually morphed from strangers to our neighbors. Occasionally, she even told us that the threat was from our father himself.

I learned very quickly that if I said something like "They're just walking down the street, Mom," she would start to interrogate me and berate me.

"You know this person?" she would ask. "You're out to get me. You're with them. You are conspiring with them to hurt me." So I stayed silent, saying nothing. And eventually, I did exactly what our mother insisted on: I allowed myself to be absorbed into her story until I believed it all.

Over the years, some of the most fearsome nights were school nights, and our mother would force Kevin and me to stay up until dawn, hiding and armed with our vacuum cleaner parts or, later, tools from the toolbox, ever vigilant and trying to protect ourselves and her. My arms would grow exhausted until I could barely hold on to my "weapon." Only pure fear ensured that I kept it in my hands. I lived in constant terror that this would be the night when the people lurking outside finally came for us. Eventually, I refused to walk anywhere in the house by myself. I wouldn't even go the few steps up to my bedroom alone; I'd make Kevin come with me.

There was a price to be paid for these years of paranoia. At school, I could never stay awake in class and was constantly in trouble for "not paying attention or following the rules." Kevin and I both developed strange little tics and odd physical ways to soothe ourselves. When Kevin was still a toddler, he began banging his head against his pillow or the sides of his crib for comfort. For years, he also bounced back and forth in chairs. My soother of choice was to rock back and forth endlessly, holding the tip of my thumb in my mouth. These forms of repetitive physical motion gave us a measure of stability, a way to physically expel the stress that surrounded us, and a route to retreat into ourselves. It was the only way that we had to solve our own problems; there was no one to tell.

I wonder sometimes if things would have been different if my mother had not been beautiful. Where my father could talk to anyone, in my mother's case, people couldn't take their eyes off her. And she knew it. Despite our precarious lifestyle, she was obsessed with fashion. She teased her hair to huge heights, adding in hairpieces or sometimes wearing full wigs. She dressed in jumpsuits that hugged her curves and in long, brightly flowered maxi dresses that made her look elegantly earthy, suggesting we were part of the late sixties and early seventies culture of "back to the land." Like one of those Wild West movie sets, where the bank and saloon and boardinghouse are nothing more than false fronts propped up by boards, she could engineer just enough of a veneer of normalcy for a parent-teacher conference or basic interactions outside of our family. She was good at getting people to engage with her and to believe that she was nice. Mostly, she got them to feel sorry for her—"poor Janice, her family treats her so horribly." While my father had to talk his way in or out of any situation, my mother didn't need to say all that much. There was almost an assumption that someone who looked that good couldn't be terrible underneath. Then, too, we were never in any place all that long for people to question what might be below the surface. My mother, as soon as she sensed that anyone in a position of authority was getting overly inquisitive, simply yanked me out of one school and put me in another.

All our family's changes, when they came, were stark and sudden. One day, we were living in our small ranch house with the big picture window where we watched the sliding cars, and the next day, we were moving to another house, with red-colored wood siding, in a completely different part of town.

Leaving was easy. The mattresses were carted out. Everything else was stuffed into big black trash bags or boxes. I remember seeing an El Camino, a cross between a car and a pickup truck, pull up to the curb. My father tossed things into the El Camino's flatbed in the back. My parents never had much stuff in any of their houses. I can still list the high-water mark of the furniture we owned: the coffee table that had been my grandmother's, a couch, the gold chairs from New Orleans, and possibly some blue chairs, although I have no idea where the blue chairs came from or at what point they entered our lives. There was also a desk with a sewing machine, another gift from my grandmother, and the Formica kitchen table with its four chairs. Kevin and I did not have actual beds with frames. Instead, we slept on mattresses that had been dumped on the floor. We did not have dressers for our clothes; they were relegated to piles, again on the floor. We would pick something up from the clean pile and eventually place it in the dirty pile. Much of our home was a series of piles and random things thrown on the floor or deposited around the room. And boxes for moving, because as I would come to know, no place or location ever lasted for long.

There was no explanation given for these moves. I don't know if my father had lost the house somehow, or if he had swindled so many people that he was run out of that part of town, or if it was partly my mother's paranoia, or even one of my father's other women. We were simply gone. New school, new street, new neighbors, new friends, but not new lives.

Not long after we moved into this new Salt Lake house, Kevin had surgery to fix his pigeon-toed feet. The surgeon broke both his legs to turn his feet so they wouldn't drift inward. Kevin spent months all but immobilized, locked in a lower-body cast. I had the same issue, but it had been corrected with leg braces. My skin had bled from the chafing of the metal. No one had thought to put any type of cloth or covering in between.

The second Utah house was one of the nicest we ever lived in, with red shag carpet in a "playroom" downstairs and bedrooms on the same level as the kitchen. While we lived there, my father must have briefly struck it rich or been bailed out by his older brother, Carlie, because I do remember that we were suddenly less poor. We had a Christmas tree with white flocking and shiny blue balls hanging from its faux branches, and come December 25, piles of presents under it. My father even bought a boat. We took one trip on the boat during the summer, which was documented in hundreds of photos, and then it sat unused, slowly rusting and turning into junk. Eventually, we moved to yet another house, set far back from the road and the neighbors. This house had a dark, damp basement that terrified me. Most of the house terrified me; I dreaded walking to my bedroom at the top of the stairs and frequently made Kevin come with me. In front of the house, we had another yard full of junk cars and machines that my father mined for spare parts for his flivvers.

My brother and I played around those cars constantly. We pretended to drive them, or we played hide-and-seek by wedging ourselves in their rusting bodies. Occasionally, we found treasures that the old owners and even the junkmen had left behind. One car had an ancient record player and a collection of Beatles records. We cleaned up the player, brought it into the house, and spent hours sitting in the dark listening to John, Paul, George, and Ringo. When my father heard the music, he made a face and called me a "hippie," which was meant as an insult. The other thing I loved to do was lie on the old mattress that sat on the floor of the living room and read books. Their pages were an escape from everything, especially my family.

In the later Utah years, my parents embraced "living off the grid." They presented it as a philosophy, but I think it arose out of necessity, mostly because my mother wasn't given much, if any, money for groceries. There was almost no store-bought food at home. In the summers, we had a huge garden with chaotic rows of every kind of vegetable, wild berries, and a chicken coop stuffed with chickens. We ate the fresh eggs from the hens and the vegetables we picked or dug up from the ground. During the winter, we ate the freezer venison.

There was an old dirt cellar where my mother stored potatoes and turnips, our winter vegetables. Chickens were killed for their meat and for soup. Sometimes, my father made me join him to kill a chicken. He'd grab the bird, hold it down, and with the other hand, aim an axe at its neck to sever its head. For what seemed like a small eternity, the headless chicken would flail about the yard, blood spurting in arcs from its open neck. The red-soaked ground looked like a serial killer had visited the place. After its dance of death, the lifeless chicken was submerged in a pot of water and soaked so its feathers could be easily plucked. The smell of dead chicken and wet feathers in that huge pot was nearly overwhelming.

I did love some parts of living off the land, especially gardening and growing vegetables. There was something amazing about planting the small, insignificant seeds and then watching them sprout through the soil, throw up their tiny shoots, and grow into something wonderful. My mother vacillated between loving and hating "the gardening," as she called it. But I always loved it. When she was in the mood to love gardening, we bonded over the soil and the plants. Mom would never pull the weeds—that was my job. But getting down on my knees and tugging their stalks and roots up from the earth seemed a small price to pay for some positive interaction with my mother, especially when my father took off from our lives for days or weeks at a time. Some afternoons and early evenings, the two of us would pick the vegetables straight from the vines and pop them in our mouths, washed with nothing more than a little bit of rainwater or a spray from the hose. One time when we were harvesting veggies, Mom got so excited about the colors: the red peppers, the green ones, the bright tomatoes, the cucumbers, and the varieties of squash. We'd collect baskets of vegetables, sit on the ground outside, and stuff ourselves with them. Then we'd pick berries from the wild blueberry and blackberry bushes that colonized the spaces around the vegetable rows. Mom would always talk about the people in her life that she hated, but I let her talk, agreeing with her as often as possible to avoid a problem. It was peaceful that way, and I could enjoy the time in the sun, just the two of us eating the vegetables and the fruit.

In those years, I spent a lot of time in conversation with, or more accurately listening to, my mother. She wanted to talk constantly, mostly about people, either those she believed were out to "get" her, or people in my life or my brother's life of whom she did not approve (invariably, all of them). Most of the time, I would listen and offer her sympathy. The sympathy was genuine. I truly felt for her and believed she was a victim of horrible circumstances. I was her therapist, really, because, although she hated "shrinks," as she called them, she needed one. I felt close to her when I was giving her comfort, and she acted like she appreciated me. She talked to me about everything—no topic was off-limits: her horrible parents, my horrible father, and how she would do anything to save us from that terrible man. I believed her. I cried with her when she said my father had tried to kill her. And I had witnessed my father yell and grab and raise his fists to try to keep her from saying harsh things about him.

Because our third Utah house sat on a large piece of land, for a long time, we did not know any of our neighbors. Eventually, my brother became friends with the boy who lived closest to us. My mother's response was to say, "I hate that family." I don't know why she hated them, and looking back, there might have been no rational reason at all, but it made me reluctant to be around my brother's new friend.

This was also the house where I got good at firing a gun and where I learned to drive.

At first, my father had me sit on his lap in the driver's seat and taught me how to steer, use the turn signals, put the car into gear, and park it. I was fairly tall, so he soon deemed me able to drive alone while he sat in the passenger seat. I was eight years old the first time I drove solo. The steering wheel felt enormous, and it took my full force to turn or to keep us from drifting on the road. But driving became something I could control and master, something where I was in charge. I could stretch my leg to reach the gas and the brake, feel the power beneath me, and feel the rumble of the road deep inside my bones.

In the beginning, I drove on dirt roads when we were camping, fishing, or hunting. But it wasn't all that long before my father had me drive on public roads as well. When I drove any vehicle to his satisfaction, he would praise me profusely, and I'd beam. I was so proud because I longed to be viewed as "responsible" and "adult." But if I did not drive to my father's "satisfaction," he would take over. That invariably meant a ride of pure fear, high speeds, off-roading up hills, where the car was on two wheels or sometimes completely disconnected from the ground so that it would nearly overturn. We'd drive into mud or bogs and feel the tires sink. Or if we were in a boat on the water, he'd throttle the engine and then turn the bow at such a sharp angle that we'd nearly capsize. I would scream until we came to a stop.

By age ten, I became a very good driver, out of pure self-preservation and no small measure of terror. Between the ages of ten and fifteen, I drove a variety of vehicles—the white Lincoln, a burnt-orange Ford Bronco, a pickup truck, a dune buggy, a boat, a dirt bike, and sometimes a rattletrap RV. It got so that I could drive anything if I could see just a bit over the wheel.

four

My father and I had one special thing that was ours: fishing. It was just the two of us, out on the water, away from the screaming and the chaos. We always went on a weekend, waking up well before dawn. He kept fresh worms inside an extra refrigerator that sat in the garage. In the dark, he'd pull out the worms, grab our poles and gear, and load everything in the car. We would drive to Strawberry Lake—often, I was at the wheel—and climb into an old, beat-up aluminum fishing boat with an outboard motor. A firm tug of the cord, a sputter and start, and we would be out on the lake before the sun rose. We didn't talk much out on the lake, we just fished. But my father patiently taught me how to do it—how to tie the hook on the end of the line after adding the sinker and the floater. How to get a slimy worm pierced onto the hook. He showed me the best places on a lake to find fish. He told me that fish love corn, so we would throw some corn onto the water once we found a good spot and watch it float along the surface before we cast our lines. Then we'd sit and wait for a fish to bite while the sun floated up.

I was always reading books. My mother had kept a collection of Nancy Drew books from when she was a child, and I worked my way through the entire set. While we fished, I would read, always once the sun came up, and sometimes using a flashlight before that. My father didn't read much; he sat and watched the lines and ate peanut butter and honey sandwiches. He was always eating those—if he was home, you could usually find him standing over the kitchen sink mixing peanut butter and honey and eating it straight from the jar with a spoon and a glass of milk. When we were finished for the day, he took out a big, sharp knife and fluidly cleaned the fish we caught, removing the heads and tails and gutting them into neat fillets. We would pack them on ice in an old Styrofoam cooler and carry them home for dinner. Sometimes, we'd catch enough fish to eat for an entire week. That was a good day.

◀▶

Both our parents believed that Kevin and I needed to know how to take care of ourselves, to "live off the land" if we had to. So, not only were we taught how to fish and grow things, but we also had to learn how to find shelter and build a shelter. I also learned how to collect dry wood and twigs for fires, how to cook over a campfire, and how to clean up. Once I could drive, my father insisted that I learn the final piece of the self-preservation puzzle: how to hunt so, as he put it, I would be able to provide food for the family.

My father loved shooting and hunting. As far back as I can remember, there were guns all over our house, particularly in closets, some precariously propped on their sides. One of the earliest photos of Kevin and me shows us amid the carcasses of dead birds. I am bent over, in my bowl haircut, cautiously holding the foot of a shot-out bird to keep it away from my red pants and especially from dripping blood on my shoes, while Kevin's nursery-schooler hands keep a firm grip on the bloody beak of a dead pheasant. Bits of blood smear his face and his shirt. The shotgun that killed them and at least one more plump pheasant rest against a bush just beyond his elbow. The gun's barrel is at least a full head taller than Kevin.

My parents took us shooting many times. Learning to shoot usually involved going to some remote place, setting up a target (cans, papers on sticks, rocks), and firing the rifle until Kevin and I could reliably hit whatever target had been chosen, not once but many times. My father's version of an incentive was to slap me when I missed the target (if no one was looking). So I quickly learned how to hit it. He was very proud of me because I was a really good shot.

But hunting was different.

The first time I felt shame with my father was when we were hunting. He had taught me how to hike silently through the woods, how to sit in silence for long periods, and learn to differentiate between normal sounds and sounds of disruption, such as a large animal moving through the growth. We always went deep into the woods, where the forest floor was soft and the pine trees fought their way up toward the sun, the older ones periodically toppling over to make way for new ones. This was the place where we could find a deer to kill and no one could hear the blast of the rifle. Eugene Smith almost certainly didn't believe in hunting licenses.

That morning, we walked far into the woods and sat among the trees for hours. Finally, we heard a noise, and he gave me the hand signal to move, to fall in quietly behind him. I was carrying a rifle. So was he. We slowly crept toward the source of the sound. As we came to a grove, we saw a mama deer with her baby fawn. The fawn was the one making the noise, moving, jumping, tugging at her mama, and trying to play. We were some distance away and frozen in place behind the trees. My father motioned to me to take the shot at the mama. I raised the rifle to my shoulder, trained the sight, and released the safety. Then I started to shake uncontrollably. I just couldn't pull the trigger. Just. Could. Not. I was shaking so hard I dropped the gun (I'm lucky it didn't discharge). My father looked at me in disgust. He shook his head, turned, lifted his rifle, fired, and killed her.

The fawn ran. My father made me help him carry the mama's carcass back to our camp. And then he made me help him gut her and skin her. He ordered me to pull out her still-warm organs and entrails and yelled at me for crying as the congealing blood stained my hands. Her butchered pieces ended up in our freezer, and she became our dinner for many, many nights during the winter. I always wondered if her fawn survived.

◀▶

By age ten, I was too old to rock back and forth and suck my thumb, but there were so many days when I couldn't stand to be in my own skin. Or at least inside the house. I had become hyperalert to every facial expression my mother made, especially when her eyes changed. Her irises would expand as if they had transformed into the vent of a volcano, and just below, lodged in the crater, a cascade of molten lava was on the verge of forcing its way out. Other times, my mother would be overcome by a furious twitch that made it appear as if her entire eye had detached itself and was visibly wiggling inside its socket. But when a look of pure hatred came over her entire face, that terrified me the most. Nothing good ever followed one of those looks.

Kevin and I had very different ways of solving the problems that were our mother and our household. Once he was able to, Kevin's answer was to disappear into a cloud of neighborhood boys. I lost myself in library books. Sometimes, I would hide among the current crop of rusting, picked-over cars that my father had scavenged and somehow dragged home, or I would make myself small beside the chicken coop and escape into the pages of my book. I also had my cats.

Curiously, my mother allowed the stray cats who wandered into the yard and eventually the house to stay. We fed them saucers of milk, and they would slink in and out of the house and between the rooms, soundless except for the slight click of their claws on the hard, wooden floors. On cold nights, they would sometimes find their way up to my room. They were generally fast enough to make themselves scarce when trouble hit—but not always.

For a time, early on, I also tried to escape with my one friend. She was a bit older than I and on the wild side, always running off with different boys. In the straitlaced world of Mormonism, she was also an outsider, even more of an outsider than I was. She didn't belong to the Church of Latter-Day Saints, and her parents were divorced. Although her mother had remarried, she remained a bitter woman. Occasionally, her mom and my mom would get together and talk about how horrible their respective husbands were.

I liked having an older friend. I still thought of myself as being mature for my age, older and wiser. After all, how many other kids could drive a car, knew how to shoot a rifle, or could find their way home from miles away? My friend had a brother who was about seventeen years old. I knew him in passing, and a few times at their house, I had been drawn into his room, with its posters depicting heavy metal bands, a beat-up dresser, piles of clothes on the floor, and a bed with huge sheets tented around it. His room was dark, and there were a lot of dishes with bits of discarded food covered in traces of mold scattered around the room. I remember that the carpet was short-piled, dark brown, and scratchy to sit on. The sheets on his bed were dirty and smelled bad. He had one of those lamps with a colorful plastic piece that sat over the bulb and spun, throwing multicolored lights onto the walls in a way that made you feel dizzy.

I remember gazing up briefly at the spinning light in that dirty room one afternoon as he held me down and raped me. I had no idea what was happening. Despite all my mother's screaming about my father's other women, I knew nothing of sex. But I knew that what had happened was shameful, and I thought it was my fault. I was about eight years old.

Slowly and gingerly, I walked back to our house. My underwear was damp and stained bright red with blood. I asked my mom about the blood "down there," and all she said in reply was "Maybe you're getting your period." That ended the conversation. But it would be years before I would bleed again. I kept quiet and told no one. My mother, I knew, never stuck up for anyone. Almost instinctively, I recognized that she would most likely blame me. When my father cut the heads off our chickens and forced me to watch, her reply when I pleaded for it to stop was only "See how awful he is?"

There were plenty of times when my father was awful, or they both were. The arguments were constant and ever more explosive. They would often begin with my mother hissing that my father was "controlling," exploding over how he kept money from her or how he cheated on her with other women. Everything would quickly escalate into yelling, screaming, and threats, with each of them unleashing a torrent of the most hateful, hurtful things that popped into their heads.

Just as she had in our other Utah houses, my mother would turn to my brother and me and tell us that our father wanted to murder her or murder us. In her words, our father was a "fucking loser," an "ugly fucker," a "lying sack of shit," a "bald-headed dick," or some other adjective that could be inserted before the phrase "sack of shit."

My father would retaliate, calling her "a lunatic, crazy, insane, psycho, disgusting cunt." I lost count of how often their anger accelerated until they came to physical blows. My father was five feet ten, while my mother was five four. He was not a big man, but he was still stronger and bigger than she was.

When my father got violent, my mother would scream at the top of her lungs at him or at me. She never defended us to him, but we defended her against him, or at least I tried to. I had the sense that, on some level, my father loved to terrorize us—or maybe it was only my mother, because that was how he could find a shred of control in their marriage. Most people get to a point where they've been terrorized often enough that they either cower in a corner or fight back. At some point in my life, I refused to cower. I decided that I would rather fight.

When my parents really went at it, I would wait until they were completely locked on each other, oblivious of my presence. Then I would maneuver my way behind my father, jump on his back, and try to pull him away or keep him from moving forward, in a vain attempt to protect my mother. Most of the time, I'd end up being tossed like a rider on a bucking bull. My father would reach around and grab me or shake me off, and in the process, I would be pitched into a wall or land hard on the floor.

During one particularly nasty fight between my parents, I ran up to my father and shoved him. Instead of hitting me, he grabbed our cat, my cat, walked outside to the backyard, and shot it dead as I watched.

"No he didn't," my mother told me afterward. "Your cat just ran away."

When I confronted my father about my cat, he said nothing and simply smirked. My brother looked at me and said, "He did it. You can tell by the smirk on his face."

Other times, when things exploded, our mom would run from our father to her room or to my brother's. One of the times that we ended up in the hospital involved my mother running to my brother's bedroom during a huge fight that started in my parents' room. It was the middle of the night, and my mother woke up my brother to tell him what a horrible "piece of shit" his father was, that he was evil, and he should be dead. My father chased after her and demanded that she leave Kevin alone and stop saying those things. My father grabbed her arm and tried to pull her away from my brother's bed. My mother screamed at him, accusing him of beating her, which made him pull harder. Either he threw her, or she let go, or wriggled free, but the resulting force sent her head into the doorjamb. The impact sliced her head open along one side. My mother took off, blood streaming down her face, and raced toward the stairs. My father grabbed her to try to stop her. Again she pulled away from him violently, or he let go, and this time, she fell down the stairs.

On the way to the hospital, I was instructed very explicitly about what I could and could not say. I learned that doctors would ask me what had happened, and I was always very careful to tell only the approved truth.

No one ever asked me if I had been hit, but I was. It happened not only at home, however. I was being beaten up at school, too. Once, a pack of kids threw me into a rosebush. That ruined roses for me for a very long time.

If my father was the king of physical threats and making good on them, my mother was the queen of emotional ones. She'd threaten us with the volatility of our father—"I'm going to tell him," she'd say. But she'd also threaten us with herself, or more specifically her absence, with her walking out and Kevin and me being left alone. "I'm just going to abandon you," or "I'm just going to leave," and "I'm sick of you and don't want you anymore" were a few of her favorite sentences. And they worked. We would stop, cater to whatever she wanted, or make ourselves disappear.

In retrospect, I see the horror of it all, but at the time, I possessed a sycophant's blind devotion and loyalty to her, the kind that drove me to throw myself upon my father's back. She was the victim; she was the one who needed to be protected. It's hard to reconcile that now with the things she did: kicking me out of the car so that I had to find my way home, or constantly telling me, "I can't stand you, get out of my house and never come back." Or how her favorite description of me was "little shit."

But I had to justify her behavior to explain it, or at least to rationalize it to myself. So seeing her as the victim, as the person in need of protection, made me blindly loyal. I was the cause, I told myself. When she did these awful things, I had to accept the narrative that I had driven her to it, that it was all my fault, that something was wrong with me. That was a workable narrative because I could always work harder to change myself. To believe otherwise meant there was no hope at all.

Then, too, maybe her threats to leave were also her expressing her own deep wish to run off. In that desire, she was not the only one.

While we lived in the third Utah house, Kevin and I started plotting how we could run away. Once, we even did it. We gathered up all the cats who had taken up residence around us and stuffed them in a big cage, because we feared, justifiably, that our father would kill them in our absence. Then, lugging the cage, we walked as quietly as we could to the end of the long dirt driveway, carefully crossing the noisy wooden boards that had been placed over a small stream as a makeshift bridge. But we didn't have a plan beyond that. In the nearby woods was an old, decrepit tree house. We hid in its tiny, splintery space for twenty-four hours. Eventually, the air grew too cold, and we grew too hungry. The cats were howling. So we did the only thing we could think of: we hoisted the cage with the cats and, walking side by side, headed back up the dirt driveway toward home.

RYAN

five

In Washington, DC, a city that is dominated by sea-level buildings and paved swampland, Sidwell Friends School clearly occupies the high ground. It is not simply on the ascendant side of the terrain; the school's main administrative building, a Georgian-style, redbrick and white-columned country house that dates from before 1827, is perched on a rise as if it's surveying the territory below. In fact, the house's original name says it all: "Highlands." It is also a building with a past.

The Highlands was built by a man named Joseph Nourse, who served as the register of the federal treasury for more than forty years, spanning six presidents. Nourse owned the nearby plot of Mount St. Alban—a portion of that land would become the site of the National Cathedral. The Highlands was designed as a home for his son Charles and Charles' wife, Rebecca. The Nourse family belonged to a social set that included Thomas Jefferson and Dolley Madison, and when Charles, Joseph's only surviving child to reach adulthood, occupied the Highlands, Joseph gifted him with a thirty-five-year-old enslaved

Black woman named Ann and her five children, whom Joseph had purchased from Walter Brook Beale for the sum of $380. One of those children, William Brooks, served as the Nourse family's coachman, pulling in and out of the outlines of the circular drive that is visible today.

After the Nourse family's many decades in the prominent spot along Wisconsin Avenue, the house was subsequently owned by both Woodrow Wilson's personal physician and, later, the legendary spymaster Allen Dulles. Sidwell Friends bought the property in 1955 and renamed the Highlands the Zartman House, after an aide to the school's founder, Thomas Sidwell. Two years later, the school enrolled its first Black kindergarten student, and in 1967, exactly 140 years after five enslaved children set foot on the property as servants, Sidwell awarded diplomas to its first five Black graduates. But that seemed like ancient history and certainly was not something that was highlighted in the school's glossy admissions pitch.

Before our family left California, I had been told that Sidwell was the best school in Washington, the one I should want for my children, Justin and Elie. But I was thoroughly uneducated in the ways of East Coast prep school admissions. I had naively thought that Justin could just walk in, after the formality of an application, and start in his eighth-grade year. I didn't realize that he couldn't apply in April, after the deadline had closed, and easily find a spot for September. Instead, we were firmly but politely told that we would have to "hold" in another school for a year and then try again. Being declined somehow made the school seem more perfect and made me more determined.

Ryan was the opposite. Until he was approached and until he set foot on campus, he had no idea that schools like Sidwell existed. Ryan had come up through the Montgomery County, Maryland, public school system. Although the county's schools had a good reputation,

Ryan was completely unprepared for Sidwell. The schools he had attended were large and crowded, often thirty-plus kids jammed into a classroom, with hardly anything in the way of individual attention. While he was by no means a poor student, Ryan had developed almost none of the organizational and academic skills required to survive in ninth grade at a school like Sidwell.

None of this was apparent during August, when there was only football practice to contend with, but once Labor Day had come and gone and classes started, the atmosphere in our car rides changed. The school workload was immediate and overwhelming, particularly the homework. Meanwhile, Justin and I were still getting home after 8 p.m. from Ryan's bus stop runs. I soon learned that Ryan's morning commute was even worse. The public buses were erratic, sometimes late, sometimes a bus didn't show up or was too crowded for him to get on, so he was often late to school. After a few nights of driving to Bethesda, the next time Ryan hopped in the car, I half asked, half told him, "Ryan, don't you think it would be easier if you just came home with us, had dinner with us, and then we'll take you home?" His answer was a quick yes.

After a few evenings at our table, Ryan relaxed. He was a joyful, happy, funny kid, the kind who brightened a room simply by walking in. Even Elie, who was in sixth grade and couldn't stand sitting between the two sweaty boys in the back of the car and pointedly said that she wouldn't wish breathing the smell on her worst enemy, declared that Ryan was the happiest person she had ever met, adding, "He loves mornings, cold rooms, and, most of all, he loves to laugh."

I don't know how Ryan thrived in football. He wasn't a fighter; he wasn't confrontational. The violence on the field, the bruising clash of bodies, never seemed appropriate for him. Or perhaps he just left every one of those impulses on the turf. He was a great football player;

he was on the varsity squad as a ninth grader. Justin was not as gifted; he was relegated to JV, although both teams practiced together.

Dinner wasn't anything fancy. I had a lot of Taco Tuesdays and rounds of grilled chicken or spaghetti and meatballs. Occasionally, I would surprise the boys with grilled steak and lobster, and they concluded that I must be the best cook in the world. Once the plates were cleared, Ryan and Justin would head to Justin's room to study, where it quickly became clear that their back-of-the-car banter had only been a warm-up. They might have opened their books, but they also talked and talked and talked—about life, girls, sports, school, and philosophical and political issues. Justin would say that Ryan understood "what goes on in my head. He gets me."

Ryan unabashedly said that he loved Justin and could "talk to him about anything."

It was great for their friendship, but not for academics. Ryan was struggling in his classes, and Justin started having difficulty, too. Justin had taken it as his own personal challenge to not only raise his grades but to get Ryan up to speed in the various classes they shared, the lockstep courses all ninth graders were expected to take: English, history, math, and biology. But Justin was a kid himself, and the academic gaps were too great, no matter how hard he tried. Justin was always like that: thoughtful, not wanting anyone to be left behind. Once, when he was small, he insisted on tearfully saying goodbye to every tree in our yard before we left for vacation—and as we drove away, I looked over and realized he was quietly crying, as if he were abandoning the stoic brown trunks until he returned.

I decided each boy needed his own space to work, and I made a study room for Ryan in the basement. But while that helped Justin and his grades rebounded, it did not help Ryan. That was the first sign to me that Ryan might have a bigger problem beyond just being distracted by Justin. After a few weeks, Ryan hesitantly started coming to me for help. The two of us would sit at the sprawling wood kitchen table every night, enveloped in a post-dinner calm, the dishwasher quietly cycling in the background.

I tried helping him with biology to start, which was doable because it involved a textbook and memorization. I lasted about one session in math. Ryan had tested into the lowest-level course section, but even so, the gaps in his math knowledge were profound. It was not as if we could identify a year or a particular area that had been overlooked; rather, it seemed that he was missing basic foundational skills. He especially didn't know how to study. He didn't know how to read a textbook or how to underline or highlight the most important information—he didn't even know how to pick out the high-priority information. He had not been taught how to memorize. Even more devastating, he also had almost no writing skills. It was as if he had never written a research paper. In fact, he probably hadn't.

For English class, I would help him memorize Shakespeare, an incredibly difficult task for both of us. Ryan had a stutter, and now he was faced with learning and pronouncing words he had never seen before in his life. Half of them I hadn't seen before, either, growing up in the middle of nowhere and changing schools sometimes multiple times in one year. "What the heck does this mean?" he'd ask me, and I'd reply, "I don't know!" I had an easier time helping him in Spanish. But he was operating at such a deficit and was struggling in so many areas that I wasn't sure what to do other than just sit beside him and attempt to be useful. Justin tried to work with him as much as he could in biology and history. But every class presented a challenge. Sidwell was a grind for even the most prepared students. For Ryan, it was overwhelming.

If Ryan's prior education had not prepared him for the demands of Sidwell, my experience was that Sidwell also was unprepared for a student like Ryan. Its underlying philosophy was one of no accommodations for any differences, learning or otherwise. Instead, in the school's view, everyone was equal; everyone was subjected to the same rule of sink or swim. However, scratch the surface, and a very different image came into view.

Over time, to me, the physical appearance of Sidwell, the school, very much came to reflect the intangible appearance of Sidwell, the community. To the outside world, the public-facing, solid stone building with redbrick columns perched on the hill sits back from the street just enough to appear self-consciously modest. A passerby could imagine all the trappings of age: squeaky wooden floors, glass doorknobs, slightly bowed wooden doors, and old, unadorned spaces. In many ways, the consistency of the main facade over the decades was the physical manifestation of Quaker modesty and plainness, the architectural equivalent of a muted, shapeless, long-sleeved, long-skirted dress with not a ruffle or extra button to be found. Because Sidwell was a "Friends" school, adhering to Quaker education, each week, the students gathered for a meeting for silent worship in a stripped-down, Shaker-style space with elegant wooden pews. There, students and teachers sat in a communal "shared silence" until someone in the room was moved to share a thought or feeling.

Only the high fence that enclosed the glistening artificial-turf field to the left along Wisconsin Avenue, flanked by a squarish, nondescript, pale brick building rising beyond it, suggested that behind this facade there might be something more. Indeed, there was a lot more. In the back, along the smaller residential street and where the elevation drops down, an entirely other school rises out of the hillside. Designed for middle school students, it has sleek modern architecture and an enclosed courtyard, complete with a wetland wastewater treatment system; gleaming glass windows, a green roof, wood reclaimed from fifty-year-old wine casks; and state-of-the-art classrooms and laboratories. It's a separate space with a completely different look and feel. It reminds me of a secret garden residing behind an ugly high wall, where the world is transformed inside, but only if you possess the key. And the key to Sidwell was a very ephemeral thing.

After months of watching Ryan struggle, Tom and I scheduled a meeting with one of the school's top administrators. His office had a small window, a sparse desk with a computer on top, and two simple chairs facing him. The walls were unadorned except for a couple of family photos and a very large corkboard. Tacked to the cork was a family tree–style diagram. Its mass of leaves and branches displayed the names of one of the school's most substantial benefactor families, winding through its successive generations of Sidwell siblings and connections. If someone on the tree called, all he had to do was look up and see what position they occupied. The tree gave the illusion of decades of familiarity and intimacy with the school.

Neither Tom nor I was a slouch when it came to making a case. Yet, the administrator dismissed every concern we raised. His attitude was, in essence: everybody's happy here. Nobody has a problem. We're all in this together. And his unflinching view, which he kept repeating, was that all the kids eventually do fine "in a couple of years."

My view was that two years of failing grades would keep most kids from getting into a good college if that was the path they wanted to pursue—and if they couldn't learn the material in ninth and tenth grade, by what magic would that material suddenly become accessible in eleventh and twelfth? Sidwell spoke very proudly of the fact that the school didn't provide grade point averages; families could calculate them on their own, but the school would not do so, because everyone is on a so-called level playing field. Except that everyone wasn't, at least not kids like Ryan. And it soon became clear to me that from the moment the members of the incoming ninth-grade class set foot on that proverbial "level" playing field, no matter where they came from, even if it was simply from Sidwell's eighth grade, families with means armed their students with private tutors. Equal was not just a misnomer; it was a full-blown mirage.

six

One of the first things I noticed, even before our homework sessions started, was how slowly Ryan packed his things in his backpack when it came time for us to drive him home. It was already nine thirty or ten o'clock most nights when we left. Justin would insist on riding along even if he desperately needed to sleep. Once we reached Ryan's apartment building, Ryan would hop out of the car and vanish inside, usually climbing in through a ground-level window. In the beginning, I assumed that he was just one of those kids who could leave in the morning, run around, do whatever he wanted, and come back at night. I had been that kid, too. But I also had never spoken with his parents; I had no idea what his family life was like. Or perhaps I did. Perhaps I recognized it almost too clearly.

Weeks passed, and I silently wondered why I had never heard from Ryan's mom or dad. Especially because, since we had moved to DC, I was used to private school helicopter moms. They would call, almost with a checklist in hand, if their child was coming over for only two hours in the afternoon. There were snack rules and screen rules. Some even sent tubes of sunscreen. I admit I was also guilty of a certain amount of this micromanaging. To be otherwise was to somehow be barely passing at parenting. But this arrangement was different. If my son had been spending hours every day at someone else's home, I'd at least want to have a conversation. Gingerly, later in September, I asked Ryan, "Is your mom or dad okay with you coming over here?"

From a very young age, I had trained myself to be hyperalert and hypervigilant, aware of everything around me. Like monitoring the slightest dip in the barometric pressure for the first sign of foul weather, I could read the tiniest changes in a facial expression. I had to if I wanted to survive. The benefit of that type of growing up is that I'm quick at discerning what is really happening with other people. I can see it in their eyes, hear it in the first few words that they speak. So, the moment after I spoke, I immediately knew that, to Ryan, it was a loaded question, and one he was deeply uncomfortable answering, even though he replied yes, it was fine with his mom. A few times, I asked him for his mother's number so I could call and introduce myself, and each time he evaded. He would get her number to me, he said. He promised to text it to me, but he never did. Nor did I see her at any of the football games—or if she was there, I did not know who she was. Then, in early October, Rochelle, Ryan's mom, called me. Ryan must have finally given her my contact information. Looking back now, I don't know what I was expecting.

After thanking me for driving Ryan home each day, she told me that it was not "safe" for Ryan to be living at her home. I listened as she explained about his father Leonard's benders, his disappearances, the drug dealers who came to their home to collect on debts, held everyone at gunpoint and terrorized her children, essentially holding them hostage, until Rochelle dug out some cash and they relented, until the next time.

"Would you let Ryan stay with you?" she asked. No mother asks for such a thing unless she is desperate. And no one who has had a childhood like mine could say no. Growing up, my family always criticized me for being a naive person. If I saw someone in need of something, I would give it to them. If I feel that you might need my shoes, I will hand you my shoes, no judgment and no questions. That's how I've always been. My mother would call it terrible or horrible and holler that I didn't know the value of money or how to manage things. But knowing when someone truly needs help versus when they are taking advantage of you—or are perhaps somewhere in between—is also something I quickly learned. Real need speaks to me.

I had already suggested to Ryan a few times that he was welcome to spend the night. But now, listening to Rochelle, I began to understand. Change a few of the details, add an overlay of pitch-perfect California sun, Utah mountains, and some flat Idaho farmland, and many parts of Ryan's world had very much been my own. I'd basically committed to welcoming Ryan the second Rochelle had asked, although I said something about having to talk to Tom. That evening before bed, I told Tom what Ryan's mom had requested. "Oh God, no," was his immediate reaction. "We have no idea what we would be getting ourselves into."

We had already added an exchange student, Ranim from Ramallah in the West Bank territories, to our household. Each week in August, the Sidwell email newsletter had asked for parents to offer Ranim a home, but no one had responded. It bothered me. I asked our family to vote—"Oh yeah, cool," Justin and Elie said—and so I signed us up. Hosting long-term guests or students wasn't new to any of us. In California, we hosted different students; I thought it was good for the kids and good for us as a family. Tom complained that I was always opening the doors of our home to anyone who asked, and even a few who didn't. My view was different—a person in need is *right here*. If I can help, I will. It was part of the deal if you wanted to be married to me, and I had said so. Besides, Tom was usually out of town most of the week. I knew it would make no difference to him on a day-to-day basis. So I asked him, "How is having Ryan here going to make your life different? You're never even here."

I was the stay-at-home mom, the driver, the cook, and the overseer of all school-related things. Tom traveled for work—a lot. He was gone so much that if you added together the number of days in a year that he was home, the time that he was present totaled at most only a couple of months. If Ryan came to live with us, Tom likely wouldn't even know the difference.

Tom wondered aloud if the people who were after Ryan's father might also come after Ryan at our home. I didn't know the answer, but I've never been one to back down from fear or a threat. If anything, I'm more likely to stand my ground. Besides, given that information, how could we not help Ryan?

I have always believed that things happen for a reason. People come into our lives, and we into theirs, for a reason. After quite a few heated discussions, Tom agreed that we should say yes to Rochelle and to Ryan. Once Tom committed, he was just as resolute as I was.

I called Rochelle and said we would help. But I wanted Ryan to know, very clearly, that I was not attempting to replace her as his mom. It was up to the two of us to carve out a separate relationship so that each of us could speak to him and to his life in a meaningful but also fully coordinated way. Rochelle and I agreed to communicate frequently and to always offer a consistent message to Ryan. We would also watch for any effort by Ryan to play us, getting me to say yes when his mother had said no, and vice versa. Rochelle noted that Ryan would in effect have two moms, and that could be both a blessing (lots of love) and a curse (two women telling him what to do and not to do). We had a long chuckle about that. Rochelle and, later,

Leonard, whom I would eventually meet at a football game, where he came and stayed in the car, also began to refer to Tom and me as Ryan's "godparents."

But that was not the end of the discussion. Tom and I sat down with Ryan in the upholstered swivel chairs in the family room and gently asked if he knew what his mom had requested. It was so quiet I could hear the slow exhale of air as the cushions compressed. Around us, in the long expanse of built-in shelves, I had carefully arranged framed family photos spanning Justin's and Elie's lives, our books, and other mementos, all the trappings of what to a visitor must have resembled a carefully curated suburban life. Outside in the yard, beyond the wide French doors and a wide wraparound deck with the professional-sized grill and an outdoor living room, the grass was still green, and the leaves were a riot of color, obscuring the neighbors and making the house feel tucked away, peaceful, and serene. I kept thinking of Ryan, hauling himself through a ground-floor window when Justin and I dropped him off in the dark. Did he think that someone else might have been in the apartment? Was he going in the "safe" way? Was there even such a thing?

We wanted to know how Ryan felt. We told him that we would love to have him with us for as long as he and his mom believed it was necessary. He wiped his eyes and said he really wanted to stay with us. That settled it. Initially, the plan was for him to live at our house for the school weeks and go home on the weekends. We had no idea how long this arrangement would last, so at first I set him up in the basement with a sofa bed and used a screen to separate his bed from the rest of the room.

He carried his clothes into our home, packed inside black trash bags and a single duffel bag he received from the school football program, just as I had moved my belongings throughout my childhood.

Ryan's moving in was more of a progression than a change. He was already staying with us until nine or ten o'clock each night, and my schedule already resembled an airport departure board.

7:40 a.m.: Drop Ranim and Justin at Sidwell
8:10 a.m.: Drop Elie at Norwood School
3:30 p.m.: Pick Elie up at Norwood
4–5 p.m.: Elie to Ms. Levin for tutoring
5:30 p.m.: Pick up Ranim, Ryan, and Justin at Sidwell
6:35 p.m.: Leave to take Elie to swimming
8 p.m.: Pick Elie up at swimming
9 p.m.: Take Ryan home

That was Monday. Tuesday was Elie's SSAT vocabulary tutoring day, with a late pickup at Norwood and a stop at Chipotle to grab dinner on the way. The rest of the week looked very much the same.

I was awake by five o'clock each morning to make Justin, Elie, and Ranim breakfast; adding one more plate wasn't a huge stretch. I don't know whether it was my own years of hunger and deprivation, love, or channeling the pent-up residual energy that had once been directed at a hard-charging, overachieving corporate legal life into the creation of elaborate breakfasts, but I fixed custom omelets or put out vast cheese boards and bowls of hard-boiled eggs and assorted fruit every morning, trying to have things that were familiar to Ranim. I went to a Middle Eastern store and stocked up on imported cheeses, hummus, and other things that she loved. I cooked chicken sausages or turkey bacon (Ranim is Muslim, so no pork products). I made breakfast sandwiches, like English muffins with an egg and cheese. The boys wanted two of those almost every morning. My signature meal item was fruit smoothies. Rather than their alarms, they woke to the sound of the blender, which told them that it was time to run downstairs because the food was on the table.

It's easy to perceive the outward structural changes to a family and a life when a new person joins you, the adjustments to a daily schedule, the complex route and carpool dance to get three teenage children and one tween from one location to another (two different schools and three separate sports), the routine questions about homework and study time, even the laundry cycle. It's the emotional needs that are subtler, the pivotal pieces that sneak up on you or that you never expect, such as when Ryan came to me on one of our first mornings and haltingly asked me to pick his Afro and to please do it the way his mom had always done.

It was a profound request. Ryan's hair was a cornerstone of his identity, and for his entire life, his mother had been the one to do his hair. Asking me was both incredibly hard and a powerful act of trust. Ryan and I went to Sally's, a beauty supply store specializing in Black hair care, and bought products, both the ones that he used and some others to try. The first time, I was terrified that I would pull out his hair, between the heat of the dryer and the pull of the sharp-edged comb on his dry hair. I was sure I was going to leave him with massive bald spots. Or worse, hurt him. I looked up dozens of videos on YouTube, and I tried to follow his directions.

Our first morning, I spent forty-five minutes before school trying to get it right. The top was okay, but the sides were awful. Ryan arrived at Sidwell looking like a conehead. The next morning, his hair was lopsided, too much on the left side, too little on the right. On the third day, I followed him to the hallway mirror. He looked up and down and pronounced his verdict: "I love it." My eyes welled up, and we hugged. That became our ritual every morning, at least thirty, but more often forty-five minutes of him sitting in a chair at the kitchen table and me standing behind him, holding a blow-dryer and the pick, followed by a trip to the mirror. Meanwhile, Elie would use the noise of the blow-dryer as a backup alarm. She knew if she didn't get out of bed that very second, she would be wearing her fuzzy pajamas to school.

There is something deeply personal about caring for another human being in that way. I came to know each curve and indentation of Ryan's head, the spots where his hair was slightly more unruly, and where I had to spend extra time. I could sense his mood by how he sat, the tension he carried in his shoulders, and their slight slump under the weight of the world. I could gauge how tired he was by how often he rubbed his eyes.

Then there was the unique familiarity of the laundry bag. I started doing Ryan's laundry, just as I did Justin's, Elie's, and Ranim's. Right away, I saw that his T-shirts and underwear were in tatters, the material had worn down until it was tissue-thin, and there were holes where the cotton weave had pulled away from the elastic and the seams, a level of disrepair that must have been hard to conceal in the Sidwell locker room. Very matter-of-factly, I said to Ryan that he would probably be more comfortable in some clothes that would last in our washer.

We went shopping for new things, but the following week, when I put his laundry in the machine, I noticed the same disintegrating T-shirts and unraveling underwear; Ryan's new things had disappeared. Gingerly, I broached the topic, saying I had favorite clothes that I couldn't part with, but why wasn't Ryan wearing his new ones? "I don't have them anymore" was his reply. It was spoken with a measure of finality as if this were the end of the conversation. I didn't press it. I replaced a few of the undershirts, a couple of pairs of underwear, and some pairs of socks for a second time.

Later, I learned that Ryan had given his new things to Kenny, his older brother, who still lived at home with Rochelle, when he returned to the apartment on the weekends. Ryan said that he felt it was "unfair" that he had new clothes when Kenny could not.

"Okay," I said, "but they are your things."

After a couple of months had passed, I uncovered a bit more context about fair and unfair: Ryan told me that Kenny had been awarded a scholarship to study at Penn State, but Rochelle and Leonard couldn't cover the rest of the costs. Kenny's scholarship offer vanished, and so did the opportunity. There would be no college for Kenny. Guilt is a terrible thing for a fifteen-year-old to cart around, far weightier than a few garbage bags of clothing. As I knew from my own life, family dysfunction is like a ripple. It is not simply the stone that drops to the bottom; it is also the wave that pulses outward, expanding and expanding, until it covers everyone and everything, including us.

I made sure Ryan had whatever he needed at our house, even an allowance. I gave him one along with Justin, Elie, and Ranim; if you were living under my roof, I did not differentiate. What I wish now that I had done much earlier was to intervene at Sidwell.

I was a new parent at the school. I was worried about overstepping, even though one of my earliest conversations with Rochelle had circled around to the question of whether I would be willing to help her with navigating Sidwell. The communication system from the school was geared toward a specific collection of parents. It relied almost exclusively on emails and newsletters, and it was weighted toward parents with constant access to computers or unlimited-data smartphones and ample time to read. It assumed that the chime of an arriving email and a quick glance to see a Sidwell return address were somehow galvanizing to all parents. Rochelle worked as the property manager for their Section 8 apartment building, which is a euphemistic way of saying that most of the tenants were low-income or in need of government financial support. She was rarely at her desk, and when she was, her inbox was already crowded with tenant requests, information from the building owner, emails from the county, and from contractors.

Her job was also quite different from those of other working parents at Sidwell. As I heard it, when one of the tenants at the complex became irate and menacing over a dispute, Rochelle had started backing away from him, and in her haste, fell hard off a curb, hurting her back and seriously injuring her ankle. She had to endure several ankle surgeries, and the time away from work and the recovery made it difficult for her to keep up with the information stream from Sidwell. She had a long list of other priorities that didn't involve her youngest son's private school. And the entire school communications system also comfortably assumed that she was well-versed in what to do next and knew exactly which person or office to reach out to and what to reply.

"Are you able to do that?" she asked me when I made the offer. "Yes, please help with the school; help him with his classes." She had seen some of the emails from the school about Ryan's failing grades. From that moment on, she repeatedly wrote her own emails, giving me permission to see his grades and to speak with the teachers and administrators to handle his academics and any other needs at Sidwell. In reply, the school said nothing. It was the electronic version of stone-cold silence, a digital disapproving glare.

I asked the school for the log-in information for Educator Online, the software program that showed Ryan's grades and assignments, so I could check on them the way I did for Justin, and the answer from Sidwell was to ignore my request, even though I had all the log-in information for Ranim, our exchange student, and Sidwell had been eager to share it. Instead, Rochelle gave me her log-in information. However, it was a fraught arrangement because I couldn't see the emails alerting her to problems, and the system periodically required her to change her password. If she neglected to tell me after she had changed it, I couldn't log in. When it came to Ryan's school needs, I was too often the proverbial "a day late and a dollar short."

I've read so much about the concept of the "white savior complex." It hangs out there, a blanket assumption over every action, every decision. But should I have refused to help simply because I feared how I might be perceived? Of course, we made mistakes in our new role; I made mistakes. But I made mistakes with Justin and Elie. How could I have offered Ryan food and shelter, but not the same level of intangible love and support that I was willing to give my own kids? As a family, we were fortunate enough to be in a place where we could help Ryan, and this was about helping someone who needed help, who didn't have anyone able to push back against the system and to advocate on his behalf.

What was unfortunate was that most of the things I did and could do to help Ryan at school came down to an equation where the constants were always that I could make the time to pursue the problem and I had the advantage of money, not simply by virtue of the significant tuition payments we made, but the amplifying all-important donations that the school counted on. "Name families" brought their prestigious names, but there were literally hundreds more who wielded the weight of their checkbooks, and that gave them position and access. I could withdraw school support if I wanted to (and at one point, I did).

I also possessed the force multiplier of years of legal wrangling: I was prepared to write, document, and argue every issue. People listened to me—and were forced to listen—because I had a seat at the table. Thus, I was in a unique position to help Ryan. My purpose was not to "save" Ryan, but to give him tools so that he could flourish on his own. Too many times, I saw the perhaps unintentional ways that the systems put into place at elite schools (not just Sidwell) pushed him down. These systems were designed to benefit students who were able to be at school on time, who had safe environments to complete schoolwork, or who had the money for tutors to help them in areas of deficiency. I wanted to help Ryan build some form of a safety net that other students innately possessed but that was nonexistent for him. Ryan worked extremely hard to change his grades from Ds to Bs, putting in long nights of studying. This was all him, his own efforts, and his own brain. I was just there as a support. If he needed something, if he asked for something, I could and would provide it for him.

A few teachers and administrators did not like that I, or sometimes Tom and I, went to Ryan's parent-teacher conferences and that I handled forms and emailed the school on Ryan's parents' behalf. One, in particular, was deeply opposed to allowing me access to any information about Ryan. She did everything in her power to set up roadblocks, no matter how often Rochelle wrote to request that I be given access. This administrator viewed Tom and me as the stereotypical do-gooders, swooping in and taking this kid away from his parents. At one point, after another round of bad grades, I said to the administrator, "Look, Ryan really needs some extra help in Spanish, and I'd like to see if we can get him a tutor. I don't know if the school will help us with that."

And her reply was "What Ryan really needs is his mother."

I took a deep breath and said, "Well, yeah, he does. And that is why I try to help Rochelle do things for Ryan when she doesn't have the time or the ability to do so."

I paused and then said to her, "Do you realize that it's Ryan's mother who asked us to have him live with us? She asked us to keep him at our house and to take care of all of this. She needs our help right now, and I intend to do what I can."

The administrator looked impassively back and said, "Why doesn't his mom call us?"

"Well," I said, struggling to keep my voice even, "she has called. And emailed. Several times. So why won't you help?" She just shrugged dismissively and said nothing. Conversation closed.

In December, after the end of the football season, Ryan had to have shoulder surgery. He had a hereditary shoulder issue, and football had added stress and injuries. He needed his tendons repaired. If ever there was a plan set up to fail, it was this one. The surgical schedule forced him to miss all his final exams in early January, and almost immediately after he was discharged from the recovery room, his family dropped him off at our house. He had a shirt slung over his shoulders, with his immobilized arm underneath. With his good arm, he was clutching his backpack and a garbage bag, balled up like a sack. I realized, without a word being spoken, that I was going to be responsible for taking care of him. He needed help taking on and off the surgical sling, getting a shirt over his head, zipping his hoodie, and even having someone cut up the food on his plate because he only had the use of one hand. He needed someone to squeeze the toothpaste onto his toothbrush, and he needed to be propped up on pillows to sleep, so as not to roll over and damage his arm. He needed someone to make sure he took enough, but not too much, pain medication. He needed help going to follow-up medical appointments and physical therapy.

After a few days, I realized that Ryan would not be going back to Silver Spring, even on most weekends. He would be living with us for at least the rest of the school year. A pullout couch would not do; he should have a permanent room. I moved the exercise equipment out of the exercise room downstairs and borrowed an extra bed from our neighbors. I bought new bedding and hung posters and other decorations on the walls. I bought a rug so he didn't have to walk on the home gym's rubber floor. I bought a new desk and chair so he'd have his own place to study. I cleared out the overflow closet. When it was complete, I said, "Okay, here's your room." And I watched him exhale.

In mid-January, when school resumed after final exams, I learned that Ryan was failing almost every class.

seven

Inside the Sidwell cafeteria, the regimented rows of bland industrial tables, utilitarian chairs, and the almost complete absence of color gave off an air of uniformity and simplicity, a kind of industrial asceticism. It was a mirage. What appeared utilitarian on the surface was, in fact, a plainness created by the highest-quality materials and illuminated by a complex lighting design artfully hung from the ceiling. Even the food itself followed this dichotomy: yes, it was a cafeteria, but it was known as "the lunchroom." The school emphasized how the kitchen served locally sourced, farm-to-table cuisine with international flavors. There were vegetarian options, a make-your-own deli bar, and a supply of local, farm-fresh milk as well as soy and almond milk. The soups were made from scratch, the granola was home-baked and sweetened with maple syrup, and the chicken was cooked with coconut milk. There was a yogurt cart. The chefs had culinary school training. It was not anything resembling a typical high school hot or cold lunch.

The arrangement of the tables themselves became a study in

student hierarchies and teenage tribalism, an inner ring of the popular kids and an outer ring of the exiles, their positions fixed and unchanging. I remember one of my first times passing by the lunchroom, glancing in and noticing that the Black football players and Justin were all clustered at one table on the periphery, while the rest of the white football players sat together, joking, front and center in another part of the room. I didn't fully appreciate this level of segregation during Justin and Ryan's ninth-grade year. No one at the school highlighted what happened after you got your tray and before the leftovers were deposited in the compost bins.

What I did see is that every time Ryan came with us into downtown Bethesda, someone from his old middle school would stop to talk to him. If we went out to eat and happened to be seated by a window, invariably a couple of kids swimming in their new, oversized high school sweatshirts would bang on the glass to get Ryan's attention. When Elie had recitals at the Levine Music school, so many people in the audience knew Ryan. He had that bright-light charisma that is seen in pro athletes and celebrities, a magnetic pull where people were swept up like filaments and happy to congregate around him. But when he entered Sidwell, all of that magnetism vanished. Ryan was starting over at the bottom, trying to find his way inside a very different ecosystem where the top spots had already been allotted and taken.

I don't need much in the way of therapy to know that I am a fixer. In a world of nail heads, I'm the person marching around with the hammer, banging away. But the impulse isn't always wrong; sometimes, there are things desperately in need of fixing. Ryan's teeth were one of them. They were covered in brown stains. Being at a school like Sidwell, where personalized orthodontics were a rite of passage, made Ryan's imperfections even more noticeable. I decided that we had to get Ryan's teeth whitened—and not just with whitening trays. The level of discoloration in his mouth required a special machine to essentially shave the brown layer off his teeth. I prevailed upon a dentist friend to treat Ryan so he could have the teeth to match his winning smile. The same was true for Ryan's speech. He had a stutter that, along with the teeth, inclined him to say very little or even nothing in class. I could afford to pay for a speech pathologist to work with him, and I did.

Fixing things with Sidwell and Ryan's academics was infinitely harder. I found tutors to try to get Ryan back to passing grades, which was vital if he was going to stay on the football team, not to mention apply to college someday. I scheduled parent-teacher conferences. I would arrive with folders with Ryan's test papers, homework, and tutors' notes as if I could somehow find the elusive answer in a document deep in the file or, more likely, as if I were the defense attorney building a case for Ryan. I routinely emailed polite requests for meetings, conferences, or additional support. When I got nowhere, I had the tutors write their own polite notes and make phone calls. Dani, the main tutor, wrote to one of Ryan's teachers, explaining why she had included me in the email. "Ryan has been living with Sandi for the past several weeks, and she and her family have been instrumental in helping him improve academically. We would love to set up a meeting to discuss his progress and how we can help him going forward." The reply from the teacher was that she would not meet with the tutor, Ryan, and me, and that, instead, I should contact her directly.

But there were a few teachers who did reach out. Occasionally, emails such as this one would arrive in my inbox: "Hi—hope all is well. A quick question . . . I believe that Ryan has been living with you (?) If yes, I just wanted to check in with you—he did not seem himself this week—do you know anything about this? He was uncharacteristically quiet, tired, and somber. Thanks—would appreciate any insight you have."

I wrote back that I had noticed the same thing, that I thought

Ryan's family situation weighed on him, and I mentioned that he was struggling "a bit" with his studies. I added, "His family situation is also embarrassing for him, so it is difficult to get him to talk much about it."

Or maybe "embarrassing" was more my word, and me projecting my past. Ryan had chosen to handle the discordant parts of his life via separation, erecting invisible walls, and trying to compartmentalize the different facets. He had started off by calling me Sandi, then he stepped back to Mrs. McCoy. Eventually, he started calling me "Mom Two."

Around the start of sophomore year, all of us were shopping at Nordstrom: Ryan, Justin, Elie, and our newest exchange student, Laixin, who had recently arrived from China. Everyone was calling me "Mom," and all the salespeople looked at me as if to say, *What is going on?* Finally, a young Black man working in the men's section nodded in my direction and asked Ryan, "So . . . who is she to you?"

And Ryan said, "This is my second mom." And the salesman was clearly astonished.

"You have two biological moms?" he blurted out. All of us spent years laughing at that one.

But there were other times that were not laughable, where, instead, for a moment, I experienced a glimmer of deeper understanding. After Ryan came to stay with us full-time following his shoulder surgery, I took him to both his physical therapy appointments and follow-up visits with the doctor. As we sat in the waiting room before one visit, an older white woman walked up to us and said that she wanted to touch Ryan's hair. By this point, Ryan had an absolutely perfect Afro. I had learned to pick it properly in the mornings; we were going to the right place to get it cut. But that did not make his hair "public property." I could feel my eyes widening in horror, and I stammered out, "Yeah . . . no."

She looked at us and said in a clipped voice, "You know, I've *been* to Africa." Ryan was staring at her as if he had unwittingly entered a freak show in the middle of a bland waiting room with rows of attached chairs.

"What does that have to do with anything?" I asked.

"Well, I've been to Africa. I've met Black people before, and I really want to touch his hair."

I could not believe this was happening. "No. Absolutely not," I replied.

She wasn't even chastened as she walked away.

Afterward, I was furious with myself for not standing up sooner and for not making more of a scene to protect Ryan, and I felt ashamed. This woman felt entitled to touch Ryan's hair. *His hair*. As if it were some kind of common property. How many people did things like this? How often did it happen? I talked to Ryan about the woman and what had happened. He tried to laugh it off but was clearly shaken. It was also an ingrained part of his experience. And if he spoke up or tried to stop her hand, Ryan first had to weigh the risk of negative consequences for himself. This moment in a waiting room changed how I saw the world. There was so much that was profoundly unsettling about this casual assumption of possession and the expectation that another human being is there for the touching.

The kitchen was the room in our house where everyone felt comfortable. It was my place of business and busyness. Often, there was a long list of repetitive cooking tasks waiting to be done: washing, rinsing, chopping, stirring. Being together in the kitchen didn't require excessive eye contact; there was simply the slow putter of familiar routines. The kitchen was where the kids could complain about Tom's extended work absences, and where Ryan could cry about how much he missed his family, his guilt over having left his brother behind, and at the same time, his guilt at not wanting to be in the chaos of his home.

Having Ryan move in with us wasn't a completely radical choice in the world of Sidwell. There were a few students with long commutes who did stay with closer-in families during the weekdays, but most of those arrangements were a bit more like Ranim's or Laixin's presence, like having a domestic exchange student, rather than assuming the role of managing the complexity of another student's learning struggles and overall life. And in each of those cases, it was an affirmative choice made by the students and parents together. Rochelle's choice was more unilateral and more one of desperation, rooted in dead ends and overwhelm, of something closer to surrender to circumstances and a school environment that made no effort to meet her where she was. Ryan didn't protest; like someone who had been washed into the floodwaters of a wide river, he was simply being carried along.

Initially, it was somewhat hard on Elie. Where was the fairness in Justin being able to have a friend stay over every night? However, the two of them gradually developed an inseparable bond. Ryan was constantly looking out for Elie, from teasingly reminding her to stop procrastinating and "DO YOUR HOMEWORK!" or to clean her messy room, or the small, heartfelt things, like sensing when she was tired and quietly saying, *It's a beautiful day, don't forget to appreciate it.* Only gradually did I begin to appreciate what it took for Ryan to find beauty in an ordinary day.

The constant fight-or-flight response that I remember coursing through me in my own childhood, the lack of knowledge and the uncertainties that I felt around my father's many prolonged absences—I could see flashes of it in Ryan. I recognized it, but at the same time, I didn't want to project my experiences onto him. I didn't want to assume that the parallels in our stories somehow made our stories similar, let alone the same. Instead, I hoped that my past would help him become more comfortable and feel safe. That he would come to trust me.

It took almost a year of us knowing each other, of me becoming

Mom Two, of the hair violation and shoulder recovery, before Ryan told me about the closet in his apartment.

I can picture Ryan standing on the landing of the stairs that led to the basement, his hand on the banister, getting ready to walk down to his room. It was a Thursday night; the next night, he would be heading home for the weekend. When he got well enough, he started going back from time to time. It was not yet football season, so Friday nights were still quiet. Ryan said something about the difficulties with his dad and mentioned what his mom had told me about their home not being safe. I set down whatever dish was in my hand, turned around, and responded with a quiet "Do you want to tell me about it?" He nodded slowly.

In a soft voice, Ryan explained how his mother would stuff him and his two brothers inside the closet when men armed with guns pounded on the apartment door, demanding to be let in and demanding that she pay them the money that his father owed. Eventually, after being instructed often enough to hide in the closet, Ryan and Kenny learned to run for the dark space themselves and pull the door shut behind them at the first sounds of balled-up fists on the apartment door. Or if Kenny wasn't there, Ryan did it alone. Ryan was a big kid. A few sentences about how much the tiny dark closet terrified him, and it was easy for me to envision the rest, to imagine the stale air, the small space, the need to be silent, even fearing that your breathing might be too loud. All these decades later, I still feel profoundly uneasy if I am inside any sort of confined space in the dark.

Ryan explained how he would have to remain excruciatingly still, with no rustling or repositioning. His foot would tingle, and his leg would gradually go numb. He'd listen to the heated voices and hear the echoes of feet as the men moved around the rooms, sometimes sounding almost catlike in running sneakers or moving with a heavy tread in thick-soled basketball shoes or tough boots on the other side of the thin plywood door. Ryan would concentrate on keeping his breath low and shallow, not making a sound, nothing to give him away. He would listen for the sounds of his mother, her voice rising and falling, her footsteps coming and going as she tried to bargain with them and then root around for enough cash to hold them off. Sometimes, he could hear a drawer being opened, but she always tried to ignore the closet door. Neither of them knew where Leonard was or what else he might be spending their limited money on at that very moment. I remember that when Ryan told me about the closet, he kept his gaze down, his soft voice dropping straight to the floor. I wondered if he had ever memorized where the closets were in my house.

Although I mostly listened, I did occasionally talk to Ryan about how it was okay for him to be his own person, to have an independent identity that did not seek to absorb the family chaos. But I failed to take my own advice to heart. My fixer-self wanted to help not only Ryan but also Rochelle. I got involved, and probably, almost certainly in retrospect, overly involved. Yet at the same time, how could I not? Especially when I saw up close how the system failed families like Leonard, Rochelle, Chris (Ryan's oldest brother, who had moved to Seattle), Kenny, and Ryan. Or at a minimum, took extreme advantage of their circumstances.

Chronically short on cash, Rochelle borrowed money from payday lenders and shady internet sites, which operated using false street addresses, where a small debt quickly ballooned with massive interest rates and hidden fees. Which was then followed by demands for money and threats. Predatory lenders have a lot in common with drug dealers, hooking you in with small enticements and easy promises, and then once they have you, it's all but impossible to quit.

At one point, Rochelle borrowed money online from a disingenuously named outfit called "CashNow." When the payments came due, she asked us for help. Tom offered to function as her lawyer, and he battled with the online services to be sent copies of the loan agreement, account statements, and a list of debts and credits. But untangling that loan mess was nothing compared to another struggle: getting the family car out of repossession.

During one of Leonard's benders, the family's GMC Yukon had been repossessed on a street where Leonard had gone to use drugs. He had stopped making the car payments, and getting the car out of repossession was going to cost close to $6,000. Rochelle couldn't leave her job at the apartment complex, so I offered to retrieve the car. It became one of the most challenging, bizarre, creepy, and awful things I have done in my life. It wasn't that I didn't understand the underlying process or the tactics. I was familiar with creditors, liens, and the risk of repossession from my childhood. Creditors were constantly chasing my father, and he never filed or paid taxes. For all I know, some of the times when he disappeared, it was because he had been arrested. He owed many people and institutions money. But I was a child; I never had to answer for anything about his financial recklessness. I only had to live with the consequences—strange food, terrible clothes, shacks, or trailers without electricity or running water to live in, and kitchen-bowl haircuts.

Now Ryan was living with those consequences. Some Sidwell families might have been carrying large sums of credit card debt or relying on home equity credit lines to cover expense gaps, but as far as I knew, no one was coming for their cars. Ryan would walk out into the parking garage and see the older boys on the football team who had their driver's licenses speed off behind the wheel in the family's cast-off BMW or an "extra" Mercedes SUV. I didn't want to make Ryan feel awkward, but I wanted to get his family car back. We had the resources, and some stability for Ryan's family was a way to help Ryan. But when I got on the phone with the repo people, it quickly became very clear that they did not want to return the car; they wanted to sell it.

They refused to accept a wire transfer—"No, we don't take wires."

"Wires are like cash," I told them.

"Well, no, we don't take them" came the reply. I asked if I could pay with a cashier's check. They didn't take those, either. The only thing they would accept was a Western Union money order, and the only way to pay for that was with cash at a physical Western Union counter inside a grocery store or gas station. There was also an additional daily charge tacked on to the $6,000 charge for each day they had to wait for the money order. My only option was to withdraw $6,000 in cash from our accounts. I called Tracy, the woman I worked with at our bank, and told her that I needed to find an ATM and withdraw $6,000. Her first response was "That's not safe."

"I know," I replied, "but I'm going to go to the safest ATM I can find. I need to get the cash to Western Union and get a car out of repossession." This problem was not something that Tracy, who worked in private banking, had ever dealt with before. My daily withdrawal limit was raised, and I ended up at an ATM on a street corner near a Safeway in Potomac, Maryland (the only place I had been able to find a Western Union service counter), making multiple $500 withdrawals in increments of $20, because this machine didn't give me any other options. A line of people waiting to get access to the ATM started to form, and, despite the upscale area, I was convinced I was going to be mugged as I kept stuffing stacks of cash into my purse. Clutching my bag tightly, I parked at the Safeway and walked inside to the Western Union counter.

Six thousand dollars equals three hundred $20 bills, and I learned that it takes a very long time to count out three hundred bills. I don't think the clerk had ever counted so many bills before, and he kept making mistakes and having to start over. At one point, he picked up the cash, and in the process of trying to move it, the entire stack in his hands fluttered to the floor. I watched hundreds of images of Andrew Jackson's face spiral down, sinking like a strange kind of oversized rectangular confetti toward the dirty, tan linoleum. All the while, I panicked that individual bills would be lost, and I would be short the money I needed for my money order. I dropped to my knees, and the clerk and I were both crawling around trying to scoop up the bills, some of which were sticking to the floor, while another line of people who needed customer service was forming.

Finally, we had the bills counted and the money order paid for and sent. But the car situation still wasn't resolved. The impound lot was 250 miles from Washington, DC, and it was going to cost another $500 to get the car released from the lot. This was where I drew a boundary; I was not traveling five hundred miles round trip to pick up the Yukon. I told Rochelle that she was going to have to take the bus to retrieve the car. I gave her money for the impound fee and bus fare.

When you are a fixer, and you are in the thick of it, it's easy to believe that this repair will be the one that makes things better or that changes the dynamic. But the situation looked different because Rochelle desperately wanted things to change, too. She prayed every day to God to "open up a door for me," as she wrote in one email. And I could see how much harder the doors were for her. Financial means and connections are guarantors of help. Tom and I knew where to find the loopholes, how to navigate them, and how to push through to the other side. I hadn't always known any of this, just as I hadn't known how to eat properly at an expensive restaurant, how to dress appropriately, or how to write a thank-you note. But I had been given the opportunity to learn. Rochelle hadn't. And payday lenders and repo companies counted on that.

Rochelle was incredibly grateful, as she was every time. The praise that she sent in her emails and expressed in person was so deep that it was almost embarrassing. "Sandi, I cannot thank you enough for what you are doing to help Ryan and my family. God has a way of working with people and bringing people together for a reason. I am so glad that this is the path for you and me. Keep smiling, keep shining, you are an angel. Love you from the bottom of my heart, Rochelle."

Rochelle and I took to calling each other "sweet sister" and "my sister." I kept her updated on Ryan's grades and even his haircuts. I copied Rochelle on the emails to the school. Ryan was back in Silver Spring for most of the summer, but in early August, when football season started up, he was returned to his room downstairs, and our lives slipped back into their old routines.

It seemed that none of the protective steps we had put in place in ninth grade transferred over to tenth grade for Ryan and his classes. When Ryan and Justin's sophomore year started, I had to try all over again to have Ryan's classes added to my Educator Online account. I wrote to one of the administrators about receiving Ryan's weekly interim grades "so we could monitor how he was doing and adjust early if there was an issue." Ryan had been getting weekly grade reports ever since he had nearly failed out the previous winter.

"Is that still happening this year?" I asked in one email. "If so, could you add my email to the recipients of those interims? I am copying Ryan's mom in case there is any question she needs to answer as part of this process." Unfortunately, the access never materialized.

Rochelle was still dealing with her injuries from the tenant altercation. I told her about back-to-school night and Ryan's teachers and classes and sent her photographs. And we prayed for each other.

In September, Rochelle wrote, "Things here at home are better. My husband is doing better, but I am still praying that this keeps up. As you know, the mood can change, and I am hoping that it will not. So, for right now, it is okay. Please keep us in your prayers as I know you do."

I replied, "I'm so glad to hear that things are getting better. I will continue to pray that they stay that way." We spoke about the two of us going to dinner and a movie outside of the times I saw her at football games or occasionally drove her when Leonard was off with the car.

eight

Like Ryan and Justin in the lunchroom, I was not part of the close-knit group of Sidwell families that had come up through the system since the Lower School. Some days, it felt like I was standing on the other side of an invisible wall. I needed to go under, around, or over. I tried all three: I started volunteering inside the school. I became the football team photographer, first using a long lens from the stands and eventually prowling the sidelines to capture images of players and the game. And I started hosting team dinners—cooking up an SUV trunkful of food purchased on massive Costco runs—that morphed into mass sleepovers at our house on Friday nights before the Saturday morning games. Air mattresses and sleeping bags were strewn about the house; almost all the available floor space was filled with sleeping boys. I had no plan when I started to do this. I certainly didn't set out to build so much of my life around the school; rather, it was more that the school was available. It and I had mutual needs and mutual space to fill.

My first stop was volunteering in the office of the dean of students, where I assisted with attendance and fielding questions from teachers, students, and parents. Here, I saw the heart and soul of Sidwell. I was able to see and visit with nearly every ninth through twelfth grader as they signed in upon late arrival or out for lunch or outside appointments. I was able to visit with teachers who would drop by to say hello or to hand-deliver their attendance sheets, which had to be logged into the computer system. I'd visit with the Secret Service agents who patrolled the halls trying to keep track of their charges (and who frequently asked if I had seen where one or another of them had run off to—the Obama girls loved to escape their "keepers"). Slowly, I learned a lot about the people who were contributing members of the school community and those who were not.

Repeatedly, I could also see the subtle ways the school wasn't prepared for students like Ryan. Almost unconsciously, expectations shifted, and there was a subtle belief that a student like Ryan would have a different trajectory. Something as simple as an email about summer writing tutoring came with a hint of disappointment, even condescension, and unmet expectations. As the ninth-grade school year had finished, Sidwell's learning support coordinator wrote to Ryan, "Ms. B___ told me that you were interested in writing tutoring this summer. Ms. S___ would be available to meet with you for 10 individual sessions. Both Ms. B___ and I think that she would be the best person for you to work with since she clearly knows the expectations at SFS. Let me know if you would like to follow up."

Tenth grade began for Ryan in an even more tenuous manner. He knew that he was attending Sidwell because of football, but due to a hereditary condition, he had issues with both of his shoulders. For a long time, he ignored his shoulder pain and told no one. After he started living with us, Ryan would have long talks with me and would end up crying—a lot—about his shoulders. I purchased a special brace that the team doctor recommended, but Ryan still couldn't play properly. Fairly early in the season, it became clear that he was going to need surgery on the other shoulder. With his ability to play limited, and thus his utility to the team minimized, the coaches and some of his teammates largely ignored Ryan. From the sidelines, he followed the action on the field with his eyes.

I generally considered Ryan to be a fearless kid, but he was terrified of needles. I learned this when I took him to the doctor's office for a flu shot and we entered the exam room. He saw the needle being pulled from its plastic sleeve and he tried to bolt. The problem was that Ryan had asthma, and he had gotten the flu once while living with us—a terrifying experience of wheezing and sending him to stand under a hot, steamy shower, as well as using multiple inhalers and medications. I did not want him to go through that again, not under my roof, and not while he was recovering from major orthopedic surgery, hence the flu shot in the fall of his sophomore year. As I saw him leap up, I ran and barred the door. Then I wrapped my arms around him, got him into a sitting position, and held him while the nurse gave him the shot.

The flu shot was fresh in my mind as Ryan prepared for his next shoulder surgery. The original plan was for Ryan's parents to take him to the hospital for the surgery, and I would meet Ryan in the recovery room and take him home to recover at our house. Then the plan shifted: Ryan would spend the night at our house, Leonard would pick him up in the morning and take him to the hospital, and I would get him after surgery. When Leonard arrived with Ryan, I insisted that he sign a special consent form, witnessed by my neighbor Joan, who was also a doctor, which would allow me to pick Ryan up at the hospital. The form wasn't notarized, it was only witnessed, because I didn't need anything more than that to drive him home. After he signed it,

Leonard promised that he would be back early in the morning to get Ryan and drive him to the hospital.

Instead, Leonard took the car and left on a bender. But I didn't know that. I got Ryan up and waited with him near the front door—no breakfast because of the surgery. He was wearing his baggy sweats and looked hungry and tired. It was as if we could hear the clock tick, minute by minute. We both paced a bit, knowing Ryan was due at the hospital in downtown DC, a trip that would take time because of morning traffic. Finally, we could not wait any longer. We grabbed our things and jumped into the car to race to George Washington University Hospital.

On the way, Rochelle called my cell, which automatically defaulted to the car's speakerphone because of the Bluetooth connection. With her voice filling the front seat, she told Ryan that she was sorry, but she could not come to his surgery because "your dad took off with the car," and "you guys"—meaning Ryan and his brother—"are the ones who said I had to stay with him." I glanced over at Ryan, who had started to cry, big, blubbery tears rolling down his cheeks. So much emotion and responsibility were being hoisted onto his literal broken shoulder. I abruptly told Rochelle we had to go and ended the call.

I parked in the cavernous concrete lot, walked Ryan through the pneumatic doors that closed with a hiss, and got us into reception. I had all the ID and insurance cards ready, fanned out like playing cards, even a credit card, if we needed one. "Where is your medical power of attorney?" the intake specialist asked, clicking away on the computer keyboard, punching in codes, as Ryan and I squeezed together on the other side of the chaotic check-in counter. I handed the paper to her. She scanned it. "This isn't notarized."

Pulling up my best lawyer voice, I answered, "Right, it's witnessed."

"Well," she said, starting to hand it back, "we can't accept anything that isn't notarized."

I knew if I allowed her to return the letter, we would be dismissed. I kept standing there, my hands on the counter, and began the story. "Ryan is scheduled for surgery, and you have no idea what we've been through to get here." I had barely begun when Ryan started to sob. He was afraid of the surgery, afraid for his football abilities, his mother had just blamed him for the dysfunctional situation with his father, now the hospital was telling him he couldn't be admitted—thanks mainly to me not thinking ahead to get a notarized power of attorney and anticipating that I might have to drop him off, too.

We stood there, Ryan crying, me trying to argue my case, as the inner lawyer in me frequently tries to do, and the intake specialist restating the rules, until finally, the surgeon appeared. I knew him because he was the Sidwell football team doctor and I was the team photographer. We had chatted on the sidelines, making small talk and exchanging pleasantries and comments on the game. He pulled me aside and said the paper wasn't notarized.

"Yes," I replied, "but it was witnessed."

"By whom?" he asked.

"By my neighbor, Joan Kristal."

"Joan Kristal? Really?" he said, giving his head a slight shake. "I know Joan Kristal. We went to medical school together."

I took a deep breath and said the next logical thing. "Well, can you call Joan and confirm that she saw Leonard sign it and that she also signed it herself?" So, standing there at the admissions desk, that's what we did, and it worked. This was another situation that resolved itself simply because of the experience I had, where I lived, and who I was. Joan Kristal was our next-door neighbor, who happened to know the doctor performing Ryan's surgery. But for that serendipitous connection, Ryan would have been sent home, and the surgery would have been delayed. Instead, Ryan was handed his gown and sent to change.

The anesthesiologist came out, introduced himself, and explained that he was going to start with a nerve block, which would be injected through an IV line that they would implant in Ryan's neck. It was like a needle on steroids (at least four inches long). They told Ryan to lie flat on the surgical table, and I held his hand as they found the vein and placed the line. I could feel his palm, clammy and cold, and the way his fingers clung to mine. I watched the needle and felt my own stomach tighten.

I was ushered out and sent to sit on the slick vinyl waiting room chairs to flip through magazines or scroll through email on my phone. Afterward, the doctor appeared in his surgical scrubs, with a white coat hastily added, and his surgical cap slightly askew. The repair had gone well, he said. He gave me the rundown of instructions, pain medications, changing the dressing, and what to look out for. Watching me trying to make mental notes, he added that I'd be given a summary of everything he was saying in the discharge instructions. It was all very routine, he said. Do the physical therapy, just as after the last surgery, and Ryan would be ready to get back out there on the field. He paused for a beat and then said, "You know, I remember his mom coming after the last one," meaning the last surgery, "and she seemed like a good person."

"She is a good person," I said without any hesitation. "She's just in a difficult situation right now. She's profoundly codependent, things became too challenging, and she couldn't be here." He nodded, and I walked back to wait with Ryan in the recovery room.

When Ryan was ready to leave, I pulled the car up to the exit and waited as they wheeled him down in a wheelchair. He grimaced as he came out, the chair's wheels bumping on the pitted concrete and thus bumping his shoulder, even with its bulky sling and stabilizer. Hospital liability concerns, I explained to him, which every lawyer recognizes, although it probably would have been less painful for him to walk out. I drove home as slowly as possible, avoiding any speed bumps or sudden braking. After we got inside, I helped him get comfortable on the couch with extra pillows and a throw blanket, gave him the pain meds that I had picked up at the hospital pharmacy, and heated some homemade soup.

After that day, Ryan stopped calling me Mom Two and started calling me by a new name: "Mama."

SANDI

nine

It was a chicken-and-egg dilemma: Was it my mother's paranoia, the amorphous thing that drove her to have us march around the house clutching our vacuum cleaner parts or send me off to ring the doorbell at the homes of attractive women, that led my father to disappear? Or did his ever-increasing disappearances create a climate that fueled my mother's fears and sent them spiraling further and further out of proportion? I had no answers. But by the time we moved into our third Utah house, he had started to vanish for longer and longer stretches, more and more often.

My parents also separated multiple times during this period, and with each separation, my mother became a bit more unhinged. She screamed at Kevin and me constantly, especially me. It was difficult to know which was worse: the times when our father was around or when he vanished, and Kevin and I had no idea when or if he might return. Because when he did return, the fights between our parents would start up again.

But the physical fighting wasn't confined only to altercations between the adults. My father's rage, in particular, was uncontained and unpredictable, which made it even more terrifying. One episode occurred because of my visit to a shopping mall. My father had promised to pick me up at the mall, but I had gone to the wrong location to meet him. He couldn't find me, and I couldn't find him, and by the time we found each other, he was furious. The moment we arrived home, I leaped out of the car and ran inside. He raced after me, burst through the front door, hauled me up off the ground, and threw me, slamming me face-first into the living room wall. My nose started bleeding. I managed to get to my feet, ran upstairs to my room, and locked the door. He followed, his feet pounding up the stairs. The lock was no match for him. He broke open the door, and as I crouched down, he seized my ankle and dragged my leg out from under me. "I'm going to break your leg," he growled, his voice laced with fury. There was no doubt in my mind that he meant it. He'd broken my nose three times.

I was eleven, maybe turning twelve. I'd always been scrawny, but I'd gotten a little bigger, and Eugene Smith was a short, dense man. I kicked him as hard as I could in the face with my other foot. His glasses splintered, the shards from the lenses embedded into his face. He screamed in pain as I ran past him, down the stairs, and out of the house without stopping.

I lost another pet over that incident. She was a kitten that I had found in the neighborhood and was nurturing back to health. I found her shot dead, her corpse collapsed in a small heap against the wall that I used to refer to as the "wall of death." My father thought nothing of killing my pets with a shotgun or picking up a hapless dog or cat by the tail and swinging it into the wall, although sometimes one of those survived, maimed but alive. But I'd learned an unexpected lesson that afternoon: I could fight back.

By the time I was twelve, I did begin to fight back. I started with my brother. Kevin and I were close in the sense that we depended on each other to survive. But we also approached survival in very different ways. Kevin was the golden child. During the times when my parents separated, they argued over which one of them would get to "keep" Kevin. If they had been asked to choose between the two of us, there would not have been a moment's hesitation. They would have spared Kevin every time. Kevin felt it. In the continuum of flight-or-fight responses, he came down on the side of flight. He was always trying to escape the chaos of the house. He often did, which meant we were often physically apart. I, on the other hand, became more of a fighter.

I wasn't an angry kid. All I wanted was to be left alone with a stack of books from the library, but I began to comprehend that I had to defend myself to survive. So I did. And I was determined to become good at it. Whether to atone for the lingering guilt of the moving-truck accident or simply my sense of responsibility as an older sister, I started out fighting for Kevin. When some middle school kids threw a baseball at Kevin, I leaped over the fence, and they were so shocked that they sprinted away. Slowly, I also started to defend myself. I slugged a girl at school when she and her group viciously made fun of me. At home, I began to fight back when my parents spun out of control, with me or each other. But with my parents, the harder I fought back, the harder they fought for control. We were due for a breaking point.

Somewhere around my fifth-grade year, whatever remained of my father's business had failed or had been lost, or he had simply burned through his investors' money and had run out of new, unsuspecting neighbors to attempt to charm, cajole, and persuade. He was now traveling to Idaho to try his hand at farming. The farming idea came from his older brother, Carlie, who had been responsible for some of our periodic financial rescues.

Carlie was the sibling who had made it out of Arkansas first and was quite successful. I'm not sure how he became responsible for bailing out Dad, but when he did, there were always strings attached. I couldn't see the strings, but somehow, they remained both taut and omnipresent. This time, the invisible string pulled us out of Utah, along the flat, long freight train routes that ran north through the red-rock-and-scrub-brush-lined landscape and across the border into Idaho, finally coming to rest in a small town named Mountain Home, south of the city of Boise.

There wasn't much at all mountainous about Mountain Home, other than it was possible to see mountains in the distance. The town had sprung up in a region of flat farming country that was bisected by the undulating curves of the Snake River. Somehow, my uncle had handed my father oversight of a farm that grew pinto beans, wheat, potatoes, and alfalfa on two separate plots of land. My mother, whose hatred of relatives was not confined to her own parents, hated Uncle Carlie with a passion, so his involvement in our move and my father's new vocation made her even angrier. She made no secret of how much she hated her brother-in-law.

My mother lived in a fantasy world of her own making. In that world, she viewed herself as the queen of the universe—a rich, successful wife and mother. The more our family was disliked or shunned, or the more my father failed, the more her fantasy was placed under siege, and the more enraged and extreme she became.

We didn't move all at once. It was a gradual process, rather like a frog being desensitized inside a slowly heating pot. My father started driving the four of us in one rattletrap car or another from Salt Lake to Idaho—a lot. We went during school holidays and sometimes even when school was in session, leaving my classroom desk empty for weeks on end. We were always gone during the summers. In Idaho, we lived not in a house, but in a series of mobile homes or shacks.

On the farm, some of the more permanent migrant workers who

tended the fields and picked the crops lived in a house. The seasonal workers, who came for the harvests, were housed in a dilapidated trailer in what might have been considered the house's backyard. We lived in a different trailer with no running water and only a generator for electricity. The setup worked except when my father didn't have money to pay for the gas required to operate the generator. Then the inside of the trailer was plunged into darkness as soon as the sun set, and it was always either too hot or too cold. Any fresh food spoiled.

Instead of having pipes and a faucet inside the trailer, we relied on a pump with a line that ran into a nearby pond for water. I lugged sloppy buckets back and forth to the trailer for cooking and the occasional washing. The trailer did have a toilet, but it used a tank to collect the waste, and that tank had to be emptied often because it was small. I was the one tapped to do it—for several years, my mother's nickname for me was "Shitty Sandi." Given the water situation, I'm not sure we ever regularly washed our hands. I don't recall any way to do it. There was always a black outline around our fingernails and burrowed into the lines in our palms.

In the mornings, Kevin and I followed a long dirt path from the trailer to the road to catch the bus for school. But I didn't go to school all the time because, according to both my parents, I was needed in the fields. My father still saw himself as an inventor, and his priority was remaking or inventing a combine to harvest the crops, so he sent me to weed.

On farm workdays, I'd head out in the early morning with the migrant workers and walk up and down the endless rows of pinto beans. Their dense, teardrop-shaped leaves unfurled from the slender stalks, but below, there was a war for domination. The weeds were constantly vying with the crop for control of the soil, sucking up the nutrients, and threatening to crowd out the delicate plants with their lumpy pods of beans. I had to crouch down to pull out the invading plants from below. It took hours to make it through a single row as the blazing summer sun climbed up in the sky. Some days, crop dusters flew overhead, ruffling our hair and even the backs of our sweat-damp shirts as they dropped down to buzz the fields and dump chemicals on the plants. The fine spray would indiscriminately rain down on everything—plants, soil, and people. I didn't think anything of it. I didn't even wash it off when I got home, since it wasn't as if I had a shower or bathtub, only the sloppy buckets carried from the pump by the pond.

I wasn't the only kid working in the fields. I made friends with Pepino, a boy close to my age whose parents were migrant workers. When we weren't working, we would run around the farm, and I started showing up with him at the house where his family lived near the migrant workers' trailers. Pepino's mother, Juanita, was often in the kitchen, cooking. The kitchen was tiny. There was barely enough room for two people, and even then, the people barely had space to turn around. The kitchen had a small refrigerator and a narrow two-burner stove, but everything that was frying or simmering always smelled amazing. Juanita would fix food for me, and I learned about traditional Mexican foods, including tripe, menudo, and mole. A constant stream of tortillas came off the stove. I would watch her rolling the thin dough and dropping each circle in the hot pan sizzling with lard. She would flip the disk at just the right moment so there was a slightly crispy surface on each side and the taste of soft, cooked dough in between. She made tamales, too, and let me help her so that I could learn how. Everything was so fresh, full of texture and flavor, not at all like our dinners of leathery, freezer-burned venison.

I would eagerly chew on my tortillas, which Juanita stacked on old, white Corningware plates that had been used for so long that they had accumulated a ring of chips around the edges. Because there was no space in the house, we'd sit outside on the ground or perched at a weathered wooden picnic table out front. If I moved wrong or slid slightly, the rough benches sent splinters in my behind. Both Juanita and Pepino's father, whose name was Junior, spoke enough English to get by, and I learned enough Spanish from them to make limited conversation possible. We would talk about food and the farm and the equipment my dad was trying to invent but that Junior could never make work. We'd talk about Pepino and whether he could go to school (he wanted very much to go to school, but he could not). Pepino spoke little to no English, and his mom would try to help me understand him. But over time, I was able to figure out enough on my own. I knew that he hated his name—it means "little pickle" in Spanish. And he did not like my parents because he didn't think that they treated his parents or me well. On that, we could definitely agree.

After my first couple of visits to Pepino's, I started to lie to my mother about where I had been. When she first learned that I had gone to the migrant house, her response had been to call me a "whore" for making friends with a Mexican. Except she didn't say migrant or Mexican, she called them "wetbacks." I didn't understand what the word meant, but it made me recoil. Pepino, Juanita, and Junior had been so kind. For many months, Pepino was my only friend. But while my mother didn't want me to visit his house, she never tried to stop me from working with Pepino in the fields.

One afternoon, a posse of border patrol agents with their brown, broad-brimmed hats and shiny badges arrived, stirring up a cloud of stray pebbles and huge plumes of dust. They had come to round up the migrants, Juanita, Junior, and Pepino included. My mother was almost gleefully happy. "We can just get more workers," she said with a dismissive wave of her hand. But I was devastated. For weeks, I would head out to the fields and lie on the ground between the rows of beans, staring up at the sky, feeling the hard dirt against my back as the sun beat down and the wind wafted over me. The fields were where I had the most memories of Pepino and Juanita, so I felt the closest to them on that ground, as if they were still somehow with me.

Without labor to weed, tend to the vines, move and reconnect irrigation lines, and pick the crop, the fields fell into disarray. It turned out that it was not easy to "just get other workers." Not long after the border patrol raid, my father lost the first farm section, and the trailer we had lived in along with it. We packed up what little we had and moved across the river to the second farm. We were supposed to be living in an old, beached houseboat that had been deposited onto dry land, but that didn't work. Our next move was into a shack that my father built out of random pieces of plywood and painted barn-colored red. It didn't even have a staircase, only a makeshift, wobbly ladder to climb up to reach the second floor. I tried to imagine that we were living like Laura Ingalls Wilder and her pioneer family in *Little House on the Prairie*. They had survived in a sod house cut into the Kansas plains, and her words made their lives seem slightly magical. But Kevin and I were not living with Pa and Ma Ingalls, and our shack was barely a notch or two above a chicken coop. By this point, our "furniture" consisted of a car's bucket seat that had been stripped from a junked vehicle. We slept on a dusty, unfinished plywood floor in sleeping bags. More dust blew in from the fields. It banked and settled and then periodically rose in puffs from the coarse wood, casting a haze over the air whenever the sun streamed in. If it was dark in the night or the morning, we had to be extra careful of the loft's gaping opening that would send us crashing to the floor below.

Like the trailer, the red shack didn't have running water. If Kevin or I wanted to bathe, our only option was a small nearby fishpond stocked with carp. Whenever one of us jumped in the water, the carp, with their big fleshy lips, would glide over and start sucking on our skin. It was awful, both the feeling and trying to pluck the slippery, slimy fish off us. But after enough days had passed, we would try to forget what it was like in the pond because we were so desperate to get wet and slightly clean.

Pinto beans required hand-weeding and picking, but alfalfa farming was a large, mechanized operation that required both planning and timing, and that made it particularly unsuited to my father, who didn't have much use for either trait. Alfalfa plants needed precisely placed and monitored irrigation lines to grow, and a full complement of tractors, mowers, and bailers when the crop was ready to harvest. None of that fazed my father. He was certain that his farmland would soon bloom with masses of pinto beans, potatoes, alfalfa, and wheat, which would be harvested by the newfangled combine that he had invented. However, the machine never functioned properly and never actually harvested anything. It wasn't many more months before that second farm was lost, too.

Leaving was easy because we had so little. I'm not sure there were even boxes, just trash bags. By this point, the only things I had were a black cat that had moved with us from Salt Lake, a few items of clothing, work boots, and whatever books I managed to steal from the local library. This time, we also didn't go far.

ten

The old Route 30, later renamed Sunset Strip, which skirted the edge of downtown Mountain Home, had a motel perched beside it. The building rose up for two stories, with a bright turquoise balcony railing running from end to end, bright turquoise doors leading to every room, and an exterior stairway for guests to reach the second floor. Taken together, the motel looked more like it belonged in the red desert of New Mexico or Arizona, not in brown-tinged and frequently cold Idaho. Built of cement and brick, the motel's two wings formed an L that enclosed two sides of the asphalt parking lot. From the upper balcony walkway, it was possible to glance down the main road and see the praying mantis–like chutes of a nearby grain tower rising into the sky. Inside the motel's rooms were a mix of single and double queen-size beds with veneer frames that looked expensive to me. I still wasn't used to the idea of a mattress sitting on a frame, and I had no idea what on earth a box spring was. The main feature that distinguished one room from another was the color of the shag carpet. Some rooms had a deep gold color, others a dark green. I knew this because I worked every day on the second floor of the motel as a maid. In the evenings, I worked in the motel's small restaurant. I was about twelve years old.

My father had charmed the husband and wife who owned the motel and had bartered my work in return for our family's room. The owners were happy to give us lodging so long as I worked for free, or at least that was what my parents suggested. I had only seen the owners at a distance, I didn't know exactly what they thought or what they had been told. All I had to go on was my father's explanation. During the days as I pushed my cleaning cart, my father did God knows what, while each afternoon, my mother put on a bathing suit, slathered on some tanning oil, and stretched out on a chaise by the pool to sun herself.

As a maid, I had a pushcart with towels and linens, little slivers of wrapped soap and cleaning cloths and supplies, and a duster and a vacuum. I'd start work around 8 a.m. and finish sometime in the afternoon. I was taught how to make a bed tightly by folding the sheet corners at the bottom (a method I use to this day) and how to clean the bathrooms using certain chemicals. The motel's second maid cleaned the downstairs rooms. She was an older Latina woman who did not speak much English, but she constantly criticized me for how I cleaned. That part I understood. She also didn't think that I worked fast enough. But it wasn't just changing sheets and cleaning toilets. The rooms were often smoky and dank-smelling from the guests. They needed to be aired out and deodorized. I would throw open the door and hope that fresh air would mix with the stale room air. Sometimes, the only thing to be done was to douse everything with big sprays of air freshener.

I had a couple of hours away from work, but by 5 p.m., it was time for me to start my work at the restaurant located on the other side of the pool. The restaurant was very dark inside. The lighting was dim, and what windows there were must have been covered by blinds or heavy curtains. It was also small, with about fifteen dark wooden tables surrounded by red vinyl chairs. I think the carpet was also dark red, and it had a mildew smell. Mountain Home is located in what's known as a high desert plateau, meaning it was generally a dry, somewhat arid place, but in my memory, so many parts of it had an underlying scent of mold. Perhaps the Snake River had come roaring over its banks at some point and left its residue around the town. The restaurant menu was a list of basic American food: baked Idaho potatoes in foil, meat and meatloaf, chicken-fried steak, chicken breasts smothered in sauce, rice, and little white side saucers of overcooked green vegetables or canned corn. But the restaurant was usually full of customers. People passing through town ate there, and Mountain Home had a surprising number of visitors, many with tight haircuts and lace-up shoes, because there was an air force base nearby.

My first task in the late afternoon was to help roll the cloth napkins around the utensils to set on the tables. When the guests arrived, I refilled water glasses and cleared plates. Once enough dishes had accumulated, I stayed in the back, working at a large stainless steel washer basin with an adjacent drying table. I'd spend hours washing dishes, glasses, and utensils, usually finishing around 10 p.m., after the kitchen closed and the last of the patrons had left. I wore rubber gloves, but my hands and wrists were small, and the water from the sprayer wriggled inside and ran in rivulets down my forearms. Periodically, I'd shake the residue out of my gloves, but between the heat and the soap and dampness, the skin on my hands turned bright red, and then became scaly and chapped. I couldn't heal it, and each night, by the end of my shift, it stung.

Like any twelve-year-old girl, I'd begun to be more skeptical and less tolerant of my mother. I still believed I had to protect her, but in the last year or so, she had found God, and her constant talk about Christ wore on me. The moment we were flush with any kind of cash, she also used it for her own physical betterment, specifically plastic surgery. She had her boobs done and her face smoothed. It didn't matter that we were living in a trailer or that Kevin and I wore mismatched Salvation Army clothes scrounged from racks and bins. There was always a doctor happy to take her cash in exchange for the promise of enhanced beauty and perfection. With each birthday, she became increasingly vain and insecure. She veered between complete, blind hatred of my father's affairs and a wounded belief that his interest in other women was due to his loss of attraction to her.

When it came to me, my mom had her own low-cost, tried-and-true remedy for my preteen withdrawal. If she saw me tuning her out when she was complaining about something, she'd toss a cup of hot coffee in my face.

Our nomadism continued unabated. Before I reached thirteen, we had left the motel, driven back to Utah, and then, in short order, returned to Idaho, this time with me in the driver's seat, attempting to navigate an old rickety RV on the interstate so my father could sleep. The summer before my eighth-grade year, the four of us moved into a trailer park in Mountain Home. I remember the rectangular interior of the trailer: the section of white kitchen cupboards that had worn to a yellow tinge and a small oven that made an incredibly loud noise whenever its buttons were pressed. Bright fluorescent lights were suspended overhead, and they buzzed incessantly. The small rectangle of linoleum on the kitchen floor had buckled under previous occupants, leaving it chipped and torn in various corners. I had to be careful to avoid the rough spots with my bare feet.

Mountain Home was located a little more than 3,100 feet above sea level, and it baked under the vast dome of the western sky. In the early evenings, the sun would set on the back side of the trailer, and the light and heat would press against the metal sides and pour in through the dirty, aluminum-screened windows until the living room felt like an oven and we were baking. There were no blinds on the windows, only ugly, dark beige curtains. The small trailer felt oppressive when they were pulled closed, and it didn't help with the heat. The thick fabric seemed to trap the broiling heat more than anything.

The heat did nothing to clear the heavy smell of mold, mildew, and dried sweat from the dozens of migrant workers who had lived in the trailer for years when it had been parked in the farm fields before it was towed to the trailer park and became ours. These smells must have infiltrated the walls and the floors, or lived like a microscopic civilization under the carpet. Or perhaps they resided behind the thin, brown paneled walls, where either dried-up glue or too many encounters with an angry fist had left the panels and the cheap veneer split and broken in random places. But I loved the fact that the trailer did not have a basement or a second floor. I was still inordinately fearful of the dark, and I hated going up or down stairs. Whenever the screen door, which never seemed to fully latch, swung in the gusty wind and banged hard against the metal frame, my heart would race. No matter how many times I heard it, the sound was always unexpected, and I would jump, primed to run.

The trailer was a good house in many ways. There was running water, and because there were no crops to tend or guest rooms to clean, I went back to regular attendance at school. I wasn't a great student, but it also seemed that my extended absences hadn't mattered all that much. I kept moving along, grade by grade, with my peers.

One day, at the end of summer, not long before the new school year opened, I came home from the library to find my father loading all our belongings into an old Lincoln Continental that I had never seen before. (Most likely, my uncle was behind that acquisition.) My father announced that we were moving back to Utah.

I looked at my father and mother standing by the doorway and at the piles of garbage bags. *I'm not going*, I told them.

So they left. Without me.

I don't recall a fight or any kind of bitter words. They just finished stuffing the back of the Continental, told Kevin to get in, and pulled away. On the kitchen counter, Mom left behind a white envelope filled with barely enough cash to get by.

For four months, I lived in a trailer park version of *Home Alone*. I walked to and from school and tried to remember to brush my teeth at night. After school, I would often sit in the library with a book. As dusk approached, I walked over to get the $1.69 Big Red burger special from the Red Steer drive-in or splurged on an ice cream cone if I was in the mood. I'd eat my hamburger outside at a picnic table, elbows propped up, as the juices and grill grease seeped into the bun. Sometimes, I bought a pizza and took the leftovers home in the box.

I went to the grocery store, too, but mostly to shoplift Butterfinger candy bars. While the summer heat lingered, I would wander the ice cream aisle. I liked that it was cold and that the big tubs stacked in the open-style freezer bins were cheap. I tried to steal one of those once, too, chocolate chip, my favorite (though I was allergic to the chocolate). Out of the corner of my eye, I'd watch moms push their shopping carts with toddlers in the folding seats and notice the little kids scuffing the floor with their sneakers, bored and trailing behind. The moms rotated their eyes from their kids to their shopping lists and ignored me. I felt as if I were almost invisible everywhere I went in Mountain Home. It was a bittersweet kind of loneliness. I wanted a set of parents to come back for me—just not my parents.

Otherwise, in the beginning, inside the trailer, I felt that I had gotten what I wanted. I had peace and quiet. No one hit me, slapped me, or slammed my face into a wall. And I was able to read every Nancy Drew mystery ever published. I read a lot of books during those months, including Mark Twain's *The Adventures of Huckleberry Finn*. Not surprisingly, I identified with Huck a lot, and I tried to create adventures and fill my days with exploration as he did. I would walk down roads and trails, kicking stones and finding cool sticks. On weekends, I would walk the train tracks for hours, mesmerized by their parallel lines, periodically singing, "Nobody loves me, everybody hates me, I'm gonna eat some worms." I never actually ate worms, but I thought the song was funny.

I liked being out of the trailer because, even though I had spent months as a maid, I really didn't have much of a sense of how to keep a home. I didn't have something as basic as trash bags. Whenever the trash can was full, I carried it to a large container that sat at the back of the trailer park, dumped the contents of the can into the container, and then carried it back to the trailer. My clothes lay in piles on the floor; I had no dresser and only a few hangers. I didn't want to spend any precious quarters on the laundry machine, so I washed nothing, not my clothes and not my sheets, although I liked leaving pennies on the railroad tracks. I'd carefully lay a penny on the track and then move to the side of the tracks and sit on the ground, watching the trains fly by and flatten and smash the copper disk. The white sheets on my mattress slowly turned slick from oil, dead skin, and sweat, and my green-and-white-checked pillowcase was an equally dingy brown. I loved the pillow and its case because Maggie, my cat, used to curl up on top. But Maggie had been packed off to Utah; I had no idea if she had even survived. My tattered old pillow was almost devoid of stuffing, but it had two strings that I liked to rub repetitively between my fingers.

I had an entire system for getting up in the morning, starting with my alarm clock, which had a round clock face and loud, jarring bells on top. I placed it on the floor on the other side of my room under the window, away from my bed, so the noise would force me to get up to turn it off. That way, I was sure to leave for school on time. Someone had left behind a huge tube of toothpaste that I rationed. I was careful to brush my teeth twice a day because I was afraid of having more cavities; I'd already had a huge number, and my teeth hurt when they were drilled and filled. The same stinky aluminum screens that made my hands smell like metal if I touched them also reacted like a magnet with my fillings. No one had thought to leave a hairbrush, so I never brushed my hair, and the strands slowly matted and knotted together over time.

There was nowhere to sit in the living room; I think my parents took the furniture and gave it to the farmworkers. There was a phone in the trailer, and occasionally they called, but mostly, it sat silent and useless. They had left the TV, with its rabbit ears pointed hopelessly in various directions, and I would lie on my back on the floor and twist my head and neck to watch *I Love Lucy* reruns and *Lost in Space*. I liked to draw, too, and I could spend hours working on a drawing.

The trailer didn't have a heater, and as fall settled in, it would get cold. I'd wrap myself in my blanket and walk around. Sometimes, to try to sleep warm, I would wrap my one towel around myself and pull the blanket over that.

There was one other thing that I remember in that trailer: a bottle of painkillers left over from one of my mother's plastic surgeries. It sat in the medicine cabinet. After the first month, I would open the cabinet door and stare at that bottle every night, wondering if I should just swallow all the pills. I didn't want to die. But I didn't want this life, either. After the initial relief of being out of the chaos and on my own, I was overtaken by deep feelings of loneliness and being very misunderstood. I went to school, and I walked through the town, but I remained largely invisible. The same mind-your-own-business attitude that cultivated cowboys and mountain men and solitary harvest combines rolling over farmland was also more than willing to look the other way at a twelve-year-old girl buying burgers or wandering the grocery aisles and occasionally buying large plastic tubs of chocolate chip ice cream. No one asked about a parent-teacher conference, and I was careful to avoid library fines if I couldn't steal the books. Either the trailer rent was paid, or the office took a while to get around to evicting anyone. The only person who seemed to be paying any attention was an old man in red suspenders who lived in one of the other trailers. I'd feel his eyes on me, and it was all I could do not to flat-out run.

But the result was that, inside, I felt as if no one really knew me or cared to know me. Occasionally, I raised my hand in class to answer a question, but on the weekends, I could go for almost the entire two days without speaking to anyone.

Most of all, I didn't know how to change my situation. Until my situation changed for me.

One day in December, as I sat wrapped in my blanket, I heard the crunch of gravel outside and a car engine cut off. I jumped up and peered out the dirty window. It was my dad. "Pack your stuff" were his first words, and just like that, in about ten minutes, my life in Idaho was over. During the long car ride back to Salt Lake City, we had our first conversation alone in years. It wasn't a long talk. He simply told me that my mother was nuts, but he loved me. We arrived at the house in the dark. No one had waited up; not a single light was on.

One of the first things that happened in Utah was that I had to have my hair chopped off. There was no way to untangle the knots that had formed after months without a hairbrush or a comb. Or no one wanted to spend the time. So off it came.

DIAMENTE

eleven

I MET DIAMENTE'S MOM, THERESSA, first. She attended every Sidwell football game. She often stood in the stands, cheering, screaming, and shouting at the referees. She didn't follow the unwritten Sidwell parent playbook of being reserved and largely unemotional during the games, and I adored her for it. She was the spirit of the team. Diamente was a Sidwell football star. He played varsity and was so fast that his legs seemed to swallow the yards of artificial turf in front of him. He was the youngest child in his family and the only boy. At six feet one, he was still the baby—his mom and four older sisters remained fiercely protective of him.

As with Ryan, Justin bonded with Diamente. Justin wasn't fast or graceful or an amazing athlete. He was still playing JV, not varsity, but something about the two boys clicked. Both were highly capable outsiders, looking for ways to fit in. And both were looking for something else: brothers.

Diamente had been playing football since he was six or seven, as well as basketball and baseball. But he was truly at home on a football field. He was also a great student. His mom had placed him in a Washington, DC, charter school, one of the KIPP academies, which she heard about from someone at a baseball practice. When Diamente was in eighth grade, a counselor encouraged a few of the kids to apply to some of Washington's elite private schools. Diamente filled out an application to enter Sidwell. What Theressa later told me was that the counselor had said to Diamente, "You're very talented and smart. If you get into Sidwell, I will do backflips down the hallway." When Diamente saw his counselor doing backflips down the hall, he knew exactly what that meant. His mom and his sisters, whom Theressa calls his "little mothers," wanted to make sure that Diamente succeeded. They helped him make the long commute, on multiple city buses and a Metro train, from their home in Southeast DC to Upper Northwest Washington.

Washington, DC, the public, visible Washington, is a very green city; its major streets are lined with trees, there are clusters of parks, and the long grassy stretch of the National Mall. It is a city of plantings and landscaping. Profusions of spring tulips are replaced with summer begonias and fall pansies. But each day as he returned home, Diamente watched the blocks of manicured, tourist-ready Washington recede through the bus window. In his part of the city, beyond the Anacostia River, the city no longer invested in showy displays. No government agency or parks department would rush to replace the patches of dried-up grass. The trees are fewer, and many are stunted, their roots constrained under the weight of concrete sidewalks. Chain-link fencing and faded plastic flowers are more the norm.

Theressa had grown up in DC in the long shadow of the Capitol. Her mom had stayed home with the kids and then worked as a school assistant and sold Avon cosmetic products door-to-door; her dad was a retired army soldier who became a shoe salesman. Now Theressa lived in a neighborhood where DC's police department deployed clusters of electronic sensors—ShotSpotters—to triangulate the sound of gunfire to locate the exact location of the shootings. Sirens wailed, and drugs were rampant. It was a rougher place than Ryan's Silver Spring housing.

Diamente knew that Ryan lived with us. He liked joining Justin and Ryan to hang out at our house. And he constantly found creative ways to do so. He started organizing regular team sleepovers at our house on the nights before the games. The first time everyone slept over, Sidwell won. After that, a night at our home became the team's "lucky" ritual. I'd grill twenty pounds of flat iron steak, and it would be gone in an instant. I'd be standing at the cutting board, and I'd have twenty large males crowding around me, grabbing the strips as I sliced them. I'd have to yell, half joking, "I don't want fingers in my meat! Get away!" For dessert, I'd make batches of snickerdoodle cookies, which they loved. To cook breakfast the next morning, I bought cart-loads of bacon, eggs, bread, and juice at Costco. The boys loved all of it. They'd jostle for position to get first dibs on platters of food spread out across the kitchen counter, or they'd simply line up to be handed their eggs straight from the pan.

After each overnight, I had stacks of dirty dishes, and I realized that I needed to buy extra pails to handle the additional trash. It was as if I were running a commercial kitchen. When it came time to leave for the Saturday morning game, Tom and I would pile as many boys as we could fit into our cars and order Ubers for the others or ask friends and neighbors to transport them. Only later would I come to understand that these Friday night gatherings were so much more than just sleepovers. In those hours at our home, there was no segregated lunchroom, with the Black players and Justin clustered at one table, the white players elsewhere. There was no team bench and no clearly defined first or second string. There was simply one unit of boys, all with their long limbs and thin or thick muscles, eating, knocking each other around, joking, laughing, and playing video games in the basement, where I had set up the Xbox and PlayStation to work on the big screen. They played Madden while their workout gear sat in piles in the middle of the entryway.

After a few times, it was clear that many of the kids had not washed their uniforms despite several weeks of hot Saturday morning games. They arrived with bags that smelled so awful that the scent permeated the house. It was as if our main floor had been turned into a locker room at the height of summer—with dozens of sweaty bodies, dirty clothing, and no air-conditioning—except we had air-conditioning.

Elie would come downstairs from her room and announce that "boys smell horrible"—followed by the question "Why are there so many penises in this house?!" Then, from the basement, the sounds would start. Crashing sounds, shouting, deep rolling waves of laughter, and more crashing sounds. The vibrations reached me in the kitchen, and there were times when it felt like the house was crumbling at the foundation. Sometimes, the noise would drive me to cautiously descend the stairs to check on them. I'd find four boys wrestling at the foot of the stairs—and more often than not, there were some bloody streaks and scrapes, even though this was supposed to be fun. The team's other favorite spot to wrestle was on the sofa beds. (One ended up broken beyond repair when two three-hundred-pound guys set out to prove which one of them was stronger by wrestling on top of it. They, however, learned that a broken sofa bed mattress can snap back, wrap you up, and never let go.)

After the first couple of times, I started asking for a show of hands of those who needed their uniforms laundered (it was so much better than living with the smell). Nearly all of them said yes, so in addition to grilling and making batches of snickerdoodles, I started the first of many loads of laundry. After dinner, Tom, Justin, and I would inflate every air mattress in the house, and we pulled every sheet, pillow, and blanket we owned from the linen closets. The beds (in addition to the sofa beds) filled the entire floor space of the very large basement. Some boys also chose to sleep in the theater chairs we had in the basement—less of a risk of being stepped on by a neighbor in the night.

After each sleepover, I would find socks everywhere—in the mattresses, in the sofas, on the floors, in the hallway, hanging from the light fixtures, in the bathrooms, outside in the flower beds, in the cars—literally everywhere. Always just one sock. Never a matching pair. By then, I oversaw emailing a weekly "newsletter" to the players, parents, and coaches. So I would post a photo of a sock in that email and say that the first person to find its match would win a pizza. I found a couple of matching socks that way. But by the time football season ended, I had a huge drawer overflowing with singleton socks that no one ever claimed.

Amid this happy chaos, Justin, my pied piper of football players and teenage men, came to me and said that one of the football players, Tareq, an exchange student from Ramallah, was having a tough time with his host family. I had noticed that Tareq was around our house a lot. According to Justin, Tareq's host family had thought that Sidwell would be providing them with a significant sum of money for housing him. But as I knew from our time with Ranim, the school offered $1,000 a semester as a stipend, which was supposed to be seed money for food and any other expenses, but it was hardly meant to cover everything. Tom and I had simply donated the stipend back to the school because it was so minimal. The dollar amount wouldn't come close to buying four months of food for a serious athlete. But Tareq's host family had a different interpretation. Without more funds, they had decided to stop feeding him meat and anything else that they deemed "expensive."

Although they had a child enrolled at Sidwell, the family lived far out in the Northern Virginia suburbs, which also made it difficult for Tareq to get to school. He was often late, and some days he didn't make it to school at all. And there were unique challenges at their home. The family expected Tareq to help care for an elderly relative, something that is not usually considered to be a proper part of an exchange program. Those responsibilities and the lack of food genuinely concerned me. After some inquiries with Sidwell and Tareq's home school in Ramallah, the decision was made to have him leave his original host family and move in with us. Now I had Justin, Ryan, Elie, and Tareq appearing for breakfast and piling in the car with all their gear each day. I was dropping off a full crew in the mornings. And I was still hosting all those football boys on the weekends.

Somehow, I just made time and space. I didn't think about the work or the running around; I thought about the situation the kids were in. At a school like Sidwell, the students' lives tended to be fantastically busy, hyper-scheduled, and demanding. But we found time where we could. We would go on adventures—at a go-kart track, or bowling, or shopping at the sports outlet stores. When I was cooking, the kids would hang out in the kitchen with me and talk (and grab bites of whatever I was preparing). We would ask about each other's days and learn about each other's challenges and triumphs. Snow days were always awesome because we'd spend the whole free day together watching movies or playing video games (I became pretty good at Super Mario).

The boys *always* wanted to go grocery shopping with me. They would pile in the car, grab three carts as soon as we arrived, fill them up with just about every type of junk food imaginable, and then ride home with piles of grocery bags on their laps. They also took to attending SoulCycle classes with me. Sometimes, three would come. Sometimes seven. We'd take up nearly an entire row in the class, with everyone else staring at us as though we were the strangest group they had ever seen. We probably were. Afterward, we'd go to a local sushi restaurant and order huge platters that barely fit on the table.

The more time we spent together, the more we would talk about our lives and parts of our histories. I said relatively little, but sometimes I would tell them bits and pieces of stories about my life that had relevance to theirs. But mostly, they needed me to be a provider. I was there to offer up everything from affection to patience, a listening ear, a bit of earnest and honest understanding, or even a short lesson or a silly joke to prod them to be less serious or lighten the mood. My life was singularly devoted to them. And before long, they were just as devoted to me.

What I also didn't know in the beginning, as a mountain of boys arrived to pile onto the blow-up beds scattered in the basement and even the hallways, was that Diamente was the kid who worried about getting home at night. Many nights, he would sleep at different friends' homes—"couch surfing"—so that he did not have to make the long trek back to Southeast DC. But after a few weeks had passed, I began to understand. I noticed that Diamente always came early to our house and stayed late, stretching out his time as much as possible. After the Saturday games, the rest of the team would go home, but Diamente would return to our house, often staying well into the next school week. Sometimes, he came over later in the week to have a family dinner with us and spend the night. One or two days at our house became three or four days a week with us. Diamente could sit with Justin and Ryan, or talk with Tom when he was home, or lean against a kitchen counter and chat with me. When he left, he routinely left some item of his behind as if to ensure a "next time."

The one person who was not thrilled initially with this arrangement was Elie. Diamente's voice was loud and his language was horrendous, probably the foulest of anyone on the football team, and Elie thought he could be a bad influence on Justin, whom she now heard using some of the same words. "Mom, do you hear what he says?" she asked me, rolling her eyes. And when I looked at Diamente's Facebook and Instagram accounts, I saw that he would sometimes post things that he shouldn't.

Yet beneath that exterior, I could also see that there was a deeply sensitive and brilliant young man. He was a softhearted kid who loved to hug and cuddle. He was quick-witted and always laughing and making others laugh. If anyone needed help, he materialized out of nowhere to offer assistance. He had a flair for fashion and a love of crazy shoes, including a pair of sneakers that looked like the feet of Tigger, the Winnie the Pooh character, with mock tiger tails springing off the heels. Everyone on the team—and probably the entire school—waited to see what shoes Diamente would wear next (some had wings, some were shiny gold, and all of them were uniquely suited to Diamente's personality, high on the swag with a dose of fun). He was also incredibly smart; he could look at a physics problem and immediately understand the concept and what it was asking. He had none of the gaps that Ryan suffered from in his education. No one needed to email teachers or set up complex tutoring schedules for Diamente. On the football field, he played wide receiver, a position that depended on a combination of speed, grace, determination, grit, and precision. He was gifted at reading both the plays and the people on all sides around him.

Although he was incredibly close to Justin and would seek out Tom, he also gravitated to me, specifically to me in the car. When I drove the boys to and from the games, Diamente would inevitably call shotgun and ride next to me. He'd tease me when I shrieked and made a face listening to the language of the hip-hop and rap songs on the radio or even to what the other boys said in the rear seats. "Did they really just say *that*?" I'd squeal, and Diamente would explode in laughter until the entire car was convulsing. He was always trying to get a rise out of me. But I found that I could talk to him, too, and ask him why, when he had sisters and a strong mother, he would sometimes use harsh phrases to describe women. The first few times, he rolled his eyes and tried to ignore me. But I kept pushing. I'd repeat my lecture about cleaning up his Instagram and Facebook feeds before he applied to college. He'd reply that he'd think about it. And then there were the moments when he pushed the door to his life open a little bit, just enough so that I could see in. He told me snatches, how hard his mom worked, how he had given up on his dad, whom he had seen maybe a dozen times.

Many months later, Diamente showed me an essay in which he had written (which he said was "just fiction") that he could almost count the meaningful times he and his dad had spent together on the fingers of his two hands. No dad at his sixth-grade graduation, even if he fantasized about it in a dream. He would ask questions, get one-line answers in return, and then they would move on. "That's all I got, small talk," he wrote. He had revealed the early bits and pieces of that story to me as we sat side by side in the front seats, buckled in. But seeing it laid out in full, I saw a sober anguish on the page, something not immediately deflected with a clever joke or shocking word.

One day, while I was driving, Diamente rotated toward me and said in a serious voice, "You know, I love you."

And I replied, "I love you, too."

As if I didn't understand, he repeated, "No, I mean the real kind of love. Not the fake kind of love."

Keeping it light, I said, "There's a fake kind?"

He answered, "I mean it for real, like I really love you."

This, I think, must be what it is like when a surgeon holds a pulsing heart in his or her hand for the first time, when it is possible to feel another vulnerable life coursing beneath your fingertips. I paused for a second, glanced toward him, and said, "Well, I really love you, too." Because I realized in that moment that I really did.

I sensed in Diamente a deep loneliness—the kind that arises when, no matter how many people you may know, you are missing a deeper kind of connection. In my heart, what I saw in Diamente was a craving for a whole family, with a father and siblings all under one roof, who loved each other. And, while I knew without a doubt that he loved me, I could see that he really craved a father and brothers. He was feeling out and trying on the life that circumstances had denied him. I knew that feeling, too.

The next time Diamente came over, I was ready. I had already told Tareq that I thought Diamente might need a place to stay and had asked him if he would mind moving to one of the downstairs rooms. Tareq had agreed. I cleaned out everything and got the now-empty bedroom ready.

All I said to Diamente was "It seems like you may need a place to stay on this side of town. If that's true, here's a key to the house, and your room is upstairs." He looked at me with tears in his eyes. He returned with a couple of duffel bags. He never left.

He started calling me Mama. I started calling him Dee, as did everyone else in the family. There were many other days when I drove him and a pack of boys to the Saturday games when he would look at me, grin, and say, "Mama, right now in this car, you are the safest person in this city." Truly, in those moments, I believe I was.

twelve

As I know from my own life, family dysfunction is like a ripple. It is not simply the stone that drops to the bottom, like a weight, dragging one person down; it is also the wave that pulses outward, expanding and expanding, until it covers everyone and everything. The effects can be debilitating, not just in the moment, but in the months and years beyond, as everyone connected to that family struggles to break free from those waves.

I guess that's why I've always been a bit skeptical of professionals who attempt to tie up trauma and challenge in neat psychological packages, emphasizing how kids can learn to build resilience and find grit as if they are pushing their way through a set of bench presses in the weight room. As if the outcomes can somehow be made the same.

The harder truth is that every family story is different. Every story within a family is different. Each parent has a story, and so does each child. And no matter how much there might be a shared language of common suffering, it is a mistake to overgeneralize across situations. Ryan's story was vastly different from Diamente's, even though both had fathers who struggled with addiction. My story was different from both of theirs, even though we could feel the emotional echoes and reverberations.

I also had very different relationships with each of their moms. Rochelle often needed a mentor, while Theressa was just as likely to mentor me. We called each other with our stories and our problems. As Theressa said, those sleepovers "turned into us finding a new family for all of us. We all joined in becoming one big family."

Just as I learned Diamente's story over time, I also learned Theressa's. She told it to me in bits and pieces, but always with love. For me, she became like the sister I never had, a special gift that came with her son. We would eventually come to echo each other in more than just the deep bond between our sons.

And long after she spoke them, her words describing Diamente's life, and her own, sat with me.

Theressa chose Diamente's name before he was born—and she did it in a church van.

When she grew up, her "grandmamma" made sure the entire family attended church. Theressa raised her own kids in her church and taught Sunday school to "the little kids" for a long time. She also drove the church van, snaking through the streets of Southeast Washington to pick up parishioners for church and then drive them home after services were done. She was driving that van when she was pregnant, and at one point, Theressa said to her passengers, "Hey, everyone, I'm about to have the baby. I haven't really felt the right name, so let's figure out names." They all eagerly offered up lots of names, but none of them felt quite right. Three Sundays later, Theressa was stopped at a light. She told me that she remembered looking out through the windshield, and "I saw a car. I said, 'That's a cute car, what's the name of that car?' And my passengers said, 'It's a Diamante.' I said, 'Diamante?

That's a good name for a baby, what do y'all think?' And they all said yes. But I changed the spelling so there were two *e*'s—Diamente—because I wanted my baby to have a name that was all his own."

In the beginning, Theressa hoped that she, Diamente's dad, and Diamente would be a family. "I didn't realize everything that was wrong. It was only after I was already pregnant that I saw the signs. It was like realizing that I had a wolf in sheep's clothing."

She still cannot talk about the addiction that tore them apart. She can only say that it was painful, and that it and the choices Diamente's dad made meant that he never had a relationship with his son. "I told Diamente's father that if he was messing around with the stuff, don't come around. And he promised me he wouldn't, and he kept that promise, which was a blessing for me." But at the same time, it broke Theressa's heart.

When Diamente's dad was there, each day was "like playing the lottery." But, so unlike my own mother, Theressa tried to create a harmonious narrative, to orchestrate individual days where Diamente could experience good times and to let him know that his father had, as she put it, "the makings of a good man, but this sickness overtook him." And there *were* some good times, months when things were happy until Diamente's dad relapsed, and the family would have to start all over again. After one bad stretch, Diamente's dad entered a rehabilitation program. Theressa didn't take Diamente to visit. She didn't want him to see his dad in that facility, in that condition. After he was released, he came by the house. Theressa remembered that she "could hear Diamente laughing—his father had the gift for gab. But he also had the gift of disappointment."

One year, Diamente wanted to surprise his dad for Father's Day. He asked Theressa, "Mommy, go get the chicken, get the greens, get this, get that." He wanted to pull out all the stops. Theressa cooked a huge dinner, and she and Diamente waited, but his father never came. Finally, Theressa called and said, "We're waiting for you. And Diamente got me to cook all your favorite foods for you."

"Oh," he said, "I'm spending time with my nephew."

That, Theressa said, "broke my heart. All I said was 'Your nephew is not your son.'" Diamente was hurt most of all.

When Diamente turned twelve, he decided to stop visiting his dad. One thing that he had noticed was how his father and his father's family all had cars, but Diamente and his mom didn't. Diamente had to take the bus both ways to visit his dad. He gave Theressa a list of other reasons: no one from his dad's family came to any of his football games, his sports award ceremonies, or even his elementary school graduation. "I don't want to go there anymore," he repeated, in case Theressa had missed the point. She nodded in reply. She didn't fight him or try to change his mind; she simply let it be.

The visits became fewer and fewer until Diamente's father all but vanished—he was living in the same city, but he disappeared from their lives. When Diamente was admitted to Sidwell, everything changed. Theressa saw her son "coming into his own man. He found himself. I believe those years were something that God had in store for Diamente."

Everything started anew on the Sidwell football field. Theressa remembers it as "Diamente's sisters and I brought the noise. Win or lose, we cheered. We hollered. We had a great time. Sometimes, I worked the chains to mark off the first downs, and once, I got so caught up in watching Diamente run that I followed him down the field from the sidelines all the way to the edge of the end zone, dragging those chains. He laughed at me and pointed and said, 'You're supposed to be back there.'"

Theressa would always tell me that Diamente thought of Justin as "my brother." And she added that Justin, Elie, Tom, and I did exactly what she would have done. We treated Diamente as if he were our own, which made it much easier for Theressa to "entrust somebody else with my boy. I knew that he was going to get his education. He was going to sleep well. He was going to eat well. It's the same thing he would have done with me, but he got a little bit more sleep. It was a cycle: he would come home, and then he would go back to the McCoys', and then he would come home, and he would go back."

Theressa knew because she had been opening her own house to other people's kids "since I was sixteen. My grandmamma always took people in. She gave them places to stay; she fed them. She was genuinely caring and had a good heart. I followed her example and started taking care of my nieces and nephews. Then, over time, I saw girls who needed mothering. They needed love, and I saw an opportunity to show love, so I showed it." Theressa and I are alike in that way. We both love to welcome people in if they need it, or as Theressa says, "That's what God has put in my heart. In the case of Sandi and me, it was like God just pulling us all together. Sandi and I have the same spirit, and it's a beautiful thing, having someone who you've found who is genuinely just like you. We filled in the gaps where the other needed it. We became inseparable. I would call her; she would call me, whatever the problem, whatever the issue. Together, we would make a plan and try to work it out."

But the best thing of all for Theressa, after those years of just the two of them, "Diamente got his own big family: two mothers, a brother, plus a little sister in Elie, his four 'little mothers,' and a dad. I always prayed for his safety and especially his happiness because Diamente really deserved it. And I prayed for God's will to be done." Having sometimes been the beneficiary of her prayers, I believe that God keeps a special ear out for Theressa.

thirteen

OUR FAMILY DIDN'T SEPARATE WITH the end of the school calendar. Ryan worked summer jobs, but he still came by to see us and sometimes stayed over. We insisted that he join us on our August family vacation, if that was okay with his parents. The summer after ninth grade, we planned a trip to Maui, a place we had come to love from our years in California. I didn't realize until I had booked the tickets that Ryan had never flown on a plane before. Now his introduction to flying would be a five- or six-hour cross-country journey, followed by another long flight across part of the Pacific Ocean. He gripped the armrests with both hands as if he might break it into two as the plane sped down the runway, lifted off, and climbed up, bouncing around.

The next summer, after Ryan and Justin's sophomore year and Diamente's junior year, we took everyone to the mountains of Colorado, where the air was thinner and cool, and the grasses and flowers and vegetation were a riot of color. Justin and Elie were adamant that both Ryan and Diamente come.

Sandra E. Smith

I have traveled all over the world, including flying across the Pacific to Japan when I was eight months pregnant. I have never thought much about flying. I've absorbed endless delays and, after 9/11, I adjusted to long security lines and constantly taking off my shoes. But other than keeping my toiletries in clear baggies and not carrying water, I've never thought much about TSA checkpoints. That changed when we began traveling with Ryan and Diamente. Heading to Colorado, Justin, Elie, Tom, and I cleared the boarding pass review and had removed our shoes, taken out our electronics, and had our bags in the bins waiting for the scanners. I looked around and realized that Ryan and Diamente were missing. I started walking back toward the TSA agent stands. Both young men had been pulled aside, the agent was scrutinizing their passes and their identification—they were not yet eighteen, so they were using school ID cards. In my lawyer voice, I asked, "Sir, is there a problem?" The agent looked shocked, and before he could start saying that I was interfering, I added, "Ryan and Diamente are with me. We are all going on a family vacation." I waved my hand toward Justin and Elie.

"Oh." He paused. "Okay."

Ryan and Diamente shrugged off the agent, but I spent the entire plane ride quietly furious. I felt both helpless and ignorant. My kids had sailed through because they were white; two young Black men were held back for added scrutiny for no reason other than they were Black and appeared to be traveling together, apparently as unaccompanied minors. But as soon as I showed up and "claimed" them, the agent allowed them to progress through the line. Who taught the agent to do this? Where was the seed planted? How many times had it happened before when I was standing in a line and I had missed it? What assumptions was I making myself?

I spent the flight thinking about all the assumptions that people make, the way Ryan and Diamente were routinely sized up, profiled, and assigned a role based on sneakers or a spoken sentence. Some veteran teachers talk about how they "size up" students by how they carry themselves into a classroom. How much of Ryan's and Diamente's lives were lived in some variation of the TSA line?

Having grown up in the West, I loved Colorado for its physical beauty and the space and freedom that it represented. I loved having the chance to disconnect from our tightly scheduled Washington, DC, and especially our Sidwell lives. Tom was also about to start a new job in Colorado and would be spending most of his time there, so visits made sense from a logistical side. The kids would have a better sense of where he was—Colorado wouldn't only be a name, it would be a real place that they could picture. But mostly, this time away showed us that we were settling into being a family, an unconventional family in the eyes of many, but a family above all.

At this point in my life, I didn't have much contact with my mother, and Kevin and I were somewhat estranged, separated by physical distance and our separate struggles with our childhood memories, so a big, rollicking extended family had not been part of Justin and Elie's experience. Diamente and Ryan changed that. They brought the joy and the rowdiness. They wanted to toss a football or race up a hill. Our days were loud and fun, and I loved every minute of it. In Colorado, we grilled and shucked corn and played games. Everyone had to clear their plates. I was not the constant minder-mom, making sure everyone was up and out the door, organizing game-day transportation, juggling various sports practices and activity transportation, or watching the clock to keep mealtimes on a tight schedule and asking about homework and exams. We could all simply be and soak in the unscheduled time.

Being on vacation was also safe. I'd make a dinner reservation for six, and when we all turned up, the staff had to treat us all the same. We were part of a package. When we traveled, I always made sure that we stayed in high-end hotels or rented homes and that everyone had room keys or electronic lock combinations. It was different at home. For years, I felt fearful when the boys, or later the young men, left my suburban Maryland house. When Ryan and then Diamente first came to stay with us, Tom and I had "the talk." It is a version of the talk that Black and Latino parents have had with their children, especially their male children, for years.

We tried to be matter-of-fact, but still impress upon them that they would be treated differently when walking or driving on our streets and even by our neighbors. "You are living in an all-white neighborhood with lots of cops just driving around," we told them, "or lots of neighbors or homeowners who are ready to call the cops. If you are stopped by the police, always do exactly what the cop says. Put both hands on the steering wheel, try to turn on the interior light, and always reply with either 'Yes, sir' and 'No, sir,' or 'Yes, ma'am' and 'No, ma'am.' And never, ever, ever argue." I knew that many of the people who lived in our area, packed with the elaborate custom-built houses that had replaced the more modest rambler or center-hall colonials, might profess all kinds of progressive values, might even these days display glossy "Hate Has No Home Here" signs, stuck into the shrubbery beds or at the edge of their gardener-service-maintained lawns, but they were and are the same people who will dial 911 if they see a young Black man walking around. So I worried. I worried when Justin and Ryan walked home in the dark through the side streets. I never wanted Ryan to walk alone. I wanted to tell the boys, *Don't put your hands in your pockets, always keep some Sidwell swag visible—a hat, a sweatshirt, a scarf—take your headphones out of your ears, and make sure that you look around.*

"Report anything that looks out of the ordinary" is the mantra from police departments and neighborhood associations. Young, muscular Black men with Afros or flattops were out of the ordinary where we lived. I introduced Ryan, Diamente, Justin, and Elie to my immediate neighbors, but I didn't know the people farther down the block. It wasn't, in some ways, all that different from Salt Lake City or Mountain Home. Lots of anonymous houses, some version of the man in suspenders, never introducing himself, only watching. Or a virtual set of eyes—I didn't know what their exterior security cameras might show or when a movement at the end of the driveway might set off an alert.

Eventually, I designed envelope address labels with everyone's face and name—Tom, Sandi, Justin, Ryan, Diamente, Elie, and Elijah (when he joined us)—and had everyone keep a label inside their wallet and in the car. I told them, if you get stopped, show this, too. Their ID card and later driver's licenses didn't have our address, so there was nothing to "prove" that they belonged in our neighborhood, nothing to say that when they were here, they were also home.

◆

After Ryan's second shoulder surgery, he held on to the slim hope that he could complete rehab and be cleared to return to the football field before the autumn leaves dropped and the season ended. He was very much weighed down by his continuing inability to play football. Athletes who came to Sidwell to play—and who received financial aid—understood and absorbed the fact that they were there primarily to contribute to the team. Ryan felt the pressure to perform and the sense of not measuring up. He was constantly worried that if he could not play football, Sidwell would kick him out of the school. Rochelle also thought that Ryan was at school on a "football scholarship," and she shared this worry.

Rochelle and I continued to develop a closer relationship. We texted and talked and saw each other. I shared what I thought Ryan needed; she shared what she saw, or what she was worried about. We were like friendly co-parents. But our relationship was sometimes tested by the lying and denial that continued in their household. Leonard still went on benders; the finances remained precarious. I couldn't count on Rochelle to show up—or Leonard—so I always needed a second set of plans. Ryan needed the certainty of a definitive plan more than anything.

Diamente's situation was different. He had a very grounded mom, who loved him deeply and had sacrificed so much. She was often my rock and my sounding board, my dear, dear friend. What he missed in the worst way were a dad and a brother. He found some of it through football, but he really wanted something more. He wanted that quiet space where men talk or simply perform the older version of parallel play, doing an activity side by side. He wanted that routine and commitment. He wanted that deeper connection. He wanted a presence.

After he had lived with us for about a year, when he was a senior at Sidwell, Diamente very specifically asked Tom to be his dad. Once, after a casual exchange when Diamente called Tom "Dad" and Tom answered back, Dee stopped and exclaimed to Tom: "You don't get it! I call you 'Dad' because I really want you to be *my* dad!"

Tom would tear up whenever he told this story, adding, "That was a moment when time stood still and the world changed, and I became his 'real dad.'"

Diamente's high school graduation fell on a hot, humid, bright and sunny day. Sidwell students have an unspoken tradition that senior boys wear jackets and ties, while the girls wear white dresses. Recently, a few students have modified the girls' dress code to include white suits. The young men pin boutonnieres to their lapels, while the young women carry bouquets of flowers, usually roses. It brims with a kind of restrained tradition. The outdoor setting gives it the veneer of simplicity, but it is carefully choreographed, always with a high-profile speaker who is connected to the school—either a famous alumnus or someone with ties to a Sidwell family or a famous parent; Bill Clinton spoke when he was president. I sat next to Theressa. Diamente's dad also attended, but Diamente remained cool and reserved toward him, not entirely sure whether he was there because of his son or because it was a prestigious event at a prestigious place.

It was joyful to watch Diamente walk up and receive his diploma. Sitting there in the warm sun, I thought back to an essay he had written earlier in his high school career, about the route that he took to Sidwell.

> *It's 5:00 a.m. and I am fighting waking up. But I must. To get to school on time, I have to leave home no later than 6:15 a.m. The distance from my home in Southeast DC to my school on Wisconsin Avenue, Northwest, is only eight miles, but it takes an hour and a half to make the trip by bus. The first bus I ride, the V7, travels through my neighborhood—a dark, cold place. My neighborhood is a place you do not want to find yourself. Ever. The street outside of my apartment building is cluttered with litter and people. Homeless men and women line the sides of the street. It is the kind of place where I must watch my back when I walk at night—or when I walk alone at any time of day.*
>
> *The V7 takes me to Pennsylvania Avenue, where I transfer to the Route 32 bus. This bus takes me through Georgetown and up Wisconsin Avenue. The environment changes dramatically on this route. I begin to see changes in people, changes in streets, and definitely changes in the overall aura. It is cleaner here than in my neighborhood. It is busier, more professional, safer, and definitely more friendly. This is the kind of place most people would consider "good."*

Sandra E. Smith

The reality of my bus ride to school each day is a metaphor for my transition from childhood to adulthood. The bus takes me from a place of great challenges to my very survival to Sidwell Friends School, a place that has provided a wholly different set of challenges. Sidwell's challenges prepare me for success in college and in life. My experience at school compels me to grow as a scholar and as a man.

Every day, when I exit the bus and walk into school, I anticipate that these challenges may be daunting. I often wonder whether having a quiet place to study at home like most of my peers would enable me to perform better in my classes, but I know that this is just another healthy challenge that I must overcome. There are days when I am nearly overwhelmed with multiple tests, papers, and countless hours of homework, in addition to football practice and sports training. But then I consider where I might be in life had I not chosen to attend Sidwell. Would I be in the streets with so many of the others I see each morning and evening? Would I be selling drugs to survive? Would I even still be alive? The first moment I set foot on Sidwell's campus, I knew that I had made the right decision. While the types of challenges I face in this intensely academic environment may feel uncomfortable at times, facing these challenges provides me the best shot I have in life. Each day I spend the long bus ride home reflecting on the amazing things I have learned at Sidwell, and how I am ready to exit the bus, and not return to the past, but forge my path to a bright future.

While Diamente was in college, his biological dad died in the streets somewhere on the other side of Washington. Diamente could outrun almost every player on the field, but his dad could not outrun the drugs that called to him. The funeral was held on a Sunday in a church in Southeast DC. People from the community brought a ton of food and celebrated a life cut short by an overdose caused by addiction—a not-infrequent occurrence in their community. Tom and Diamente attended the memorial service together.

Around that time, Diamente gave Tom a Father's Day card, in which he had written, "Thank you for loving me even though I don't know what I'm doing." I didn't have that kind of love when I was his age, but I knew exactly what he was saying—what it meant to be searching for your purpose and your path.

SANDI

fourteen

I DON'T REMEMBER WHAT I expected would happen when I returned to Salt Lake City. Did I expect the dysfunction of the four of us to peel away like a scab, revealing a patch of bright, slightly shiny skin underneath? Because it didn't. We—our parents, Kevin, and I—were back in the same dark house, with the same assortment of junk cars spreading across the front lawn, except each one seemed to be in a more advanced state of decay. What had started out as small, rusty scrapes had continued to oxidize and had gradually infiltrated the paint. Ultimately, the ruptured paint was no match for rain, snow, or sun. So the rust had spread across the hoods and wheel covers, down the trunks, and along the roofs, if the roofs still remained.

As before, my father was there, but he was also gone, more chapters in the lengthy series of extended separations. No one announced the beginnings of these departures or the endings. It was like "unexpected turbulence" on a plane. Kevin and I, as passengers, just had to ride it out. There was less fighting during those periods when he was absent, but ever more paranoia from Mom.

Living alone in the trailer in Mountain Home had taught me a few things. I realized that I no longer had to be dependent on my parents. I still needed them for some necessities and money, but I could survive on my own. And I could remove myself from their orbit when the time came. Leaving had been a two-way street: by leaving me, they had also inadvertently taught me the lesson that I could leave them. Meanwhile, I had learned to live with silence. I didn't need to talk; I didn't need to say anything. Silence became the thing that defined me the most as I moved through school and navigated the erratic world at home.

I was initially pushed partway into silence by my deplorable teeth. I never visited the dentist when I was young, and toothbrushing was hardly stressed when we were marching around the house wielding vacuum cleaner parts to ward off intruders and murderers. By sixth grade, my mouth was a mess of misaligned, crowded teeth and lots of decay. The cavities had to be filled, but more important to my mother was how I looked. She wanted my smile to be perfect, as if somehow the position and quality of my teeth reflected directly on her. Before we moved to Idaho, she had packed me off to a Utah orthodontist, who pulled my errant teeth and, for a year, had me sleep in headgear, a huge contraption that wrapped around my head and had a thick wire band directed into my mouth to push back my molars. I don't know where the money to pay for all this orthodontia came from, just as I didn't know where the money came from for my mother's various plastic surgeries, but somehow, she found it. I, however, became self-conscious about my teeth. It was easier to keep my mouth shut. Then, alone in Mountain Home, it was easier to say nothing. By the time I returned to Salt Lake City, silence was my art form.

◆

Salt Lake City was founded by Mormon pioneers—members of the Church of Latter-Day Saints—who sought to create a utopian colony where they could practice their religion. After a brutal westward trek, they settled on a remote location beside a mineral-laden lake, ringed by the Wasatch Mountains, a sawtooth set of peaks linked to the Rocky Mountain chain. Some of the summits reached above eleven thousand feet. Salt Lake City was designed to be a different community—and a communal one. Joseph Smith, the Mormon Church's founder, devised a city plan based on a rigid grid that stretched from north to south and east to west. He created large blocks, a massive 660-square-foot spread, with the idea that families would farm inside the city limits. In fact, he envisioned an array of city farms, but not anything resembling a central business district. Streets were wide; at 130 feet across, they were more than twice the width of New York and San Francisco's streets, and they were sized that way to allow for easily moving horses and transporting cattle. From almost the beginning, Salt Lake was divided between Mormons and non-Mormons. Mormons lived in separate neighborhoods; they fielded their own local political candidates; and most important for me, Mormonism dominated the public school system. Non-Mormons mostly sent their kids to private schools. My parents had chosen to live in a largely Mormon neighborhood and to send me to public schools.

I returned to school in Salt Lake in the middle of eighth grade. But back in the house, the wild ways that I had accumulated on my own in Mountain Home didn't change. In our home, there were no rules. No curfew, no regular mealtimes. No one ever knew where I was or what I was doing. Social norms or general rules of living also didn't apply. I didn't know to chew with my mouth closed or how to be polite when I asked for something. I didn't know how not to point or not to grab at what I wanted. I didn't hear the phrase "thank you," so I didn't say it. The lack of knowledge about how to brush my teeth and comb my hair extended to how I dressed and when I needed a bra.

Every student had to participate in PE in school. I was required to change into my PE uniform, a tank top where my bouncing breasts and clumps of underarm hair were on full view. The other girls pointed and laughed and talked mercilessly about my "boobies" as I tried to cross my arms over my chest and hug them close to my sides. I had to beg my mother to buy me a bra and a razor so that I could shave under my armpits. When my mother finally relented and bought me a bra, it was several sizes too small. Decades passed before I was fitted for the right bra size; my mother was "competitive" with me and had been adamant that I had "small breasts," and I believed her, so for most of my life, I wore bras that were too small. I didn't know about deodorant, either, until I saw that some girls kept spray cans in their lockers.

In school, aside from the horrible display I made of myself during PE, I sat in the back of the classrooms and stayed quiet. I didn't care about learning, and my grades showed it. They were a mix of Bs, Cs, and Ds. My mother had always told me that my grades didn't matter until I hit ninth grade. That was the year when everything counted, she said, if I wanted to go to college. So, in the fall of 1975, the start of my ninth-grade year, I hit the books. I had decided that school, specifically college, would be my way out. Other kids equated independence with cars and driving and a later curfew. To me, independence was leaving my family behind as far and as fast as possible. I also did not want to end up like my mother, completely dependent on a man for my economic survival, unable to fend for myself financially, and without the skills of a well-paying profession. I was determined to be self-sufficient above all else. At night, lying in bed in my room at the top of the stairs, with its mod-girl hot-pink wallpaper, I would try to imagine living on my own for real.

Sometimes, I would sit up in bed and look out my window, gazing at the driveway, which was just a dirt path that snaked to the unseen road. Off to the left was a barnlike building where our chickens coexisted with my dad's scrap heap of car parts and the other crazy stuff that he hoarded and stored. Like a movie running in my mind, I would picture myself leaving down that driveway, not with a cage of cats, but carrying a suitcase and leaving for real.

Similar to the house it sat in, my room was a mix of the familiar and the fearful. The bed, the dresser, and the wallpaper were all standard, but then, at the back of the space, there was a small closet, a storage area tucked under the eaves that ran the whole length of the room. And it scared me to death. I was still terrified of small spaces; my palms would sweat, and my heart would race if I just looked at them. I would not enter that closet unless Kevin went with me. I kept what clothes I had in my room or a small linen-type closet with shelves, and tried to ignore the closet.

At school, my teachers were shocked by the sudden change in my performance. Overnight, and without explanation, I was earning straight As. Because it was a junior high school, seventh through ninth grades were in the same building. All the students had the same teachers and administrators. The adults could not believe the transformation. And I could not believe how easy school was once I started to apply myself. I began to wonder if perhaps I was kind of smart.

I also had nothing to keep me occupied other than schoolwork. After returning to Salt Lake, I had briefly made one friend, Stephanie. I don't know why she befriended me, but among our family collection of vehicles, we had a dirt bike, and she would come over and we would ride the dirt bike down the path leading to the road, spewing up a small trail of dirt and pebbles as we went. But after we had an accident on the bike, her mother refused to allow her to come over anymore. The lesson I took from Stephanie was that there didn't seem to be much point in adolescent friendships, so I stopped trying to make them.

We were loners in general. No one in our house saw much of our neighbors. Our family's disappearance and return seemed to have only confirmed our strangeness to them. Too many people still hated my father for his schemes, and most of our neighbors' lives were organized around the Mormon ward, what they called their churches. Mormonism was exotic enough to the rest of the country that *National Geographic* ran a feature article on Mormons and Salt Lake City in April 1975, not unlike how they might profile cultures in Africa or the Amazon or run a photo essay of life in the Pacific Islands. My parents also didn't have an interest in creating friendships if they weren't using them to try to advance my father's business dealings. They didn't host dinner parties or cookouts, and it seemed that they weren't invited to attend any in the neighborhood. Instead, Eugene and Janice lived in their own self-contained world of chaos until it reached the point that they couldn't stand each other.

Despite our conversation in the car ride from Idaho, my father disappeared again not long after I arrived, leaving me alone with my mother and Kevin in what I now began to understand were more "separations." During these months, he lived another life in another home, in an apartment where he owned a white crushed velvet sofa, which mysteriously accompanied him on his return. The older we became, the more Kevin and I learned that it was best to stay somewhat ignorant of the goings-on between our parents and, even more important, to stay out of the way.

While our father was, from time to time, seemingly aware that he and my mother had made Kevin's and my lives very hard, that awareness cycled in and out—and mostly out. It was my mother's moods that ruled our house, and as a result, there was a lot of terror in our lives. If not terror in that individual moment, then I was possessed by a feeling that I had to be constantly alert, waiting for the inevitable terror to return. And for causing that excessive vigilance, I blamed my father.

When he was home, my father frequently spent most of his day in bed, attempting to plot some new moneymaking scheme. But, more likely, he stayed in bed because he was depressed. Downstairs, my mother would hold me captive for hours-long conversations, which were monologues where she would vent about my father, veering off into subplots involving her mother or Uncle Carlie. Nothing less than my complete, rapt attention was acceptable. My mother wove elaborate conspiracy theories about how my father's family was out to get her, making up long stories about how they planned to hurt her financially—she would launch into detailed descriptions of how they were gathering evidence against her to deprive her of money, or even to kill her. She would yell and scream and wave her hands. And when the final, definitive piece of proof necessary for her story was missing, it was invariably due to a mistake I had made or something that was my fault.

The younger me, who had been completely absorbed in her fantasies and had willingly tromped around the house and crawled army-style across the floor, clutching heavy aluminum vacuum cleaner parts, would have believed it all. Now, at ages fourteen and fifteen, it wasn't as if I doubted her, it was just that I had had enough. But I still believed the essence of the story that she wove: that my father was a monster and she was his helpless victim.

When she wasn't obsessed with conspiracies about my father or his family, my mother was obsessed with my appearance beyond my teeth. She was hyper-focused on her weight, staying slim by counting calories and periodically fasting, and she made constant comments about my size and worried aloud that I was not staying slim. I was already awkwardly tall and lanky, having grown about six inches between fifth and sixth grades, until I towered over most of the other kids in my class, which was mortifying. It was as if I were a walking billboard calling attention to my irregular teeth and Salvation Army clothing. Even as the other kids began to catch up, I still walked and sat with my shoulders slumped in a permanent slouch as if that would make me disappear.

I couldn't control my height, but I could control my weight, and I began to monitor everything I ate, choosing the flimsy iceberg salad, no dressing, instead of an order of fries, carefully measuring how much cereal I put into a bowl, and counting every calorie, to the point that I calculated the calories in the vitamins that I swallowed as part of my daily allotted total. It never crossed my mind that perhaps all those years when Kevin and I had been hungry when we were shooting our food in the woods or pulling it off vines in the garden, there might have been more to our deprivation than money. The narrowness of our choices also removed all possibility of temptation—not for us, but for our mother.

By the time I started tenth grade and Kevin was entering eighth grade, our parents decided that they wanted to get out of Salt Lake City. Kevin and I were told to pack what we had; we were going back to Idaho, with our small assortment of furniture trailing behind our old brown Bronco. Compared to the polarized world of Salt Lake, Idaho remained, for me, a calm and accepting place. During the years that we had lived in Mountain Home, I had felt accepted, even though I really didn't have any actual friends beyond Pepino. Mostly, I didn't feel disliked and looked down upon the way I did in Salt Lake City. Even though Idaho has the second-largest per capita Mormon population after Utah, I didn't feel the religious divide. To me, Idaho people were simpler, with more of a live-and-let-live philosophy. They did what they needed to take care of business, and most of that involved hard work. On the land, that meant to sow the crops, pull the weeds, irrigate, and watch the fields until it was time to bring in the harvest. When someone needed a hand, they were quick to lend it, knowing that they would more than likely need a hand one day in return.

But we didn't return to Mountain Home. The farm had been lost in foreclosure or reclaimed by my uncle. Instead, my parents moved us to the capital city of Boise, up the highway from Mountain Home, and into a three-bedroom condo rental perched on a hill on the outskirts of town, near a small, par-3 golf course and at the base of a road leading to a ski hill. The condo complex had a clubhouse and tennis courts. I'd never seen a tennis court before. After I watched a few people bat a fuzzy ball around with their racquets, I thought the whole idea of the sport was strange. Why change into special clothes, short white skirts or short white shorts and matching tops, just to play a game?

Once I stepped outside of the condo complex grounds, construction hummed all around us; the bright stamp of Boise Cascade on lumber being hauled on flatbeds, the rumble and whir of concrete mixers, and the screech and thump of saws and hammers traveling through the high desert air. Homes and complexes seemed to sprout up overnight. Boise was a city on the move.

The neighbor who lived next to us was a young woman with a job in downtown Boise. Both of us liked to "lay out" on the units' small, adjoining decks, our skin slathered in oil, trying to turn our pale legs, arms, and bellies bronze. I'd talk to her sometimes; I'm sure she could hear my parents' raised voices through the flimsy walls. I'd tell her about them, and she would offer advice—about how to deal with them and, especially, how ultimately to get away.

Our condo was cheaply built, with plywood doors and a pressed bathroom washbasin. The drywall was so thin that once, when my father punched a wall in anger, his fist busted right through it, leaving a huge hole and a trail of powdery, crushed talc and gypsum. No one ever bothered to fix it, so bits of the wall would continually flake off in a slow disintegration. Our unit had two levels. On the first was a very short, narrow galley kitchen. A small room off the kitchen was designated as the "family room." My parents never bothered to put any furniture in the space, but they placed a small TV with rabbit ears on the brown industrial carpet. I used to stretch out on that carpet, lying on my side or propped up on my elbows, my spine curved in a reverse C, and watch whatever was on, mostly black-and-white reruns of *I Love Lucy* and old Westerns. The place was so newly built, the dirt still disrupted, that lying on my back like that one evening, I felt something on my belly. Looking down, I came face-to-face with a scorpion. I screamed.

After that, I began sitting on the kitchen counter to try to watch a second television that had appeared out of nowhere. We so rarely had a television in our house that I didn't know anything about many of the popular shows; I had spent my time reading instead. When kids at school talked about series like *Happy Days* or *Laverne & Shirley*, I would stare blankly. The names meant nothing, and I didn't even know what time or what channel they were on.

Our living room had the same brown carpet as the den, on top of which sat one of our gold chairs that had survived countless moves from as far back as New Orleans, and the more recent white crushed velvet sofa. My bedroom was upstairs, along with the single, shared bathroom for the four of us, just as it had been in Salt Lake City. But a shared bathroom was far better than jumping in an irrigation pond. At least when I went to school, I was clean.

I was enrolled at Boise High, the oldest high school in the city, built of tan brick, with an imposing carved pediment and four massive Corinthian columns stretching two stories in the front—not that I knew anything about the architecture. I just knew that it looked imposing and that it was a very long walk from our condo. Sometimes, the young woman who lived next door dropped me off at school on her way downtown. Eventually, my dad presented me with a very old

Chevy Vega. The heavily worn interior was brown, and the seat cushions had massive cracks and creases, but it ran, and fourteen was the legal age to drive in Idaho. After that, each morning, I'd sputter off to school in the Vega.

Boise High was a mix of old and new—to save money, someone had decided to add false ceilings that hid the pipes and supposedly reduced heating costs. On cloudy days, fluorescent lights buzzed and glowed. Boise High was the first school where I felt that people were nice to me. I even made friends, although I tried to be as inconspicuous as possible.

Just as I had in my classes in Salt Lake City, I stayed slouched and silent in my seat. But teachers noticed that I was tall. Boise was and is a place that breeds sports stars; many of the high school's notable alumni were football players. Fall Friday nights were spent on the bleachers as strapping players crashed into each other on the turf below. I didn't go to the games, but I couldn't avoid the pep rallies, the hand-painted posters in the hallways, and the marching band practices. The cheerleaders wore their hair in pigtails tied with ribbons in the school's colors and floated through the hallways in their soft-soled saddle shoes. By Friday afternoon, the air inside the building was electric with anticipation. Sports and sporting rivalries drove the high school and, seemingly, the entire city.

One teacher kept suggesting that I should try out for the basketball team. I wasn't totally sure what that meant. I'd never seen a basketball game, let alone played in one. But the female coach was very patient and tried to teach me how to play.

For years, I never considered that my height (I was now five feet, ten inches) would be an advantage for anything, or that my latent strength built from all those months working in the Idaho fields, cleaning motel rooms, and walking wherever I needed to go had any benefits. I never thought that for a girl height and strength might be a powerful combination. But they were. And basketball offered another advantage: it got me away from the condo in the afternoons.

In the 1970s, at least at Boise High, girls were still taught to shoot underhanded, just as softball pitchers threw underhanded or volleyball players served underhanded. It was very old-school. But the basketball coach and her assistants were kind, and I enjoyed the other girls on the team. Where I excelled was at running track. The track coach was also the PE teacher, and he convinced me to try out. We met on the school's field to train, running on the circular track and doing drills.

My first big race at an official school meet was as the anchor leg of the mile relay. (In today's terms, it is the equivalent of a 400-meter 4×4.) The lead runner for the other team was a good two hundred yards ahead of me when I started, and I almost caught her. My brother was watching in the stands, and once the meet was over, he told me that most people hadn't really been paying attention until I started running. By the time the two of us got close to the finish line, everyone was screaming and hollering for me. The problem was that I'd never run that far or that fast before. By the end, my legs gave out, and I could hardly breathe. Once I crossed the finish line, I staggered and fell to the ground, lay on my back, and tried to catch my breath. The coach raced over to help me up. He was astonished and excited to discover that I could run that fast.

My fastest race time was just over fifty-nine seconds—I remember the whoops and cheers from my teammates; breaking sixty seconds was a very big deal. Our team was good enough to reach the state finals, and I was entered to run the 440-yard dash. But I had developed shin splints—from all that running—and I came up lame about halfway through. I finished the race, but basically at a walk. Although everyone cheered when I finally crossed the finish line, I felt like I'd failed the team. One of the few things I saved from that year—or any of my years in high school—was a photo of our team standing on the podium.

For the first time, I wasn't sitting alone during lunch—I had friends to sit with, the girls on the track and basketball teams. I also wasn't always hungry because lunch at school was free. I could load up my tray, and no one thought much about it.

In the classroom, I gravitated to math and history. Math came easily and thus was usually an easy A. History was interesting to me because it was more unexpected—I didn't know what had happened, so each era was a new adventure for me. I loved learning about other cultures and was fascinated by the stories of the past, especially the powerful mix of heroism and cruelty. Having entire countries change their direction on the whims of one individual or bloody wars erupt over petty slights and differences were also experiences that I could relate to inside my own home.

English was more difficult. Having missed chunks of elementary school meant that my knowledge of grammar was spotty. But I loved to read, although sometimes I didn't see the point of the old nineteenth-century books that the teacher called the "classics." Their characters could feel outdated and arrogant. I preferred newer novels, where the characters wandered through life slightly adrift and alone. I also didn't necessarily enjoy writing English papers, an irony now, considering that I would go on to choose a profession that involved a significant amount of writing, and my entire career as a parent at Sidwell was spent carefully crafting legions of emails.

Ironic, too, because it was my tenth-grade English teacher who took a special interest in me. She nominated me for a spot as a People-to-People Student Ambassador on one of their two-week overseas programs. People-to-People was started by President Dwight Eisenhower as an outreach program for the Cold War. In the 1970s, it still sent a few hundred students abroad each year.

I can't recall now if she even told me that she had proposed my name. I simply received a letter informing me that I had been selected, and I believe that I also received a stipend to cover a large part of the cost, although my parents had to pay either a small administrative fee or some part of my plane fare. (I don't know if the money came from a scholarship or possibly from my uncle; I think if my parents had paid for any significant portion, I would have heard about it for years after.)

Both my mother and father were less than thrilled initially by the program and the prospect of me traveling abroad. During his years in the navy, my father had apparently been stationed on a military ship, floating somewhere in the Pacific during the Korean War, but in general, he was not a fan of "other countries," as he called them. My mother didn't see the point. But my teacher persisted, saying that this would be a good experience for me, and it would cost them almost nothing. Shockingly, they relented. I applied for a passport, and my mother even took me shopping to buy a pantsuit to wear on the airplane because this was back in the day when people dressed up to fly. Although we had crossed thousands of miles of road back and forth from New Orleans to California and up and down the stretch between Salt Lake City and Idaho, I don't think either of them had ever been on an airplane.

I was excited for the adventure, but mostly I was thrilled to be leaving everything familiar and especially my family behind.

I thought I knew what speed was until the plane thundered down the tarmac and, with a slight thump, lifted up and rose into the sky. I watched in wonder as the ground receded and Boise became nothing more than a speck. It was as if my body was learning the ability to leave, that in an instant, it was possible to pluck yourself out of one life and move completely and irrevocably into the next. Our student ambassador group spent two days in Washington, DC, being briefed, and then we boarded our different international flights, with our name badges pinned to our jackets, for our trips overseas.

I had three homestays scheduled for the next two weeks. The first homestay was with a family in Austria. They lived on a remote farm, in some ways not too dissimilar from what I had experienced in Mountain Home. It was a husband and wife and their daughter, who was a few years younger than me. They spoke no English, and I didn't know a word of German. To communicate, we resorted to gestures and pointing, and the mom would sometimes repeat what she had just said to me, only in a louder voice, as if the volume would somehow magically enable me to spontaneously understand German.

What was familiar was the farm, a modest farmhouse with a variety of outbuildings, barns, pens, and coops, where they raised cows, chickens, and pigs. I woke up early each morning to help with the chores, cleaning out the animal enclosures and collecting the still-warm eggs from the chicken nests. When the chores were finished, their daughter and I would run around the farm and play. Her friends came by to join us and, most likely, to get an up-close look at the American.

The mom spent much of her day in the kitchen, and I would help her bake various breads and sweet things. She was happy to have me measure the ingredients and knead and roll the dough. I tasted everything she cooked, and no one in the house counted a calorie. I was not prepared for Austrian farm food, the dense dumplings, potatoes, and breaded and pan-fried meats—called schnitzel. But I was determined to try everything and to pretend that I liked it. One evening, the family took me on a long drive to a restaurant as a special treat.

I didn't need to worry about how I looked or what I wore while I was on the farm. The mother spent her days in a housedress with pockets and wore sensible shoes. The father was dressed for farming, in canvas coveralls, a heavy shirt, and work boots. Their daughter wore pants and shirts, with rain or work boots, depending on the weather, which was dreary and cloudy almost the entire time I was there. After years in a semiarid desert and blazing blue sky, I was surprised by the rain and cool dampness of summer in this part of Europe, by how the clouds hung in a heavy, low layer as if sealing us in. The ground was green with little bursts of flowers, but the backdrop was a relentless gray.

I loved that time and the family because, in their house, there was a complete lack of pretense; they made me feel right at home. When we said good night, I headed off to my own small room and burrowed under the thick down comforter that stretched across the bed. I had never slept under such fluffy warmth. I was also surprised by how quiet everyone was. Except for the mom's few efforts to get her German to penetrate my brain, they spoke in calm, low voices to one another and to me. At first, I wondered if this was an act, a front they were putting up for my first or second day. I had assumed that most, if not all, families operated at some level of chaos, that raised voices were the rule and not the exception. But their behavior didn't change, and as my shock subsided, I began to wonder if my assumptions had been wrong.

From Austria, I traveled to Germany to join another family for a few days. This family lived in a small German village. They had one teenage daughter who was my age, and we spent a lot of time walking the village and meeting people. My last stop was Greece, with a loud, boisterous family who lived in a house that was located across a highway from the Mediterranean Sea. There was a boy about my age and his younger sister. The father was a typical Greek patriarch. Each night, he drank ouzo, sharing small glasses of the fiery liquid with the kids. The food was very similar to the Syrian meals that my grandmother had made, and I loved it. After we finished dinner, the brother and sister would take me to join their friends in the village at the local pub/disco, where everyone crowded the small dance floor, moving to the music that blared over the speakers. Our days were spent at the beach and in the sea. I had only seen the ocean once before, and I was thrilled to learn how to boogie board and bodysurf in the blue waters.

While other ambassadors might have been homesick, I dreaded each hour that drew me closer to the flight home. The entire trip opened my eyes. The different cultures were almost secondary. My own family was part Syrian. I had lived as an outsider among Mormons and had become friends with migrant farmworkers who spoke Spanish. What surprised me was how normal and kind everyone was. For two weeks, I watched families who started as strangers to me treat each other well. I watched them simply enjoying their lives and enjoying being with each other. To me, that was the exotic experience, after a lifetime of nonstop conflict and complaint. And although I had to travel halfway around the world to experience it, I believed I could find it again much closer to home.

For the first time, I had experienced what it was like to live with a giving family that was full of love, and for the first time I promised myself that when I got out of my own household—because I was going to get out of it—I would be giving, and I would welcome people into my home, too.

RYAN

fifteen

THERE IS A VERBAL LINE of demarcation for private schools in Washington, DC. They are almost universally abbreviated. The self-identified elite are St. Albans, NCS (for National Cathedral School), GDS (for Georgetown Day School), Maret, and, of course, Sidwell. No one bothers to append the noun "school." It is something that anyone familiar with elite education is expected to know. Like Princeton, Harvard, or Yale, these private schools are educational brands unto themselves. If you don't know what Sidwell is, perhaps it is something that you do not need to know.

The students who attend these schools are made aware of this status in a variety of ways, some visual, some intellectual, some visceral. Their position is reflected in college admissions statistics, in notable alumni and speakers drawn to the campus, in the connections of parents, but mostly it's reflected in how the students carry themselves and in the hierarchy of place and identity. But in subtle and not-so-subtle ways, it is also reflected from the school upon the students.

There is a school of thought that insists and even argues that equality of opportunity is enough. The problem is that it is not. There are deeper discrepancies and foundational skills that sheer hard work and bootstrapping cannot somehow magically overcome. Out of necessity, our academic support for Ryan had progressed from the two of us sitting in the kitchen, going over homework, to an array of fully engaged professional tutors who were trying to close holes, teach foundational skills, and bring Ryan up to speed on the voluminous new material so he wouldn't fall further behind. My concern was the level of stress Ryan was experiencing and the clear way that these "deficits" were impacting his self-esteem. But even with the tutors, the educational deficits Ryan faced were challenging. No matter how fast he tried to run, the pace set by the school and the overall academic environment kept accelerating. I had been able to "catch up" because I came of age in a different and easier time; the large public high schools I attended did not have the exacting standards of Sidwell. The level of competition wasn't even close.

I had initially thought that if we brought in tutors, if I fixed teeth, if I was there for surgical or injury rehab, if I cooked enough, drove enough, did enough laundry, if I brought everyone together, we would pull through. Our memories would be light and funny, like Elie's of the way her "brothers" would simultaneously burst into her room and bounce her mattress, shaking her awake in the morning. And the rhythm of our internal home life was largely enough for us as a family during those years. But it wasn't enough to equalize the outside metrics of achievement: academic grades and scores. In these measurements, there appeared to be two separate scales, one for Justin and another for Ryan. The differences entailed recognizing the subtle, or sometimes not-so-subtle, changes in narration, where the underlying tone of the message was transformed, the praise receded, and the expectations were shifted until, inch by inch, the door that once looked so wide and welcoming was ever so discreetly closed.

It was just as I had thought back when the boys were in ninth grade: things did not even out after a year or two. Instead, they became further divided and stratified. And there was no middle ground when it came to the weight of staggering expectations: a student either shouldered them and moved forward or faltered under the load and was slowly crushed.

◆

In the fall of Ryan and Justin's junior year, I did what private school parents across Washington, DC, did—I engaged a tutor to prepare them for the SATs. And I did it for both boys. For two years, I had avoided having them evaluated or compared side by side. I knew Justin was generally enrolled in more advanced classes, and in what core classes Justin and Ryan shared, they did not overlap in a common classroom. But now they did. Our SAT tutor wrote me in December, "So far, Justin is doing beautifully with most everything I've given him, though I'd love it if he can make more time for vocabulary. We haven't look[ed] at the ACT, in part because the SAT looks so strong . . . For Ryan, it is less clear. His numeracy is not what it might be. But he is working hard and picking things up. The math on the ACT is more advanced, which may not help him, though it (and other sections of the ACT) may seem to him more straightforward. For now, we have been working on content that is (except for vocabulary) relevant to both tests." The tutor was profoundly generous, offering me a discounted rate for Ryan based on his family situation—the owner of the tutoring company was a Sidwell parent whom I knew and thus could ask for help.

In this email from the SAT tutor, and in countless other emails and interactions, the conventional narrative of Ryan's life indelibly wrote itself into the separate narrative of his education and into the stories that we were told about him—and that he was told himself. It happened in ways that I saw and, most likely, in hundreds of more ways that I didn't. When a student is in survival mode at home, as Ryan was for many years, it can be extremely challenging to see beyond the week or even beyond the weekend. But, despite this huge mountain of challenges, Ryan did not give up. He persevered, he worked hard, he woke up every day with a smile and love for the world. He is and was the most genuine person I have ever met. It broke my heart that he internalized these comments and opinions on his abilities. He was so much more than the comments. We had countless conversations about how he was so smart, and wise, and strong. He was like me. I had to fight, too, which helped me see this truth in Ryan. He was more than other people's opinions. I had succeeded, and he could, too. I was immensely proud of him. I still am.

Once, Ryan wrote a thank-you list for me. It enumerates some stunningly ordinary tasks—the types of things moms (and many dads) do every day without thinking. But in his situation, they were anything but ordinary to him. It wasn't that his mother didn't want to do these things, but it was that she could not find space or time where she could do them. Chaos is the enemy of good intentions.

Doing my hair everyday
Making delicious smoothies every morning
Making a great breakfast every morning
TAKING ME SHOPING
TAKING ME SHOPING FOR SHOES
Treating me like your second son (for better or for worst) :P
The love you give me everyday

The amazing dinners you make (besides the beets) :P
The love you put in with whatever you do
How hard working you are
Your positive encouragement you give me
The wonderful mother you are
For taking time out of your day to pick us up and do our clothes
Always knowing how to put a smile on my face
AND EVERYTHING YOU DO FOR ME

If another mother had done something similar for me when I was growing up, I might have written a list like this. For Ryan, the pivot was enormous: moving from fending for himself and honing his survival skills to suddenly entering a world of elite education, where the expectation was that families could and would cultivate a smooth path devoid of all obstacles so that the student could concentrate on achieving in class, on elite performance in athletics or extracurriculars, and on their social life. The vast majority of full-tuition-paying Sidwell students were not doing their own laundry or making their own meals. Someone was making sure they had football tights and new pads and jerseys, or freshly strung tennis rackets and outside coaching. They were readying emails and filing all the necessary school forms. The sinuous, expectant pickup lines after practices were a daily reminder of the pinpoint organization of transportation. To be a Sidwell student was to enter a life of highly functioning competitive pressure, supported by an almost military level of precision coordination of all the other facets of teenage life. And in navigating this terrain himself, Ryan was grateful just to have new underwear and shoes.

It's hard to overstate how much of modern education is dependent on the filing of school forms. There were sign-ups, questionnaires, checklists, and official forms. By late sophomore year, I thought I had finally bested the gauntlet of the Sidwell online portal and school administration to be copied on vital emails and be seen as a point of contact for Ryan. I had a medical power of attorney as well. But there was always something that slipped through the cracks.

The summer before junior year, what slipped were the school medical forms required to be filed before the players started football practice. We were on vacation in Maui with Ryan when I received a general notice sent to football players about missing medical forms, with no student name attached. I checked the website that Justin's had been submitted, and they were, but Rochelle had been sent the forms for Ryan. I wrote the athletic department asking if perhaps this email applied to Ryan. The reply arrived the following week, two and a half days before practice started. It was from the school nurse, and she began, "I wasn't aware of you needing access to his health information. I will need to get the ok for that before I can add you as a proxy to view that info. In the meantime, emails have gone home as a reminder for mom to send health forms, but I have not received the remaining forms as of this morning."

I sent a cheerful reply as we were stuffing our suitcases and preparing for the eleven-and-a-half-hour flight back. ". . . there's no reason for you to have known about the communication piece of this. Sometimes I get emails, and sometimes not, but I'm not sure why . . . I'll work on this when I return. Thank you!!"

Constantly, I was humbled and embarrassed by Ryan's gratitude. I saved all his notes, including a note he typed me one Mother's Day—

> Sorry for the lateness
>
> But my research paper was my weekend.
>
> I couldn't even buy my 1st mom a card
>
> Luckily my brother bought one

> But I'm pretty sure what I want to say can't be found on a Hallmark card
>
> Because our relationship means more than any card can say, including this one

He had a list of things he appreciated, and he ended with:

> I've been thinking about what to say in this card for a while
>
> And it still doesn't appropriately show my appreciation for all that you do
>
> I just hope you know no matter what happens
>
> That I, Ryan, am very, very grateful for everything you've done and everything you will do.
>
> Love,
> Your second son,
> Ryan

In their senior year, Ryan and Justin were finally placed in the same class, a science course on astrophysics. After several attempts by me to reach out, the teacher responded to one of my emails with a very lengthy one of her own:

> Sorry I didn't respond to your last two emails! Of course, I have intended to, but . . . no excuse.
>
> Here's an update from my end.
>
> Ryan did set up a weekly meeting right before break . . . I'll use it to check in on their progress with coursework [another football player has joined Ryan at the meetings] . . .

> there's not much that they can do at this point to significantly change their homework grades or quiz/test grades (I think we'll have one more quiz, and maybe a couple of homeworks but not many).

Then she turned her full attention to Justin.

> As for Justin, he has definitely continued to improve! I gave him the test back yesterday, and yes, his grade was low, BUT this was THE hardest test of the year, and I structured it just like the AP (time-wise) . . . So I'm having them do test corrections, and he can early [*sic*] up to 2/3 of the points that he missed back. He knows what grade he COULD get (and will get, I think!), assuming that he does perfect text [*sic*] corrections (which Aaron and I will make sure he does, as long as he keeps up the great streak he is on!), and he seemed pretty pleased! . . . I think he's still in a little bit of a hole from earlier this semester in terms of knowledge, but far less than before and he is keeping up well . . . next week, I'll assign him some extra work that can stand in for those homeworks that he missed . . . I can replace those homework grades.

The email went on to discuss college visits and logging into the school information system, now called euphemistically "Haiku," to access missing work. "(The last test is on April 20, but I'll gladly give him an extension on that if he needs it.)"

The thing is, I had not once asked about Justin in my email. The subject and focus of my email had been Ryan and his football teammate, Elijah, not Justin. I appreciated the kind and encouraging words, but there was often far more encouragement given when it came to Justin. Students like Ryan and Elijah were seen as being at Sidwell to contribute to the sports team, but their lives were ultimately destined for a different trajectory.

Fortunately, not everyone at the school responded in this way. There were a few teachers who wanted to look beneath the surface perceptions, who managed to put aside any preconceptions and to genuinely see the boys themselves. One, who had helped Ryan as a writing tutor in the summers and whom he sought out for help and additional thoughts during the school year, wrote to me, "Years in the business of teaching has made me appreciate the good eggs so very much. Ryan is a joyous, kind, curious young man who I hope I get the chance to teach. Simply being who he is has made our school better . . . his integrity and cheerfulness shine."

As I watched Ryan progress through Sidwell, I had another worry—would a college admissions office be able to see Ryan for who he was? I believed if he could just get to the stage where he could be given an alumni interview or speak directly to someone in admissions, he would have an excellent shot at being accepted, but, otherwise, he risked being lost in the pile.

Two things had happened during Ryan's junior year that suggested the path to higher education might become easier. After undergoing two excruciating shoulder surgeries and months of rehabilitation that fall, he was finally back on the team, playing. When Ryan suited up in his pads and pants, put on the team jersey, laced a fresh pair of cleats over his feet, and walked onto the football field to scrimmage, tears of joy streamed down his face. The coach asked if he was okay, and Ryan blubbered back, "I'm just so happy to be here." He was happy.

I don't know that I ever fully appreciated until that moment the power of football in Ryan's young life. It gave him an identity, it gave him purpose, it gave him a place of belonging, and it gave him something that was his. Casual fans may not appreciate that it is impossible for a player to get dressed solo. There is an entire ritual around preparation simply for practice. Yes, players can pull on their tights, girdle, and padded practice pants solo, but when it comes to the shoulder pads, they need a teammate or a coach to tighten and fasten the buckles and belts that secure the device around the outlines of the rib cage and chest. The armor of the game, and in Ryan's case, the equipment that would house his surgically repaired shoulders, cannot be worn without help. Players need each other before they ever leave the locker room.

Success on the field also required its own unique set of skills. While Ryan loved being in school and didn't miss a day unless he absolutely had to, in the classroom, he was fighting for every inch of success. Nothing seemed to come easily to him, and he always knew that he had not been admitted to Sidwell because of his academic promise. However, that seemed to spur him to try harder. He was determined to earn A's every semester, no matter how challenging his classes were. Falling short didn't deter him. Instead, he just regrouped to try again. But on the football field, when he felt the sting of the ball in his gloves or displayed the effortless way that his feet executed the play patterns or how he intuitively knew how to read an opponent, sensing that first subtle shift to the right or left, Ryan was in his element.

The football coaches wanted Sidwell to win, and the assistant coach, in particular, was a tough taskmaster. He assigned Ryan to field positions that Ryan did not much like and hadn't played before. Sometimes, he didn't play Ryan at all. But Ryan never complained. He studied the team's playbook and films to learn what he needed to do in whatever position he was assigned, even if it wasn't instinctual. When he wasn't on the field during a game, Ryan jogged up and down the sidelines, offering words of encouragement to his teammates. Given the smallest opening or opportunity, he built a role for himself.

A second milestone event happened during Ryan's junior year. Leonard decided to get sober. Slowly, some of the fear, anguish, disappointment, and chaos began to recede from Ryan's life. At the same time, however, for Justin, a new round of suffering on the gridiron was just beginning.

JUSTIN

sixteen

As a little boy, Justin loved every toy with a face. He would notice the slightest change in the expression of another person and respond with delight, empathy, or concern. One year, I bought a collection of Demdaco angels to symbolize everyone in our household, and for Justin's angel, I selected a little boy holding a heart of gold, which perfectly captured his heart. But sensitive hearts feel pain so deeply.

Growing up in California, Justin lived in a sheltered environment. He had attended a school affiliated with a church; he knew everyone around him, and they knew him. He was completely unprepared to enter an elite K–8 private school in the Washington, DC, suburbs, as the new kid in eighth grade. Almost from the start, he became a target for bullies. Online, they wrote malicious posts, even encouraging him to commit suicide. But the worst moments came after he suffered a horrible head injury at school. He was running down a hallway, and his thirteen-year-old hormonal brain concluded that he just *must* leap down an upcoming stairway. Unfortunately, in mid-leap, he hit his head on a low steel beam. The blow knocked him unconscious; he needed ten staples to close the gash in his scalp, and he awoke with a severe concussion. When he returned to school, a group of boys in his grade started throwing balls at his head. Post-concussion syndrome left him struggling in class. At the end of the year, one of the administrators held a party for the graduating class and invited every student except Justin. So I was thrilled that Justin would be starting over in a totally different environment at Sidwell Friends.

Justin wanted to play football at Sidwell because he had played in California and loved the game and the camaraderie of his teammates and friends. I agreed because I wanted him to be happy, to feel like he fit in, and to form those bonds that sports can uniquely forge. He wasn't a top football player—what he accomplished was due almost entirely to hard work and repetition. I did not expect him to have much playing time on the field, which actually comforted me, given the head trauma he had experienced in eighth grade. His dream was to play tight end and to play on the varsity squad. But the coaches largely ignored him, and no one attempted to teach him how to play better.

After his surgeries, Ryan had also been relegated to the junior varsity team with Justin—his shoulder problems meant that he had missed the period when he could be kept on the varsity squad. Both boys were dealing with frustrations. It was another way that football further cemented their bonds.

Toward the end of Ryan and Justin's sophomore season, a new coach appeared on the scene. Football is a year-round sport. It is officially played in the fall, but the training and skill development require a year-round commitment. This man was a retired NFL player who lived very close to Sidwell. He started by walking over to watch the practices—the field was visible from the main road. He would offer the coaches bits of advice on how to improve the team, which the coaches were grateful to have. Within a couple of weeks, the man had moved from bystander to assistant coach, and beyond his NFL credentials, no one seemed to have vetted him as a suitable person to work with teenage boys.

In the beginning, Coach R was an inspiration to Justin, Diamente, and Ryan. Justin was particularly thrilled to be taken under a former NFL player's wing and to finally be taught fundamental skills. Coach R seemed to believe in him, and Justin thought Coach R was a hero of sorts. After the season ended, several times a week, Coach R would pick Justin up at our house, take him to nearby fields to run drills, focus on building his skills, and also have long conversations about life. Justin set up weights and rope ladders at home to improve his muscle strength and practice his agility. I'd never seen Justin work so hard for or be so devoted to anything. It seemed to work because Justin was told at the end of the year that he would be able to play on the varsity team. Justin was elated; he really had found a hero in Coach R.

During the spring, Coach R organized "unofficial" preseason practices with his "favored" players. Justin was included in these initially. But when the preseason started in August, inexplicably, Coach R turned on Justin. Coach R's language became abusive. He began calling Justin names, telling him that he was pathetic, incompetent, and stupid, and labeling him with a variety of profanities. Justin was devastated. Diamente and especially Ryan grew increasingly worried for Justin. This began to feel like a crisis for Justin's well-being.

In August, when his birthday came around, Justin told me that he just wanted a "family day" and to skip football practice. We told Justin to text Coach R that he had a family emergency (which we believed that he did), and Justin and I did what we loved to do whenever we could—we spent the day together. We shopped, went to lunch, and talked, and then stopped at the grocery store. Unfortunately, Coach R saw the two of us together at the grocery store that day. He concluded, based on nothing but the text as his guide, that

Justin had lied to him about a "family emergency." It is not an exaggeration to say that Coach R plotted a vicious, public revenge.

The next morning, Justin reported dutifully for practice. Coach R proceeded to humiliate Justin in front of the team, saying, "You are a lying shit who doesn't deserve to be on the team." He called Justin some of the same names that the eighth-grade bullies had used against him—"loser," "baby," and "worthless." Coach R made no attempt to ascertain the truth, and the team's head coach ignored what was happening on the field, possibly for fear of alienating or losing Coach R. After the verbal tirade, Coach R demanded that Justin roll on the ground over and over until Justin was so hot and disoriented that he vomited. Then Coach R told Justin that he would never allow him to play in a single game the entire season. In the days and weeks that followed, Coach R trash-talked Justin to the other players, something they would quietly tell me when they stayed over at our house or out of earshot on the team's sidelines, where I was taking photographs. And he made good on his threat—Justin was not allowed to play in a game during the entire regular season—even if Sidwell was ahead by forty points or more.

In one moment, Justin's overriding high school dream and his identity were crushed. We still hosted team dinners and sleepovers. We went through the rituals of the game. But the magic was gone. Some Saturday nights, after another morning spent benched on the sidelines, Justin would shut the door to his room, go to bed, and stay there all Sunday.

Ryan tried to do everything to help. He already always contributed to household work and helped Elie, whom he called his "little sister," with her homework and attended all her events outside of school. Now he tried to draw Justin out of his shell and encourage him to branch out beyond football and make new friends. I'd find Ryan and Justin at the kitchen table, with Ryan looking at the Sidwell Student

Me in my crib, and the first of many hot coffee burns at the hands of my mom.

Our dad believed Kevin and I were never too young to hunt and barely too young for a rifle.

Our front yard, which was my dad's junkyard.

Fishing wasn't a pastime; it was about catching food. But these were my best memories with my dad.

The exterior of our Idaho shack house and the pond where Kevin and I bathed.

The interior of our shack house. The center opening was how we "got downstairs."

One of my dad's Frankenstein-esque flivvers—I'm at the wheel and my mom is along for the ride.

Super Mom with Justin and Elie—except it wasn't quite so super to be trying to do everything.

Justin and Elie traveling back-to-back.

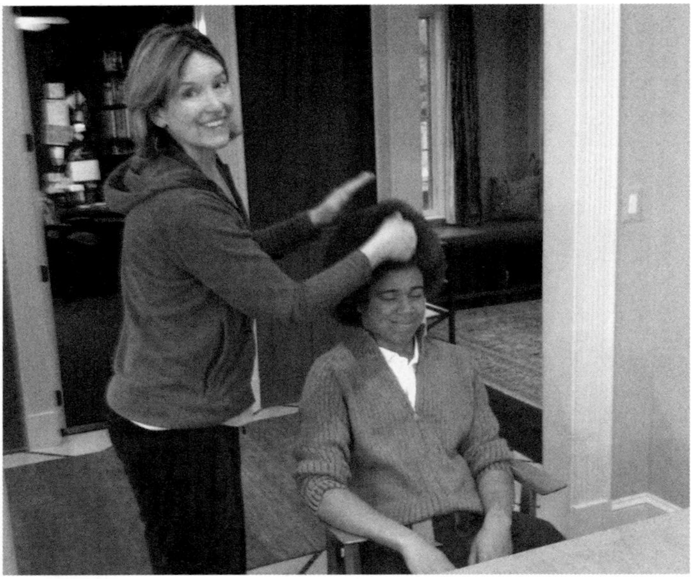

Morning home hair salon.

My favorite memories are of everyone just "chillin'." They always had to sit on one piece of furniture—all of them.

Our mass trip to Maui—all of us soaking up sun, surf, and sand.

It's not easy being green. Home spa green tea facemasks for Elie and Diamente.

Diamente's Sidwell graduation day. Mom 2 bursting with pride.

First day of school, ninth and twelfth grades.

Diamente excelling on the college gridiron.

Elie, Justin, and Elijah catching up on a school break.

Elie and her "bonus brother," Diamente. As she says, "We laugh at everything."

Justin and Diamente. Laughter joins us at every table.

Our home, our family: big, merry, and bright. Christmas 2021.

Directory and quizzing Justin about basic information regarding the kids in his class, coaching Justin on how to get to know them.

Because he felt that he had responded with character to the "punishment" that Coach R had dealt him over the entire season, Justin reached out to Coach R after the playoffs ended and begged him for a chance to try again during his senior year. Coach R said that all would be forgiven and that Justin would be allowed to participate on the team. Unfortunately, those words turned out to be false.

That spring, when Coach R once again organized his small clique of favorite players for unofficial practices, Justin texted Coach R multiple times to ask if he could participate. At first, there was no response. After many attempts by Justin to connect, Coach R finally texted back, "Who is this?" He was making the point that he had deleted Justin's contact information from his phone. To Coach R, Justin was now a "nonperson," someone to be shunned. Next, Justin asked several of his best friends on the team, friends who were Coach R's favorites and starters, to intercede on his behalf. Those friends met with Coach R as a unified group. They told him they wanted Justin to participate and asked Coach R to please give Justin a chance. Instead, the coach merely scoffed at them and walked away. The incredibly tight bonds Justin and these boys had forged survived everywhere but on the 120 yards controlled by Coach R. It was devastating for all of them.

I had a small window into the situation with the coach and the team while I took photos on the sidelines during games. I couldn't help but hear snippets of the "conversations," and it was difficult to listen to the way that Coach R talked to these young players. He could cut a kid down with two words. The insults were withering, and I'd look over afterward and see boys crying. Often, they would grab a towel and bury their face in the cotton loops to try to hide their tears.

Coach R's multiple seasons of abuse were repeatedly reported to

Sidwell's administrative and athletic department leadership, as well as to the head football coach, by us and other parents. Each time, the school and the head coach acknowledged that the parents speaking up were right, that we were not overreacting, and they agreed that it was unfair—but they said that they could not control Coach R—the very person they allowed to have authority over children without any real type of vetting or background checks by the school.

The only option left for Justin was to quit the football team. The impact this situation had on Justin, Diamente, Ryan, Elie, and the other players on the team was awful. The atmosphere was tense, and players were being divided from their families. It had become the team against the parents. One team mom told me that her son was "acting like an abused spouse," inordinately concerned about what Coach R thought or might think. Players were threatened with being benched unless they revealed to Coach R the names of any parents who had complained about him to school administrators. Coach R also made it clear that if a parent complained, their child would be punished. It created and enforced a code of silence across the team.

In addition to opening our home, Tom and I had always donated generously to Sidwell's scholarship fund. The goal was to make space for another child to attend the school by paying Ryan's full tuition and thus freeing up those funds for the school to offer another financially challenged family a scholarship for their child. But after Justin left the football team, we stopped. I felt that we could not take the risk that our funds would be used to support another child who also wanted to play football and who would end up being mistreated. If anyone had asked me: *Should my son play football at Sidwell?* I would tell that family to choose another school. No parent should endure a similar agony for their son as what had happened to mine and the other students on that team.

Yet, week after week, our lives still revolved around football.

Justin took on the role of the team's videographer. I was incredibly proud that he had refused to run away or cower in the face of extreme adversity. Instead, he found a way to contribute and support his teammates and his school. Watching him find his footing after so much mistreatment and abuse, I saw the strongest, most courageous and loving young man I've ever known.

However, while being the videographer put him on the field, he was still separated from the team. With a recorder in hand, he had become the ultimate observer. That role also meant that he was no longer officially part of the football community, even though many of the players continued to show up on Friday nights for sleepovers at our house, a ritual that no one wanted to abandon. The remaining team parents begged me to continue photographing the games, so I did, but it was very difficult to be out there knowing what Justin had been put through. If my teenage son could do it, however, then I decided that I could, too. As the season drew to a close, and with it the last fall of Justin's high school career, his sadness over what he had lost did not abate. If anything, it intensified.

I struggled to help my son. Diamente, who was in his first year of college in Pennsylvania, came down on weekends to try. Ryan tried. But it was as if, along with the sadness and isolation, there was a physical anger that had built up inside Justin, an emotional overload that had to be let out. Once, while we were driving in the car, he got into an argument with Elie, the type of silly sibling disagreement that happens between two teenagers in almost every car at some moment. But, despite my pleadings, the fight would not subside. Furious, Justin demanded that I let him out of the vehicle. When I refused to pull over, he reached over and grabbed the steering wheel. The car started to swerve into oncoming traffic at the height of rush hour. I was able to hit the brakes and steer us to safety, but as I slowed down, Justin released his seat belt, popped the door lock, and jumped out of the still-moving vehicle, sprinting away from the road on foot.

That terrible moment was like a metaphor. Justin just wanted to bolt, to free himself from the entire environment created by the very adults who were charged with caring for him, until the impulse to run became overwhelming. I understood this urge to run. But it didn't make it easier to witness it in my own son, or to help him.

It was December. The day was already dark, and a dusting of snow was falling. In the back seat, Elie was hysterical. She was scared. Justin wasn't wearing his coat, and she imagined him freezing to death.

I put my head on the steering wheel. I felt like a failure. As the open-door notification dinged on the dashboard, I felt the intensely painful, paralyzing opposite of all the times my mother had kicked me out by the side of the road and told me to find my own way home. Justin cooled off and came back. But I blamed myself.

Tom and I sent a final letter detailing Justin's treatment by the football coach to Sidwell's new head of school. Other parents wrote strongly worded letters to him as well. Ultimately, Coach R was separated from the school. But for Justin and the other boys on that team, the damage had already been done.

SANDI

seventeen

There is a principle in physics that is often applied to larger truths of human life: water seeks its own level. As a scientific shorthand, it means that water tends toward equilibrium or balance, that two connected vessels will eventually equalize their contents due to the force of gravity. In life, the underlying meaning is that like is often drawn to like, or that no matter how far the pendulum swings, it always must return to the center, to equilibrium. The personal version of this principle in my own life was the return of two volatile and broken people to what might be regarded as the scene of the crime, Southern California. This time, though, they were dragging a ninth grader and an eleventh grader with them.

After more than a decade spent careening between Salt Lake City and various points in Idaho, we were returning to the land of palm trees and perpetual sunshine: San Diego. The return went about as well as any nominally observant outsider might have expected. For us, the larger truth of water finding its level was that our family's problems reliably traveled with us, no matter how many times we changed locations. Equilibrium, in this case, might as well have been a synonym for hitting bottom.

The closest I ever came to an explanation of why we went back was some kind of purchase of part of the failed Idaho farm by my father's older brother, which left us flush with cash and able to fund the move. I don't recall ever complaining. There didn't seem to be much point, and by this time in my life, being uprooted was more familiar than staying put. My parents never agreed on much of anything, but they did seem to share a giddy love for a "whoo-hoo, we're leaving now, scoop up what you can and put it in the trunk of the car" life. Whatever was left behind or left on the side of the road—things, animals, people—it was only the opportunity cost of being adventurous nomads. Embrace the thrill of change. So I didn't think too much about leaving the condo rental with the slowly unraveling drywall hole, although I was very sad to leave Boise High School and my friends and teammates. But my eyes were also fixed on the finish line of graduating from high school. And I knew that after Idaho's bone-chilling winters, at least the Southern California weather would be warm.

After so many years away, California was downright strange to me. There was a thread of rugged commonality between the people in Salt Lake and the people in Idaho, a kind of mountain persona and a slight bit of aloofness that I had grown accustomed to. California was something else to navigate. The people were nice and friendly, but very superficial. The social codes of hair, makeup, and clothing were like speaking another language. I had felt less like a foreigner during my People-to-People homestays abroad.

The only thing that still made sense was basketball. I joined the school team. Back then, sports, especially girls' sports at a public high school, were not as highly competitive with carefully regulated tryouts. If you were interested, the coach would try to make room. And I needed a team. Basketball is also not a sport that you can play alone. It had taken me three tries to settle on a high school—I tried one, transferred to another, disliked the second one more, and transferred back. How much of that change was due to my mother's own insecurities and ranting, I'm not completely sure. It feels now as if she had a role, but perhaps it was only my indecision.

When I wasn't at school, I was playing basketball, joining games at local gyms, going to extra practices at school, practices at the local community college, and basically playing in any pickup game that would have me. The laws of basketball are such that practice is the surest route to getting better. A modicum of talent helps, but there is no substitute for taking thousands of shots at the net and dribbling your way around a guard.

If I was quiet in Idaho, I was all but silent in California. I hardly talked with other people except for the girls on the basketball team. Even then, we mostly talked about basketball or sometimes other kids. And I mostly listened. I heard them refer to one girl as a "stoner," and in hushed tones, the other players conveyed that they were worried about her. For all my family's volatility, no one drank or used any kind of drugs. I was woefully naive and inexperienced when it came to both. Mormons are not supposed to drink or smoke or even ingest coffee—caffeine is forbidden—so I saw nothing of drinking or drugs in Salt Lake and hadn't paid attention in Boise. From my ironically sheltered upbringing, I did not understand much about kids who did drugs, or used marijuana, or drank a lot. Anything with substances scared me.

Some of the team's conversations revolved around boys or other girls. I listened, completely unaware up until that moment that some people were gay and attracted to same-sex partners. I'd never been exposed to that or even heard that it existed. But a couple of the girls (one on my team and two on another team) were very open about being lesbians and talked about what it was like. When they talked about how they felt ostracized, I very much understood what they were saying. But at the same time, I didn't want to give them the impression that I was also gay. So, mostly, I continued to stay quiet and listen, and probably periodically, I stared, a bit wide-eyed.

Our rental house came with a pool, which I liked. But I did not often invite my basketball friends over, or anyone else for that matter. People knew where I lived. It wasn't the physical house that was embarrassing, but the household inside that only operated on one setting: chaos. Using the money that he had gotten from his brother, my father toyed with some type of real estate venture, but, like so much else, that effort seemed to go nowhere. Increasingly, he stayed in bed all day, every day, spinning multiple get-rich schemes and otherwise flailing around with nothing to do. When he ventured downstairs, I also couldn't trust him not to hit on my friends or do something crazy or violent to a pet in front of them.

As I entered my late teens, my father started leering at any girls around me and making inappropriate comments as if he were some kind of Don Juan character, which made my skin crawl. In a fit of rage, he had already killed another of my cats in the backyard. My mother was prone to talking to herself, carrying on heated conversations with the loud voices she heard in her head—she claimed these voices were God, talking directly to her. When she wasn't holding these dialogues with her "voices," she continued to trap whoever was home and try to absorb them in a conversation that was mostly a monologue. The topic was always the same: how my father was an ass and was trying to kill us all. Kevin made sure he was hardly ever home, but any time I was around, I would be forced to sit for hours and listen to her paranoid musings—although I didn't know that they were paranoid then—or a minute-by-minute recounting of the things that the voices in her head would say often about me and what I was or was not thinking, feeling, or doing. She would say, "I know you did *x*" (fill in the blank). I'd look at her in astonishment because *x* had never happened. But the voices in her head had told her that *x* had happened, so as a result I'd be grounded for a week. It was a constant theme. Her need for my participation in her delusions was intense, as was the expectation that I not only sit and listen but also hang on to her every word.

If I wanted to spend time with any friends, I would go to their houses. It was simpler and far less stressful. But mostly, I lived my life at the gym and on the basketball court or holed up in my room doing homework. If I did any talking, I preferred to keep it about basketball.

Even basketball, however, was not entirely safe. Our male coach would insist on the importance of back massages. The girls had to lie on their stomachs, and he would straddle our backs, sit on our bums, and run his hands up and down our backs. It was perverse, and no one said a word. We just tried to avoid being "massaged." He went on to marry one of the basketball players in my class (who was at least thirty years younger). His assistant coach married another teen player. So it was not all that surprising that everyone looked the other way when it came to what might be going on in my home.

To escape my house and everything around me, I went to the beach. I loved the feel of the warm sand pressing between my toes and watching the gentle Pacific Ocean stretch out to the horizon, although I was afraid to go very far out into the water. The only way for me to reach the ocean was by car. My father still kept one or two parked around the house. It became easier to take off after I turned sixteen and could legally drive—I had driven on the roads at age fifteen, using my Idaho license, until I got into an accident, and when I handed my driver's license over to the police officer, he took one look at my birth date and told me I wasn't allowed to be on the roads in California, and I had to stop.

As much as I wanted to leave my house, it was also almost too easy to walk out the door. My parents were highly disengaged from my life and my brother's. There were no curfews or bedtimes or house rules or set meals and mealtimes (the only thing keeping me at home was when the voices told my mom something that prompted my "grounding" or when my mother cornered me with a monologue). Otherwise, Kevin and I were left to create our own structure, or lack thereof. Our parents were focused on other things.

The anger and put-downs that the two of them traded were constant, like the steady drip, drip, drip of a faucet, until the endless drips collected into a raging flood. Their fights became increasingly physically violent, and it was very difficult to be near either one of them. Kevin and I stayed out of the house or in our rooms. But whenever we were home, even with the doors closed, we couldn't drown out the sounds of breaking plates and glass. They hurled whatever they could get their hands on. The marital fighting was so intense that I didn't immediately recognize all the other ways that my mother was becoming increasingly dangerous.

San Diego is ringed by cliffs, cliffs on the way up to the mountains that divide the temperate coastal area from the arid desert of Death Valley, and cliffs that overlook sandy beaches and the ocean, where the drop is sheer and deep. The roads cut into them were often steep and needed shoring up with rock and earth. One afternoon, for some reason that I cannot remember because everything after eclipsed it, Kevin and I were in the car with our mother. We were on a road perched alongside an edge. Mom was turning the wheel in exaggerated rotations, swerving from side to side, like we were reenacting a car-chase scene in a bad B movie. As we careened along, she had begun ranting about how our father had cut the brake lines on the car to kill us. A final turn of the wheel, and we literally sailed off an embankment at the edge of the road. Miraculously, there were scrub trees lining the edge before the drop. Somehow, the car's undercarriage caught on the tree branches, and we came to a suspended stop, the tires spinning but the car going nowhere. I vaguely remember my chin smashing into the dashboard glove compartment—the only thing between me and the windshield in the days before it was compulsory to use seat belts.

Kevin and I sat there in our seats, shaking, probably sobbing. Finally, my mother shut off the engine. We could still open the doors. Kevin and I, and eventually our mother, climbed down, holding on to the branches and scrambling back along the wild roadside grass and dirt. Possibly, we walked to a pay phone. I have a recollection of my father coming and using a winch to pull the carcass of the car back onto the road. But perhaps it was just a roadside tow truck and an unknown man in coveralls.

My mother was so convincing in the depths of her hysteria that it was quite some time before I was sure that she had invented the whole thing and realized that my father had never cut the brake lines. She had many other "proof points" of my father's attempts to end her life, "proof," she said, that he was trying to poison her. Or "proof" that his family was gathering evidence against her to deprive her of money, or "proof" that he was planning to have her killed by some nameless, faceless third party.

But it wasn't just the evils of my father. Increasingly, my mother harbored a variety of delusions outside of our immediate family.

Dealing with my mother's delusions was a constant negotiation with reality, one that I was ill-prepared to make. Because our family was largely alienated from other people for nearly my entire growing up, I had no real templates of functional homes and no outside confidants. I felt compelled to decide on my own what was reality and what was not. My mother had a way of describing her beliefs about what was happening in a way that there was just enough truth in what she said that it was believable. Did my father's family try to help him get away from her? Yes. Were they trying to kill her to make that easier? Well, maybe? The way my mother would put things together, I could not be sure whether what she was saying was delusional or not. Did I believe that my father was crazy angry at her and would then get physical with her? Yes. Did I believe he was going to kill her? Well, maybe? The dilemma was whether to join my mother in her reality or to reject that world and accept that there was something wrong with her. Either alternative had serious consequences attached to it.

Recently, looking back on everything that has transpired in my life, I had a moment where I wondered about my mother's voices again—was it possible that she occasionally heard things that were true? Had she seen the things that she claimed had happened, or did she have some kind of expert intuition? In later years, she would say that the voices told her Tom was cheating on me. Was he? At the time, I was certain he was not. Toward the end of our marriage, I was not so sure. Perhaps she did have some larger insight, and there was a deeper reason why, unlike Kevin, I did not immediately tear myself away.

There was also a price to be paid for not believing what she said. When I wasn't sufficiently solicitous and patient while my mother ranted to me about my father, she would throw a cup of hot coffee on me, just as she had done since I was a toddler.

My father, with his eighth-grade education and his own serious issues, lacked the skills to cope with my mother's fixations. His response was to snap. Hence, the sporadic violence. At some point in between their separations, my father tried to run my mother over with a pickup truck—or possibly my mother tried to run over my father. But my mother maintained that my father had tried to kill her, and that is what everyone "believed." But in hindsight, even that statement feels uncertain.

My grandmother, my mother's mother, came to stay with us in a vain attempt to help. Using the money that remained from my uncle, my father rented a motor home, and he took my grandmother on some kind of brief, two-day road trip. I think my father had convinced her to travel with him to look at a piece of property, making a pitch that they could buy it together and turn a quick profit to "make money." Like every other scheme, from the concrete pump to the farm to the harvester, those promises of quick riches did not happen. Whatever did happen caused my grandmother to lose a lot of money.

When they returned, my mother just screamed at both of them and again accused her mother of having an affair with my father. This incestuous affair, she screamed, had one goal: to take my mother's family from her and force her to be put out into the street and kill her. No amount of reasoning from my grandmother could convince her otherwise. I don't recall seeing my grandmother for twenty years after that. We did not write or call; she simply, like so many other parts of my life, vanished.

Month after month, the money my father had received from his brother passed out of his wallet like water through a sieve. Before the motor home, he bought cars, including one for me. It was a new vehicle, and I kept that car going for a very long time. I realized that if I kept the car functioning, I could be independent. By indulging his car lust, my father had inadvertently given me the gift of leaving. But he was gone first.

Sometime during my senior year in high school, he gassed up the motor home and drove east to Arkansas, the state where he was born. He had apparently convinced Uncle Carlie to help him buy some property to build a hotel, although it's also possible that this scheme was as much of a mirage as my mother's fervent belief in the severed brake lines. My mother joined him in Arkansas from time to time, and while living there, she started to believe that a local doctor was in love with her. It was irrelevant to her that the doctor was married. My mother also insisted that this doctor was part of the Mafia and engaged in child pornography, but at the same time, she said that he was rich and that he wanted to rescue her and take care of her. She would launch into long rants about how the doctor was having her constantly followed by men who were members of the Mafia and who also worked for the doctor.

It seems incredible to repeat these stories and think that anyone could have believed them. But when you live with someone in the throes of a mental illness, and when you have been negotiating with this illness since you were a child, the climate and the behavior are familiar. The hard wiring is that this is your parent, and the first impulse you have is to believe them. Indeed, for years, the schooling I pursued was in part with the goal of becoming a lawyer so I could represent my mother in a divorce and get her away from the "monster" in our lives—my father. I thought doing this would finally make my mother "normal."

◆

In all our months together in California, I don't remember my father ever coming to one of my basketball games. My mother would attend occasionally. I think Kevin came when we were enrolled in the same school, but that did not happen until my senior year. While I tried to outrun and outshoot the difficulties of living in our family on the basketball court, Kevin protected himself by becoming a surly teenage boy and immersing himself in music. He played the guitar and was constantly forming bands. He also ran track—somehow, we had both been given the gift of speed—and he was very good. Our skills kept each of us away from home for as many hours as possible.

As in Boise, it was teachers who came to my rescue. Two teachers in San Diego took a special interest in me. The first was a history teacher, Mr. Scott. I always sat in the very back of his classroom and never said a word. I had somehow mastered the art of performing on tests and completing all the homework and papers, but remained a complete unknown otherwise. I had decided that it was easier to be invisible; I had convinced myself that I was "shy" and that I preferred it that way. One day, Mr. Scott gave our history class a "problem" to solve; he did it as an experiment. What mattered was not the substance of the problem, but illustrating the larger role of group dynamics. It is basically impossible for a group of thirty people to solve any problem unless someone steps forward to guide and lead the effort. From the back of the room, I watched my classmates talking over each other, starting to shout, and generally flailing around. I looked to the front and saw Mr. Scott growing increasingly frustrated.

Finally, my annoyance got the better of me. Generally, orderly classrooms and clear expectations were the antidotes to the complete disorder I experienced at home. Because I had not spoken before, perhaps the impact of having me rise to my feet and talk was sufficiently shocking to make everyone else pause for a moment. Once I started speaking, I assumed control of the exercise and quickly guided the entire class to a solution. Mr. Scott told me afterward, "You blew me away." My era of silence in his classroom was officially over; he started talking to me.

I'm not sure if Mr. Scott spoke to the teacher of my humanities class, but this teacher also began to talk to me. Both teachers engaged me in serious discussions, not only about school but about my future. I was very certain that I wanted to go to college, attainable through good grades and basketball, but at the same time, I had only a faint notion of what college was and, more important, how to get there.

The high school's guidance counselor didn't offer much advice on what colleges to consider, but my two teachers insisted that I apply to a series of California system schools. Back then, interested students in California had to call the college admissions offices and request an application form, which was sent in the mail. I don't remember having to pay anything, so either my teachers wrote the check for me, or the application was free. I filled out the forms myself, and my teachers wrote my recommendations. The college counselor then helped me send the applications to the schools.

For once, my mother was not a source of resistance or a roadblock. She wanted me to go to college—she was the one who had impressed the importance of high school grades upon me. My mother believed quite strongly that, had she been allowed to attend college, she wouldn't have been stuck in her disastrous marriage. There were not many moments of goodness between us, but one of the best things she did was convince me that I needed to become educated to be financially independent in my life and never have to depend on anyone. I took that advice to heart.

My father didn't really care much about the idea of college or going there. He preferred that I leave school and go into "business" with him in Arkansas, where he said he was building a hotel on the property that Uncle Carlie helped him purchase. If I didn't want to do that, then I should attend college in Arkansas. Somehow, he managed to get me a tryout with the University of Arkansas women's basketball team. But I did not want to live anywhere near my parents, either of them. I enrolled at UC Irvine, whose campus was located in South Orange County, south of Los Angeles. Irvine was a newly developed, planned community centered around the university. I didn't care about any of that. All that mattered to me was that it was a solid drive north from San Diego and sufficiently far from home, not as far as Mountain Home was from Salt Lake, but enough. And I had been asked to play basketball; I had been good enough to play on the San Diego high school all-star basketball team. I graduated from high school with honors, and Kevin and our mom cheered as I got my diploma. It was as close to normal as I had ever come.

At the end of the summer, I packed my things into my little car and headed north. Kevin was left in San Diego with our mother to finish high school. Our father stayed in Arkansas. First, our father had abandoned us, and now I was abandoning Kevin. He had to endure our home life and our mother alone. Kevin also had a very different view of our mom. He was her favorite, and she tended to blame me and look out for him—I took the brunt of the physical violence. But Kevin also saw our mom quite differently and, in many ways, more clearly. He believed she was the cause of our problems, and our father reacted and acted out so horrendously in large part because of what our mother did. I was caught in a different cycle. And each of us behaved according to our very different assumptions. Kevin and our mom moved into a rental condo, where, in a flashback to our childhood, my mother complained bitterly that my father did not send enough money to pay for food. When the money didn't appear, my mother finally found a job as a receptionist in a doctor's office.

At UC Irvine, it was too expensive for me to live in a campus dorm. On a bulletin board, I found a listing for an open room in a group house with five other girls in Newport Beach. It was a typical setup of an old couch covered in a thin cotton throw, a kitchen with a fridge, stove, and microwave, and a bathroom where someone's bras and panties were always hanging on the shower rod to dry. Someone had dripped colorful wax in strips that ran down the sides of old wine bottles to make candleholders. Inside the group house, I tried to stay largely out of the way. I still found it challenging to have anything beyond the most minimal conversations. About a month into the semester, I realized that one of the girls in the house was addicted to methamphetamine. But I didn't understand exactly what that meant.

I came home one afternoon to find that she'd taken all the knives in the kitchen and had stabbed them into the underside of the wooden cabinetry—except for one, which she was gripping in her hand and threatening to cut me with. I didn't even try to run for the door. I jumped out of a first-floor open window, landing hard on the scraggly bushes that lined the side of the house. I hauled myself up and sprinted away. For hours, I crouched in a neighbor's side yard, hiding, as I watched the front of the house. Eventually, I saw the girl walk out the door, get in her car, and drive off. As soon as the taillights on her car had disappeared, I dashed back inside the house, packed up everything I had, which wasn't very much, and left. From a pay phone, I dialed the number of a high school friend of my mother's, whom she rarely spoke to and disliked, but who lived in a wealthy LA suburb.

I stayed with this woman and her family for nearly the entire second semester, sleeping on their couch until one night when I woke up to find that the woman's husband was on top of me. I was stronger than I looked from playing so much basketball, and I managed to quickly extricate myself, but once again, I had to pack up and leave. With nowhere else to go, I wound up with my mom and Kevin at the condo in San Diego. It was a different kind of awful at home and too far from school in Irvine. I had no choice but to go crawling back to the couch at my mother's friend's home. I simply had to watch my back. But I already had a lifetime of doing that.

eighteen

I DID NOT LIKE UC Irvine, even though I played on the basketball team, so I put in an application to transfer to UCLA. The school accepted me, and I started in the fall. At the same time, my father reappeared in California, and my parents moved north to the La Crescenta area of Los Angeles, again with help from Uncle Carlie, who also lived in La Crescenta. I was so poor that I tried to save money by living with my parents again. But the place was small and owned by my uncle, and none of the problems had changed. I'd be trying to study at the kitchen table, and in a fit of anger, my father would suddenly seize the table and hurl it across the room, sending all my books and notes flying. My grades sank, and I moved out again. To pay my rent, I packed my nonclass hours with jobs. I worked at a Hallmark store in Westwood, ringing up customers and pointing them toward the birthday or condolence cards. I also got a job waitressing at Sizzler, a steak house chain. The tips were good until I dropped a tray of fully loaded plates on the floor and was fired that night. But I refused to return "home." I survived by eating cans of Campbell's cream of mushroom soup. I'd pour a handful of couscous into the pot to thicken the congealed soup as it warmed on the electric stove. On campus, I used to watch people go by in their fancy cars and think, *Gosh, if one of these people, out of the goodness of their heart, gave me one-hundredth of what they probably have in their pocket, I'd be set for life.*

My first two years of college were demoralizing academically. I didn't know how to study, and I didn't have time to learn. I'd highlight everything in the book and try to absorb all the material. I didn't know how to break up the material into chunks and learn just what I needed for that week or for the exam; I believed that I had to master everything. I'd arrived planning on being premed, but I quickly discovered that I couldn't stand the math classes. My next field was psychology, mostly because I thought if I studied it, I could help myself. I completed every credit needed for the major except the lab work. I refused to do the experiments because they involved killing rats. I couldn't bring myself to kill any animal. I dropped the lab class and changed my major to political science, as much of a nomad in my education as I had been during my entire growing up. But I was largely unfazed by the switching, even thriving a bit in the chaos, and I discovered that I was very good at political science.

I could connect with people in the classroom, but I didn't have the skills to build much of a social life outside of academics. Bit by bit, I was learning how to dress and have basic manners, but I struggled to have a conversation. It was especially difficult to relate to friends who had normal relationships with their mothers. I didn't go to lunch or go shopping with my mother. My mother and I did not talk about boys, parties, or gossip on the phone. She didn't ask me how I was. I never attended a dinner party until I was in my late twenties, and when I finally did attend one, I was terrified. I had never learned how to order in a nice restaurant or where the napkins and silverware should be placed on a table, let alone how to handle a reception line or how to dress for an interview. And even though I learned some of these things from magazines, the occasional movie, and watching other people, I always felt like I was playing a part. To this day, I never feel natural doing anything that takes social awareness or skill.

But it wasn't only in social settings. On my first trip to New York City, a business trip, I went to Bergdorf Goodman, the department store whose gleaming white facade and impeccably designed window displays graced Fifth Avenue, just below the fountain at the Plaza Hotel and the entrance to Central Park. Bergdorf was the fanciest place I could imagine. But after five minutes of walking around inside, I was covered in a cold sweat, and I wanted to leave. I was dressed like an average, young professional woman, but I felt overwhelmingly as if I didn't belong. Today I can afford almost anything in that store, but I still can't walk in and feel comfortable. I get that same uncomfortable feeling at the sight of a bread plate on a dinner table. For years, I did not know what it was for and used it incorrectly. To this day, I wait for someone else at the table to place their bread on the plate so I can be sure which plate I am supposed to use. If no one takes bread, neither do I.

I also didn't date. If the volatile example of my parents' marriage wasn't enough to dissuade me, I was also terrified at the thought of a boy coming to my house to pick me up for a date—what if he met my mother or my father? So I never dated in high school; I hadn't even gone to prom. College was no different. Between classes and multiple jobs, I was too busy for a social life. But I also didn't want a romantic relationship. I was certain that I was never getting married—no one had ever loved me, and it never occurred to me that anyone would. And I knew for certain that I would never have kids.

My closest friend was a Russian Jewish woman who had immigrated to the US in the late 1970s to escape persecution and injustice in the Soviet Union. Her story had a gravity that I appreciated. It stood out from the college frat girl party scene, where I felt every bit as much of an outsider as I had years ago in Salt Lake City.

And I still hadn't found a way to escape the continuing problem of my parents; this time, my father. I think my father did, at various points, feel remorse and realize the impact of some of the things he was doing. When I was finishing college, he essentially became homeless. He drove around in an old, beat-up, clunky white Lincoln Continental (the same one my mother had tried to drive off the cliff in San Diego). All of his belongings were stuffed inside that car. He would frequently show up drunk at my apartment, crying and sorry about everything. In those moments, he was almost apoplectically apologetic. He seemed aware that he and my mother had made Kevin's and my lives very hard.

But this remorse was transient; he remained a man with no real moral compass and no boundaries of any kind. When we were in high school, he claimed that a family diamond had been stolen and filed an insurance claim. Kevin found the diamond in the toe of a boot. My father just shrugged; he was looking for the payout. The truth was only useful when it was useful to him.

Once, when my father showed up at my apartment and I was not there, he hit on one of my roommates, Joyce. She was a tall, Slavic, lanky, blond, beautiful woman, and he did not even try to restrain himself. All my roommates considered my father to be creepy, and they were very clear that they wanted me to keep him away. The best way for me to do that was to graduate and move on.

Although I was thriving in my major, by my senior year, I was running out of money, and I was in danger of having to leave school to work full-time. The chair of UCLA's political science department called me to his office. I didn't know him, but he gave me the $500 I needed to stay enrolled and finish my degree. In the end, it took me five years, and I graduated with the highest honors in my department. My parents didn't attend my graduation, but on the day of the departmental honors ceremony, my thesis advisor came to my apartment to escort me to the event. My plan had been to work as his research assistant; I had been accepted into a master's degree program in international relations at Columbia University, with a full scholarship and a stipend. I could begin my studies and have enough income to pay for graduate school.

That plan came to a crashing halt when my advisor invited me to lunch at a Los Angeles hotel. In the dining room, amid the white tablecloths and smartly dressed servers, he didn't talk about our upcoming work plans. Instead, he ended our association. As our entrées arrived, he told me, "Regretfully, we won't be able to work together." I must have looked completely confused because he added that he had "developed feelings for me." My food sat untouched; it had been nerve-racking enough just to place my order for the most basic sandwich. I'd had no idea that there was a sexual component to his attention. I was completely naive about these sorts of things. I had just assumed that he liked my work. Now I couldn't even extricate myself without calling attention to our situation and otherwise making a scene. I had to plaster a neutral expression on my face and wait out the agonizing moments until a server discreetly brought our check. I immediately fled through the lobby and was halfway down the block before I remembered I had left my car at the hotel.

Desperate for money and out of options, I deferred my enrollment at Columbia and started working as a "backup" secretary at a law firm called Finley, Kumble, Wagner, Heine, Underwood, Manley, Myerson & Casey. They were the fourth-largest law firm in the country, with seven hundred lawyers and eighteen offices, and they had a reputation for paying well, not only massive salaries for their partners but also for the support staff. I thought maybe I would learn about the law—becoming a lawyer could become a "backup plan" if graduate school seemed too out of reach, especially economically.

Ever since high school, I'd thought on and off about being a lawyer. Now that I was working in a firm—my job was essentially typing all day—I realized that I liked the law. Whatever cases, legal statutes, or articles that the lawyers gave me to xerox, I would read and try to absorb. I had told my bosses that I did not want to be a professional secretary, and, to emphasize that, I dressed up for work in stockings and pumps and blouses and skirts—I scrutinized other professional women, and I read the workplace bible of the era: *Dress for Success*, which preached a combination of sensible pumps, A-line skirts, and demure tie-neck blouses.

Increasingly, I began to wonder what a master's degree would do for me. How could I earn money and be employed? And would I like the jobs available? My answers to these questions came in the form of an assignment at the firm: I was asked to research a legal issue and draft a memo based on what I found. It seems ludicrously simple now, but it was my first chance to prove myself. I threw myself into this two-page memo. I had read enough standing by the Xerox machine that I knew I needed to write something that addressed the laws at issue and apply them to the facts under consideration in a full and balanced manner. I walked to the firm's law library and wandered around, lost, until finally, I asked a librarian for help, and she pointed me to the relevant sections of the case law books.

I scoured every bit of case law I could find and wrote my memo out longhand. When I sat down to type it up, I was so nervous that I continually made mistakes. Each time, I had to pull the paper out of the roller, line up a new clean sheet, and start over from the beginning. I was even more nervous when I finally turned in my two typed pages. In my mind, I had visions of the lawyer reading what I wrote and storming out of his office, throwing the papers in my face, and calling me an idiot. My default expectations were always dark—I believed that I would fail a task or be humiliated in some way. I still didn't understand that my mother and father had programmed those expectations into my brain, and that they were false. Every time I didn't fail, I told myself that the reason for my success was not because I was good; it was because I somehow, at that moment, got lucky.

Once again, with this memo, my luck held. The lawyers liked what I wrote, enough that they offered me a job as a paralegal, even though I had no formal training. I quickly worked my way up and was placed in charge of a large case, supervising other paralegals. The firm gave me a large office with rows and rows of shelves to store books and files; my main tasks were to manage, organize, summarize, and prepare exhibits. I could find almost anything on those shelves; I had a near-photographic memory of what document was stored in what box.

Several years later, I appeared in court to support a lawyer at a trial. Together, using small dollies, we lugged and wheeled dozens of cardboard banker's boxes filled with exhibits into the courtroom and laid them out along the bench seats. During one cross-examination, the lead attorney turned to me and asked for a specific exhibit, and I responded, "It's in box 87." I stood up, plucked the document from the hundreds of others crowded inside the box, and handed it to him. The judge raised an eyebrow and told us to approach the bench. As we stood below him, staring up, he leaned forward, his robes rustling slightly, looked at me, and asked, "How do you *do* that?" My default assumption was that I was in trouble, but instead, he wanted to know if I had a system and what it was. I almost laughed. Somehow, I thought that everyone around me knew how to remember minute details. From a very early age, I had trained myself to pay attention, to notice even little things, the small tics or subtle change in inflection that signaled that my mother's mood was about to change, or a funny-looking tree or yard decoration that I could spot if I needed to find my way home. I would commit them to memory, ready to access them when necessary. It was a matter of survival. Stay alert, remember, and survive. I had simply applied those same skills to the exhibit boxes.

I took the LSAT, applied to law school at USC, and was accepted. I continued to work part-time at the law firm, but the tuition would be more than I could afford from my wages. I called the bursar's office at the school, and they suggested that I apply for financial aid. So I submitted a financial aid application. I filled out the pages of paper forms, or at least as much as I could, and mailed them. The rejection letter came back the same way, by mail, just as classes were scheduled to start.

I took off from work and walked past the manicured Southern California plantings and elegant fountain and into the law school's old-fashioned redbrick tower building, with its vaguely Spanish-style arched windows and design. Not far from admissions was the financial aid office. The staff were a bit perfunctory, and on the most basic level, my request must have seemed naive and ridiculous. I had sent my forms in without any documentation, and they told me that I would need my parents' tax returns from the previous year to be considered for financial aid. There was just one problem: my father did not pay taxes. Not ever. His position was that he never made any money, so he didn't need to file returns. Of course, the IRS would not have agreed with him. It also wasn't true that he didn't "earn" any money. He sold crops on the farm, and those generated income. But as soon as he received any money, he spent it. He claimed that every dollar was a loss because he had to spend money to get the crops in the ground, grow them, and harvest them. While it may have been true that he operated at a loss, the only way to know whether that was, in fact, true was to do the math and file the taxes, which is exactly what thousands of other farmers across Idaho did. But not Eugene Smith.

I explained to the financial aid officers that my father did not pay taxes (a great start for a future lawyer!), and asked if there was some way for me to be considered "independent" from my parents—and thus only my money and my earnings, which were fairly meager, would be considered for the application. I was not yet familiar with the concept of being emancipated, and apparently, neither were the people at financial aid. Their answer was no.

I walked out of the postcard-perfect building into the perennial California summer sunshine, not sure whether to scream or cry. It was as if the universe was playing a cruel joke: I had been emancipated for almost my entire life, except in the one way that mattered to my future—legally and thus financially. And I knew there was no way in hell that my father would ever file a tax return.

Still, I tried. I called him and told him that his refusal, once again, to "do the right thing" was making it impossible for me to go to law school. He didn't budge, but he did go in search of a solution, the same one when his Salt Lake cement-invention business went bust or when the Idaho farm failed, the boom-and-bust bailout that had spanned my entire conscious life: Uncle Carlie. For all his financial presence in our lives, Uncle Carlie was not a physical presence. I had only the vaguest picture of Carlie in my mind, having seen him just a few times. He was at most a distant voice on the telephone, and the barbed images of a devious manipulator conjured by my mother. But perhaps she had been partly right. Carlie wouldn't help me, though. He would only help his brother.

Carlie's proposal, delivered via a phone call, was a "loan" with a promissory note that I had to sign. And he charged me an exorbitantly high interest rate of about 20 percent—a bank mortgage at the time was a little over 12 percent. He had structured the loan and the note like a balloon mortgage, so I would be making interest payments constantly and never touching the principal. Carlie's terms were that I had to pay him $1,200 a month once I had a job, which was more than half of what I earned after taxes. But without a financial paper trail from my father and no way that I knew of to secure a loan on my own, the only option I had was the bank of Carlie. Seething inside, I took it.

I kept working part-time at Finley, Kumble while I was in law school and applied for a summer associate position at the firm after my first year. I was assigned to work on the case of a doctor who had multiple complaints against him and needed to have his license reinstated. Almost as soon as my summer position ended, Finley, Kumble imploded. The firm had been borrowing to meet its office and payroll expenses—my salary had probably been paid by a loan. With more than $100 million in debt, the firm entered bankruptcy and folded. Eventually, its furniture, art, and office supplies, down to the electric pencil sharpeners, would be sold for pennies on the dollar by liquidators. But the firm's loss was my gain. The doctor hired me to continue working on his case directly (as a paralegal)—and he offered to pay me what he was paying Finley, Kumble for my services. That was enough to cover nearly all my tuition, which meant I could start trying to free myself from Uncle Carlie.

Although I enjoyed my classes and the intellectual challenges, law school for me was a means to an end. I did the best that I could while working long hours to pay for my classes. Along the way, I discovered that I liked to argue, and I was good at it. I signed up for moot court, made it to the finals, and ultimately represented the school at the national moot court competition at the end of my third year. It was a sign pointing me toward litigation.

I graduated from USC law school in 1989 and took a job at O'Melveny & Myers, a prestigious white-shoe law firm. I earned my first permanent legal position due to my work as a summer associate before my final year of school. For weeks, I had applied myself around the clock to write a memo on eminent domain, and the final product was good enough to receive a permanent job offer. Slowly, I realized that it was not my dysfunctional family that had gotten me to this point, it was me.

Up until this moment, everything that had happened in my life had taught me that I had to solve my own problems because no one else would do it for me. But when I achieved some stability in my day-to-day world, I understood that I needed to learn to ask for help. I could not file away more than two and a half decades of family baggage along with my completed legal briefs. So I started seeing a psychologist. I had tried therapy in college when I was studying psychology and for a little bit after graduation. But this doctor was the first one to help me. And the timing was right for me to really hear what he was saying.

His office was in a strip mall in North Hollywood, a nondescript office in a low-rise stretch amid hair salons and dry cleaners, underneath a few palm trees. Inside, beyond the waiting room door, was a desk, a sofa, and two chairs. I scheduled my appointments for the evening after my workday, although most other nights, I would still be at work. In that anonymous space inside a strip mall, I began piecing together a narrative of my life and my own story.

I talked about the constant fighting and how my brother and I spent years hiding nearby, listening to make sure that nothing horrible had happened. I recounted what our mother said about our father, how she yelled at us for even speaking to him after "all that he has done to me" or "to us." I recounted how she constantly told Kevin and me that our father hated us, that he didn't care about us, and that was why he left so often. I talked about how my mother could present a near-perfect veneer of normality to the outside world, how she could hold it together, but as soon as the front door closed, she turned into a monster. What I couldn't articulate—it would take me years to find the right words—was the part of what made home so scary was that it was as if I were watching a performance. The thought that her behavior was performative has, in many ways, been the deepest wound. Because it felt as if my mother could control her behavior for others, she ought to be able to control it for us.

I had been seeing the therapist for about a year, when, exasperated, I explained how I was trapped with this family, and no matter how hard I tried to get away from them, they'd always be my family, and I'd always be theirs. There was a pause and then the doctor spoke. "Not necessarily," he said, adding, "You can't choose the family you were born into, but you can choose *your* family."

His words hit me like a thunderbolt. It was such a simple idea, and yet it changed my entire life.

RYAN

nineteen

As much as Sidwell was a destination, it was also a way station en route to the ultimate goal: college. If I wandered through almost any Northwest DC or suburban Maryland grocery store parking lot, the rear windshields and back gates of high-end SUVs sported elite school decals, like tribal tattoos—orange-and-black-striped *P*s for Princeton, a navy and red shield for the University of Pennsylvania, and a white *H* on a crimson background for Harvard. It was a not-so-subtle confirmation of a particular status, a dynasty where the children would be following in the same footsteps as their parents. This is not something I'd seen in any other place where I'd lived. But the path to these prized college spots had grown narrower and more fraught. Where a decade or two before, private schools like Sidwell could almost command their pick of slots in the coveted Ivy League or other similarly exclusive schools, those guarantees had shrunk, making the college process incredibly competitive and fierce.

Sidwell was ripe with stories of parents who actively attempted to sabotage the chances of other students, sharing damaging information with the school's college counselors, and even going so far as to reach out to college admissions officers themselves, in an effort to derail other applications. The year after Elie graduated, two of Sidwell's three college counselors resigned following what Sidwell described as "verbal assault of employees." The head of the school wrote to senior parents to discuss the "newly implemented policies in the College Counseling Office (CCO)." The message went on to repeat that "the CCO prohibits the recording of conversations with our counselors; will not consider anonymous and/or unsubstantiated claims made about student behavior; will not respond to calls issued from blocked telephone numbers; does not respond to any inquiry for student records unless that request is made by the student or an approved family member or guardian. The new policies," the head of school explained, "stem from a handful of unfortunate and uninformed interactions, some of which have been unkind to students, others that have disrespected our counselors."

I was woefully unprepared for the Sidwell college process. Diamente had gone first, and his route had been easy. He was a recruited athlete. Among his teammates, Dee was known as "a fly kid—wings on his shoes. He's fast. He's cool." A wide receiver, he raced down the field; sometimes, his feet barely seemed to touch the turf. He could stretch out his body, raise his hands up, and grasp even an imperfect spiral. Sidwell football wasn't the big leagues. They didn't have muscular kids who could explode on a Division I or even many of the Division II fields, but they were solid Division III. College coaches came to watch Dee's games; he had game films, and a recruiting rating on the athletic website Rivals.

Dee was accepted by Temple University in Philadelphia, but not for football, and with only a minimal scholarship offer. Still, that was his first choice. But he ultimately committed to playing football at

Susquehanna University, a 2,200-student liberal arts college in Pennsylvania with a D3 football team. They offered him a full scholarship. But aside from making sure that he had his "reels" ready—game film for the recruiters—from there, not much was required of any of us—Theressa or Tom or me or even Sidwell—to help Dee secure his academic future. He did it on his own.

For the other boys, however, the path itself was hard. I began to see just how difficult it was in the months before Diamente's graduation during Ryan and Justin's junior year.

Sidwell, like many other schools, seemed to be almost completely unable to grasp how to get financially challenged kids, like Ryan, into college. The football coach didn't try to get Ryan into a Division II or III school, where he could have played on the team. And from what I saw, there was very little motivation in college counseling to support students already on financial aid, especially if there weren't parents behind these kids pushing the college office hard. It was easier to ignore them, given the demands and attention required simply to placate the parents of kids with more financial stability.

In the spring of junior year, Sidwell asked parents to complete a questionnaire for their child. It asked for three adjectives to describe each student, and why the adjectives "fit." It asked for a description of the student as a person, including strengths, weaknesses, and aversions. It asked for major life events and an assessment of each student's "high school career." And it asked what was something the counselor needed to know. Then the questionnaire pivoted to preferred college environments, lists of schools, and why those schools were a good match, and whether financial aid would be "a factor" in the decision. And, finally, what information did the school counselor need to convey in a recommendation letter? After answering the questionnaire and having initial meetings with the students, parents were brought in to meet with the college counselor assigned to their child.

Lawyers are trained to keep fighting when there seems to be no chance, and I found myself doing just that. Ever since I left law school, I've fought like a lawyer in every part of my life. I bring up exhibits, evidence, and receipts. I hate injustice. And when something unjust is wielded against someone I care about, I'll fight. When, in response to Ryan's failing grades early on, the Sidwell academic dean had said, "They all kind of get back into the C range when they are juniors," to me, that answer was both unacceptable and a challenge. I pushed back when teachers refused to work with Ryan's tutors because they said that if Ryan had tutoring, he might have an unfair advantage. But tutoring was the only way to attempt to catch him up. Even his SAT prep had hardly moved the needle on his test performance. I had to gently remind the college counselor of Ryan's story and who we were to Ryan, even though this college counselor was only responsible for around forty students. "Ohh yes!" she wrote back. "I do remember. Thank you for the clarification. Ryan share [*sic*] the story of how he was 'adopted' by you and your family. He is just wonderful and lucky to have two caring families." But she would still jokingly ask me if Ryan was coming with "the posse" when we made an appointment to see her.

Sometimes the forces arrayed against success are the ones you would least imagine.

But one positive change was enormous for Ryan: Leonard continued going to Narcotics Anonymous meetings and was staying sober. The end of his drug use transformed him. I had known Leonard from the fall of ninth grade because he would sometimes pick Ryan up for the weekends, and he sporadically attended the football games when he wasn't on a bender. Now Leonard began to attend more school events, and we began to talk much more often. Leonard had become increasingly religious, and he would often speak about how God brought us into his family's life. When Leonard and Rochelle answered the college counseling department's parent questionnaire, they wrote: "Undoubtedly, we believe thus far in Ryan's life two major events that have been turning points for him are the opportunity to get a Sidwell Friends School education and the relationship that has developed between him and the McCoy family." About our relationship with Ryan, they added, "The second turning point in Ryan's life is a direct result of the fore mentioned [*sic*] exposure of Ryan at Sidwell. The development of Ryan's relationship with the McCoy family is a direct result of attending Sidwell. Ryan lives, during the school year, with the McCoy family during the week and comes home on weekends. Ryan's living with the McCoy family affords him intimate exposure to the lifestyle, customs and values of an upper-middle-class family. It also exposes him to their cultural activities and their socio-political network of friends and associations. This exposure helps him to assimilate into Sidwell and our larger society.

"We believe that his relationship with the McCoy family is divine guidance, which is why we consider Tom and Sandi McCoy Ryan's God (sent) parents. Further, we believe this relationship has enhanced Ryan's experience at Sidwell and it will have a lifelong impact upon him. He is truly blessed to have two sets of parents he can share and receive input, thoughts, and opinions."

Leonard had graduated from the University of Maryland, and Rochelle had also graduated from college, so Ryan was not the first in his family to apply to college. But their economic and personal struggles made the application process difficult. The entire process had changed radically in the more than two decades since they had applied to college. It was difficult for even highly engaged parents to keep up, let alone parents who were trying simply to navigate the day in front of them, especially when it came to ensuring that Leonard did the thing that mattered most: stay clean.

To the Sidwell question of "What information would you deem vital for your son's or daughter's college counselor to communicate in the school recommendation letter?" Leonard and Rochelle replied with one sentence: "The most vital information we would like the college counselor to communicate in the school recommendation letter is the need for financial assistance to cover tuition, room, and board."

The problem was that when it came to locating assistance, Sidwell was in unfamiliar territory.

I began researching options. I learned that some schools hosted what they called "multicultural weekends" and offered "fly-in opportunities" for students to visit, but the programs were selective, meaning Sidwell would need to nominate Ryan as one of its participants. The counseling office responded that after Ryan had created his school list, it would be best to determine if any schools on his list offered this option, "OR [Ryan] can also always reach out to a school and ask if they would financial [*sic*] support a visit. I would do this once he has determined that he does have a strong interest in the college of course." Sidwell did not believe that Ryan would be a compelling enough applicant for QuestBridge, a program designed to help high-GPA students with serious financial challenges. Another program, the Posse Foundation, which valued leadership and academic potential rather than just a high GPA, required a nomination from a community organization, not a school. Sidwell could not nominate Ryan.

All juniors at Sidwell were required to conduct a search on the College Board website to develop a list of schools. Ryan did that, and he also attended a college fair, where he spoke with representatives from a wide range of schools. But what he really needed was a personal checklist: here are the steps to take with your football coach to explore being recruited; here are the steps to build a college list around financial aid; here are the steps to build a college list around accessible visits; here are the steps to build a college list around likely acceptance, given your profile. But Sidwell was not used to that type of personal coaching. The college counselors expected to be pushed by overly involved parents who were asking every possible question and looking to gain every possible advantage for their student. It was a complete misalignment. And Ryan was the one who suffered as a result. It was as if he had been given a room full of IKEA furniture pieces, but not the directions, the rubber mallet, or the Allen wrench required to successfully build the final product.

If Ryan was going to have a college process and make an informed decision, I realized that I was going to need to take him to visit schools. We flew to Ohio to tour Case Western Reserve, where a former member of Sidwell's football team was attending, and Ohio Wesleyan, and then we visited Oberlin College, which to both of us seemed as if it had been built in the middle of nowhere, but Oberlin's football coach was interested in Ryan. At each school, Ryan would attend the "kid" events, while I went to the "parent" events. Ryan, with his magnetic personality, always made a huge impression. By the end of the day, when we would meet up and walk across the campus to our rental car, it seemed as if every fifty feet, someone would call out, "Hi, Ryan!" It took us forever to reach the car, not because I had parked far away, but because so many people wanted to stop and chat with Ryan. When we visited Syracuse University in upstate New York, Ryan felt as if he might have found his place. For the first time, he wanted to come home with something from the school's "swag store."

I made sure Ryan's applications were submitted on time—I signed Sidwell's required school transcript release form just days before the first application deadlines after Sidwell's college office wrote noting that the paperwork had not been completed—but there was one overriding issue for a kid who needed financial aid to attend: Ryan had to file the federal government's Department of Education's student aid form, FAFSA, and also a CSS Profile from the College Board. Not all schools required the CSS Profile, but filing the FAFSA was nonnegotiable for aid. And the aid was calculated from one essential piece of financial information: parental tax returns, just as it had been when I was attending law school.

I had promised Ryan we would make up the difference in whatever aid he received and the cost of the school, but we did not have an unlimited budget, and Ryan needed to receive aid. Weeks passed, then months. Ryan's parents assured me that they were gathering documents that were "somewhere else." Then they began telling me that "the accountant has them." The December 31 deadline passed, and the FAFSA and CSS forms were not filed. The last, hard deadline was February 1. On January 20, the Sidwell college office wrote to Ryan, telling him that Oberlin had not received his forms. "Last week, you mentioned that you and your parents were completing the CSS Profile for Oberlin (and your other schools). Could you update me on the progress of completing this paperwork, as well as the FAFSA? I contacted XXXX at Oberlin and she indicated that they have not received the CSS Profile (a requirement)."

The night before this email was sent, I had spoken again to Rochelle. She suggested to me that they hadn't paid their accountant, which is why the forms were taking so long. With the new deadline approaching, I had another very unpleasant conversation with Rochelle and Leonard. I had already told them, "Ryan needs the tax returns because he needs to complete the FAFSA form, and without the FAFSA form, he's not getting any financial aid. Yes, we will help him, but it does not make sense for us to pay the full freight when he is actually entitled to aid." Now I said, "Okay, where's your accountant? Give me the address, and I will go and pick all the stuff up and have somebody else do this." That ultimatum broke everything wide open.

There was no accountant; there never had been. Leonard and Rochelle had not filed tax returns for twelve years.

It was even more staggering when I considered that Ryan was a scholarship student at Sidwell—had Sidwell never asked for tax returns from Rochelle and Leonard to process Ryan's financial aid package? Did being an athletic recruit mean those issues were overlooked? At one point, I asked Sidwell's offices how they could not know that the family had failed to file taxes for so many years, but I never got a reply. In fact, to the question of how you could not know that this family hadn't filed taxes for twelve years, one of the college counselors simply said to us, "How is this my problem?"

In many ways, the response to the tax issue was a window into how Ryan's family had been paralyzed by other dynamics—Leonard's addiction struggles, the threats of violence in their home, or not showing up for events like Ryan's surgery. Excuses became the easiest path, rather than telling the harder truths. It was more like choosing an acceptable truth, even if it wasn't true, and then circling the wagons. When Ryan first came to live with us in ninth grade, his older brother, Kenny, was a senior in high school. I'd heard from Ryan that Kenny had been awarded a scholarship to Penn State, but his parents couldn't afford the rest of the costs. I thought at the time that it was a very sad situation. But now I had finally learned the truth. Kenny couldn't accept the scholarship because Leonard and Rochelle couldn't produce the necessary forms to receive the money from Penn State. Kenny had not attended college because of a failure of parental paperwork.

In some ways, there was an implicit decision that because Kenny had been denied his opportunity, Ryan should face the same consequences to keep things equal. But I refused to accept that answer. Their refusal to file taxes was also a repeat of the situation I had found myself in with my father when I was in law school. I was angry and indignant, not only for Ryan but also for the continuation of the same system and, all these years later, for me.

I emailed a friend who owned an accounting firm and asked for help. I promised that we would pay the fees to have Ryan's parents' back taxes filed and that we would also cover the costs of any penalties or interest. Tom and I stayed true to our word. After a forensic accounting process, the family's back taxes were filed in late February. The accountants also oversaw the completion of Ryan's financial aid forms.

On March 20, as Ryan and Justin were waiting by the side of the road for a tow truck after Justin's car had broken down, Ryan received an email from Syracuse University. He sent me a screenshot. Ryan had been admitted to Syracuse and had received a full scholarship. When I saw the amount listed in the letter, I let out a whoop and immediately texted back, "That, sweet son, is a full-ride scholarship!"

"Wait really?!?!?!?" Ryan replied.

"Yep: take a look," I typed. "You will not have to pay any tuition. Just living stuff. And that's for us to take care of."

Ryan responded with a crying emoji, adding, "Thank you guys so much. It really means a lot to me that you guys would do that." He continued, "Thank you so much for everything I truly mean it . . ."

I replied, "You are family—love you forever. And, you are welcome J."

"I love you too momma!!" he answered.

Once we had completed the family's back taxes, Kenny was also able to attend community college in Maryland. It wasn't a perfect solution, but it was something.

There are thousands of opinions on "the system" around college admissions and the quest for equitable treatment. But when it comes to financial aid, the system rests on an expectation that families, no matter how dysfunctional or how much they are struggling, will complete a preset list of paperwork. It is based on the assumption that these families will have filed taxes and have maintained bank accounts; in fact, the supplemental CSS forms from the College Board up until a few years ago even required families to list the makes and models of cars. If the parents have not done this, or if there is only a single involved or responsible parent, and a student cannot prove their total estrangement from the other parent, then the system simply wipes the student from its rolls. You do not exist to us. You are incomplete information and uncompleted forms. The path forward that was promised to you is a dead end. In this instance, it is not the parents who pay for this dysfunction, it is the student who has done everything possible to climb the ladder. I had to ask myself, How many other Ryans are out there in the world?

It turned out that at Sidwell in the senior class, there was at least another student in as great a need as Ryan.

Dear Mom & Dad

This birthday I wanted to do something different. I wanted to take the time to thank both of you. Not many people would take in a kid let alone an African American kid, but you all did. You both saw something in me that I did not see in myself. As the years have gone on living under your roof and under your wings you have opened my eyes to the world and given me the tools not only to see what you all saw in me, but to actually be the best man I can be. I cannot express to you both enough how grateful and lucky I am to call you my parents. You guys literally gave me another life, you all have opened up so many opportunities for me. Opportunities that I will no longer take for granted. I am 21 years old and it's time for me to take my life by the reins and really be the best I can be.

This birthday all I want is for both of you to know that you are as much a part of me as my biological parents are. As I get older I am seeing more of both of you in me, and that is because you all have taught me how to be successful. More importantly Dad you showed me how to be a man and what it takes to be a father, and together you both taught me what family really is. As I look around and see the many blessings in my life I cannot thank God enough for the both of you. You both have been apart of some of my happiest memories that will last a lifetime. So I just wanted to say thanks and I hope you both always know How much I appreciate everything you all do for me.

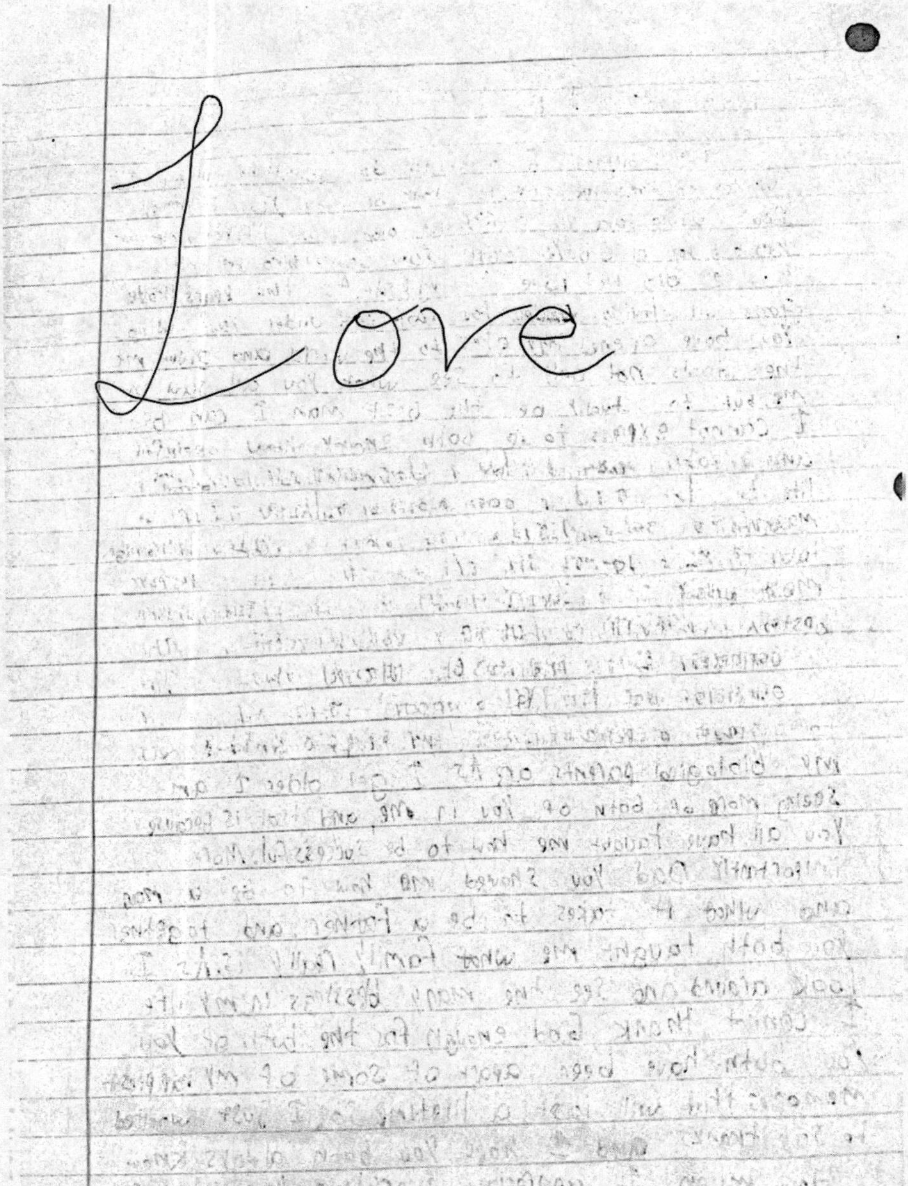

Love

[illegible]

my biological parents ... as I get older I am
seeing more of both of you in me and that is because
you all have taught me how to be successful. Mom
unfortunately Dad you showed me how to be a man
and what it takes to be a father and together
you both taught me what family really is. As I
look around and see the many blessings in my life
I cannot thank God enough for the both of you
You both have been apart of some of my happiest
memories that will last a lifetime so I just wanted
to let you know and I hope you both always know
how much I appreciate everything you've done for me.

ELIJAH

twenty

Every problem at Sidwell eventually wound its way to the Dean of Students Office. The dean's office took up a large room as if to convey the position's importance. Adjacent to the office was a small reception area that held a desk, two chairs for visitors, and two narrow sets of bookshelves. There were some clever motivational quotes in frames hung on the walls, but otherwise, the room was nondescript, its walls painted white to emphasize the "plain" Quaker way that was meant to characterize Sidwell. Over the years, the dean's various assistants had added small decorative touches, a tiny rug here, a lamp there, to give the cold space a slightly warmer feel. But they never blunted the overall impression of starkness. It wasn't a public space, given its location relatively far from the main entrance. Instead, it was close to the parking garage—tucked away as if to suggest that a visit should be a quick in and out.

Shortly after Justin started at Sidwell, I heard that the dean's assistant, Susannah, was seeking volunteers to watch her desk during lunch or during the school's weekly Quaker silent worship meeting. I volunteered. Susannah and I became very good friends, and gradually, my volunteer duties increased. I covered the desk when the dean's office needed help, or if Susannah had to be out of the office. I learned how to input the attendance into the computer system, handle the visitor's log, answer phones, and assist with student issues and questions.

I was at my post one January morning during Justin and Ryan's senior year when Elijah shuffled into the office. He had eaten dinner at our house with the football team numerous times, but I knew very little about him or his home life apart from briefly making small talk with his mom at football games. But I did know that he lived far away in Prince George's County, Maryland.

Like Ryan, Elijah was another scholarship student who understood that he was attending Sidwell because he was a sports recruit, even if that wasn't his official classification or what had been written in his admissions letter. He played offensive lineman on the football team. The O-line consists of players whose job is to protect the quarterback. They create a safe pocket for the quarterback to hand off the ball or throw it. But whenever I saw him, Elijah struck me as a quiet and introspective person. Interestingly, Elie saw him as wickedly funny. It's true that his jokes detonated like a stealth weapon, out of nowhere, when you thought he had simply been listening. But funny, quiet, or introspective, what I didn't see was any of the punishing brute force that the O-line required. I did notice that he was always hungry—it was common for him to eat three full dinners when he came to our house.

That morning, I said hi and asked him why he was there, and he answered that he was there to see me and that maybe I could help him. Elijah told me that he had a nearly two-hour commute each way on a mix of trains and public buses, which were unreliable and often late. As a result, he was often late to his first-period class. As I knew well, the Sidwell tardy system was unforgiving. Each tardy was quantified as "misbehavior points," and the more points a student accrued, the more the student's privileges were removed. Elijah had a mountain of misbehavior points. As a result, he could no longer leave Sidwell's campus for lunch. During his free period, he had to report to study hall. He was constantly being disciplined, but the points kept growing, and now the school had threatened to suspend him—if Elijah didn't give up and decide to drop out first.

My methodical, gather-all-the-facts lawyer brain clicked on. Why was he late? Could he take an earlier bus? Was there another route he could use? I sat him down and started asking questions. Elijah explained that his mom had given birth to a baby boy eighteen months before. The financial cost of a baby had been a hardship. Behind on rent, they had been evicted from the apartment where they were living. Elijah had arrived home from school one night to find their belongings piled on the street. He was back at Sidwell the next morning, walking from the public bus stop through the snaking lines of BMWs, Mercedes, and Lexus sedans and SUVs sitting bumper-to-bumper in the school drop-off lane. He told no one.

His mom also needed Elijah to help her with the baby. One of his current household jobs was to get his toddler brother ready for day care each morning. No one could leave home, including Elijah, until his baby brother was ready.

It turned out that I was the only person in the entire school who had ever asked Elijah why he was late, and what was going on, and what they could do to help. Everyone else had simply punished him. The more I listened, the more appalled I was at how he had been treated. And I told him so. I thanked him for trusting me enough to come and ask for help. Then I asked him what he thought I could do for him. He said that he'd really like my help in getting to school on time so that he could avoid getting suspended. Realizing how far away he lived, I understood immediately that there was no way for me to drive out to get him each morning and still manage to get everyone in my home to Sidwell on time. I explained this and offered that I didn't think I'd be able to help much unless he wanted to come and stay at our house for a while until his attendance situation was fixed. Shyly, he nodded yes.

"Okay," I told him. "So call your mom and make sure this is okay with her. Then, today, after school, go home and get some clothes and, if your mom agrees, have her bring you back to our house." Diamente was away in college; we had enough room.

As soon as I finished my volunteer shift at the outside desk, I marched into the dean's office. I explained to him why Elijah was late every day and asked why, on earth, no one had ever tried to learn what was going on with him and offered to help. I told the dean, "I will take responsibility for getting Elijah here on time, but I need you to erase every point and remove all disciplinary action against him. No points, no suspension, no having to go to study hall." I kept my hands balled in fists. I was worried that if I unclenched them, they would start shaking.

I drove away from Sidwell and called Elijah's mom from the car. After a two-hour conversation, we agreed that Elijah would stay in my house until he got back on track with attendance and was not at risk of suspension. As soon as I hung up, I started clearing a space for him.

The young man who arrived at my door was and is a gentle giant. His voice was soft and sweet. He was six feet six, wearing a size 15 sneaker. By the second day, I realized that Elijah was a soft-spoken, artistic, gentle soul who ate all the leftovers. He loved to create, whether drawing on paper, making graphic designs on the computer, or writing music tracks or spoken word poetry. Not long after he arrived, Elijah drew a picture of Tom as a spontaneous gift. In it, Tom was dressed as Superman, complete with ripped muscles and a cape.

Elijah's coming to live with us changed the dynamic in our home. For one, Sidwell wasn't entirely wrong, he *was* chronically late. After a couple of days, I remembered that the few times he had slept over at our house before football games, not only had he eaten three dinners, but it also took four other players to wake him up in the morning so that he could be ready on time to leave. Now, each school morning, the kids would stand at the top of the stairs and yell at Elijah to hurry up. He frequently ran to the car still in his bare feet, his shoes and socks in one hand, belt in the other, wet hair spraying droplets everywhere. But the kids kept each other in check. They, including Elijah, were never late to school.

A week after Elijah arrived, I walked into the house, and Tom, who happened to be at home instead of in Denver, where he was working, told me, "Well, Elijah's now living with us full-time, for good."

I responded, "What?" and he said, "His mom just moved to a one-bedroom apartment in Baltimore." Baltimore is about fifty miles or more from Sidwell Friends. When I called her, she explained that she needed to find a less-expensive place to live, closer to relatives who could help her care for Elijah's brother, since Elijah was no longer there to help. She also needed to work and was able to get a good job there with childcare nearby. So, for all of us, Elijah included, it was sudden and total immersion. One week, Elijah wasn't a member of our family, and the next week, he was. In those early weeks, as he settled in, he seemed so sad. It was clear that he missed his mother and his little brother and that he had not expected or been prepared for this outcome.

Elijah was quiet, but when he felt ready, he also loved to talk, especially to have deep, philosophical discussions on topics like the state of the environment or the question: Is world peace possible? Invariably, he found me when I had just sat down by myself to do something. I would be distracted and tempted to tell him we should talk later. But then I would remember that whatever I was planning to do would still be there, but this moment with Elijah might never happen again.

Elijah was also an example of the divide at Sidwell. Scholarship kids were provided with clunky, black laptops, not the sleek silver Apple computers that other kids brought from home. And these laptops only worked for Sidwell materials, meaning that to access college information or anything else on the internet, Elijah had to use his phone. Neither he nor his mother had a computer—his mom read the Sidwell emails on her phone as well. Once I realized that Elijah was relying on his phone, I bought him a computer—he no longer had to lug around the heavy laptop that all but announced: "I'm at Sidwell on financial aid."

At some point that winter, probably in February, it became clear to me that Elijah processed his emotions not through words, but through music. So the two of us went to the music center, and together, we found equipment that would enable him to mix his own music. I had no idea how much this simple gesture meant until he told me, "It's because I can make something really pretty out of something that is really ugly. I like that."

Elijah's calm demeanor and presence were also a balm to Justin after the very difficult fallout with football. The two of them collaborated on a spoken word senior project with a musical component, something that mattered deeply to both of them. The project was called "Aberdeen," after the street on which we lived. The general themes were being teenage boys and having fun while also coming to learn and understand some harsh realities. They covered race relations in the world and the difficulties of growing up Black. They made an EP, and its cover was a photo of them standing together on the roof of our home. Watching Elijah, Justin, and Ryan together, and also Diamente when he was with us on school breaks, I saw a support system unfold. Several times, Diamente would come home from college, collect Justin, and take him to his dorm room for the weekends, just to change his location and get him out of the Sidwell fishbowl. When

Leonard, Ryan's dad, completed Narcotics Anonymous, he brought the NA book to us because of its positive outlook and perspective. He thought its words might help Justin look at his situation at Sidwell differently. When Justin had days when he couldn't get out of bed, Elijah understood. He explained that he had days when he was equally paralyzed. In high school, he had shaved his head because he couldn't stop pulling out his hair—a disorder known as trichotillomania. The three boys hung on to each other, sometimes physically. They didn't flinch from anyone's sadness. It didn't fix everything right away, but they helped in ways I could not, no matter how much I loved my son.

Bit by bit, the longer Elijah stayed with us, the more he shared not just his philosophical thoughts but his personal story. It took a very long time for Elijah to feel comfortable enough to share all of it. In the beginning, when he started a story, he would often stop and leave it hanging. He'd say, "It's like . . ." and then trail off. I'd listen, and when he stopped speaking, I'd suggest, "Is it like this?" and explain, telling him a little bit of my story. And he would nod thoughtfully and say, "Yeah, that's it." There were points when he would start to cry, and I would cry along with him. We would both just sit there and cry until we had gathered ourselves again. These conversations became another form of bonding. Coming from poverty, I know it when I see it. Elijah's path and mine were remarkably similar on a variety of different levels. Poverty doesn't discriminate; it doesn't care what color you are.

Later, I asked him to tell me his story, from start to finish, and he did. I recorded every word. It sounded so matter-of-fact when he spoke, not as if he was tired of telling it, but as if the only way he could get through the telling of it was to strip what happened down to the barest of facts, removing all trace of emotion. That first spring, I didn't get the story in full, but I had enough to know that he needed our help and for our home to be a safe place for him.

Elijah was born when his mom was nineteen. On Elijah's birth certificate, the space for the father was left blank. His biological father was skeptical at first that he was Elijah's dad. But he eventually came around. Even then, father and son "did not see each other very much." His dad had been twenty when Elijah was born. Elijah's mom was always on the move, a step ahead of losing her home or in the process of being evicted—Elijah attended four different elementary schools. At age five, he would walk home alone from the bus and use his key to let himself in. That was the starting point, but this is Elijah's story, in his own words, as he told it to me.

My birth certificate does not have my dad's name on it.

He was unsure at the time—he was messing around. He accused my mom of messing around. He had just had another kid—my sister. After a little while, people realized I looked like him. He would stop by my grandma's house—to check up on me. He went into the military and was in Iraq. When I started kindergarten, I really don't think he was that present. I lived with my grandmother a lot. My grandma's house was my mom's home growing up, so that's where I went.

Before I was five, I was in school. After school, I stayed at my grandma's house while my mom was at work. So that's why I was there all the time with my cousins. I'm not sure when my mom got her first apartment. I was at my grandma's all the time, in Temple Hills, Maryland; my grandma was my primary caretaker. That's the only house that I can think of that's been consistent. My step-grandfather still lives there. My grandmother passed away during my first year at Sidwell.

In high school, I stopped liking to go over there. They tried to start having family dinners in my junior and senior years—they invited some relatives from my step-grandfather's family, but I didn't have a connection with them. I also knew that I had to stay away—that my grandma's old house was not safe and stable. Growing up there, people would get in fights all the time. There were drugs, but no one wanted to talk about it. Some of my relatives introduced me to a lot of bad stuff like pimping—a couple of them did it. They got messed up by other family when they were teenagers.

My first memory is that my grandma was a foster parent, so there were always a lot of new kids around the house. Kids kept moving in and out, and I didn't really understand why. People would come into my life and then they would just disappear. It was confusing. I didn't understand what a foster kid was. The foster kids would mix in with my grandma's older kids. Everyone would be playing video games, eating my grandma's food, watching movies.

But I witnessed some messed-up stuff. At my grandma's house, sexual things would happen to kids. I witnessed one of the older guys making one of the younger girls give him head on the bed—he was about seventeen, she was about six.

I was molested in my grandma's house—by an older boy, a foster kid. A lot of the kids she had were kids from bad situations. I don't remember this boy's name. I was maybe somewhere around five to eight years old—I really don't remember. It happened just once. It was a memory that I had suppressed for a while. At a certain point, not long after that, I started to pull my hair out. Pulling your hair is a compulsive disorder. I was struggling with what happened and with anxiety. I had a bald spot in the center of my head. I pulled out my eyelashes, too, for a while. I started eating a lot, and it impacted my social experience. It was probably uncomfortable for my mom to talk about it. My mom took me to a therapist; I remember going to see the therapist one time—it was one of those meetings where they say point with the doll, point to where you were touched.

Whenever I'm growing my hair, it is a sign that I'm doing better.

Grandma was trying to maintain a positive household—but she couldn't do it on her own. She always tried to teach me right from wrong. But she had two boys with my step-grandfather; they were my mom's half brothers, they were about ten years younger than her, and they never fully grew up. Another relative, he was a pimp. The music he listened to—hip-hop—and the violent video games he played influenced me, and I'm still working through that. He had a brother who was very laid-back. Both of them had a lot of girlfriends. There were women who came over all the time, but not all of them were girlfriends, some were the women they'd pimp out.

These guys had guns stored in the house, in the walls—I remember everyone shooting stuff in the backyard. We used to shoot BB guns, too. They sold drugs as well—weed, pills, and probably cocaine—but pills more so than the other stuff. They also grew weed—I definitely saw weed plants. I'd always see a bunch of different faces coming in and out—and they knew there was a limit to what they should show me. I think they would steal cars. My extended relatives were a huge influence; they'd come into the house late and get in fights—they were each in a different gang. One was a Crip, another was a Blood. They had different bandannas for the two gangs. Once, they put each other in the hospital. They also liked to sick the dogs—Rottweilers—on us, the younger kids. They thought it was fun. They'd let the dogs off the chains and make them chase us. I was fast back then. I always got away.

My youngest uncle and one of my close cousins—there were two of them from the same mom, but different dads, like my little brother and me—were the most consistent kids who were there growing up. One time, my younger uncle slammed my cousin's wrist against a wood ladder. The wrist was bent, and I could see the pink inside. I remember thinking, Why would you get that mad at a kid? I was their blood nephew, their sister's son—they knew better than to do something like that to me. I did get beatings sometimes, but those were because I was bad.

But something was always unsettling around that house—and I tried to stay away. Most of my "stuff" from that time is from the emotional pain and mental confusion.

My grandma lost her foster care license after a while.

Eventually, my mom put me in day care and aftercare, and I went to my grandma's less and less as I got older. I went to four different elementary schools. There was a lot of instability. I might stay in a school for only half a year. We would change apartments a lot. Once, my mom bought a home, but it got foreclosed on, and we had to leave. We also got evicted from a rental.

My mom struggled hard to be independent, and whenever it was just the two of us in an apartment, I saw a very peaceful side. That's why I like my peace now.

I hated school, and I still don't like school. I always thought I was dumb. I remember I went to Benjamin Foulois Elementary for kindergarten, and one afternoon, I was like, I hate this. I was like, fuck it, and I just left the building. I thought I knew how to get home, but the trip was much longer than I realized. I ended up walking by myself along a highway, confused. Some lady picked me up and drove me back to the school because I was able to tell her which school I attended. I'm very blessed that she didn't kidnap me or that I didn't get hit by a car.

When I was five, I had my own key to our apartment. There was bullying in school, mostly by older kids. I remember I rode the bus alone and walked back, alone, to the apartment. I'd unlock the door and then lock the door from the inside and wait for my mom. Eating became a compulsion—food always tasted good. I'd have two dinners—but kids started messing with me when I started getting bigger. I was constantly bullied when I was younger.

Sandra E. Smith

I remember being in kindergarten when it was wintertime. I was getting off the bus, and they bombed me with snowballs. The bus dropped us off at the top of the hill, and I had to walk down and up again to get home, and all the way, I was pounded with snowballs. It seemed fun to them, but it was painful to a little kid like me. During the summers, I would go to summer camps. I got choked out on a bus once going to Christian summer camp. The guy held his hand on my throat. My cousins were going to the camp, too; I was always with them back then. But my cousins were young and probably scared. The kid who choked me was probably one of the counselors. But why would you choke a kid on the bus? I didn't understand that. That was one of the main points when I stopped trusting people.

I stayed in one school, Longfields Elementary, for a few years, but then by fifth and sixth grade, we were moving around again. We lived at my grandma's house for a year, and then we moved to an apartment somewhere else. I also got into a few fights during those two years of fifth and sixth grade. There was a chubby African kid I didn't get along with. But I learned that I don't like to fight, and I realized it's not worth it to have a lot of drama, so I stopped fighting back. There were times in middle school when people tried to mess with me, my stuff was stolen, and I was pushed at the bus stop. I was always alone.

I also stopped liking all the moving around. Each time, I'd have to meet new friends. You lose touch with the friends you make. Even if you go over to a house and try to maintain some contact, you still have to meet new kids again in a new school. I didn't have many close friends in middle school. My closest friend was John. He was also a quiet kid, a loner, and we were the calmest kids in our grades. By late middle school, I was huge—six feet two and three hundred pounds. That's when I started playing football. Playing football gave me a new focus and something to do after school. Otherwise, I would just play a lot of video games, watch movies or cartoons, and eat a lot. I actually hated watching sports—it doesn't interest me that much. In school, I also met other kids who liked football. It was hard when I first started. I was out of shape, but I tried to be macho.

My dad emerged in my life when I was around five or six. He had come back from a tour in Iraq. I remember he brought me a camouflage backpack with Spider-Man on it. After that, for a number of years, I would visit him during the summers. I was seven when I first went with him. In the beginning, he lived in Columbia, Maryland. He had married a woman who was eleven years older than him, and they had a house and a car. I went to their house on a few weekends. Then I didn't see him for a while because he went back to Iraq. I remember he made me a photo book showing him in Iraq. After that, my dad and his wife bought a large house in Plainfield, Illinois, about thirty minutes from Chicago. There was a cornfield and train tracks with trains running in the back. I'd fly out in the summers to visit him.

I thought everything about being out there was cool. It was so different from my life growing up at my grandma's and my mom's place. In Plainfield, I saw a very peaceful spot and better food. My dad and his wife were vegetarian. The house was one of the biggest houses I'd seen at the time. I always liked going to my dad's place because it was more stable. Until one year, when I didn't want to go back because he kept getting on me about my weight. He'd make me do military stuff if I got a punishment. One time, I had to sleep in the cold, dark, unfinished basement—in a cardboard box on the floor, with a pillow and maybe a blanket. It was very scary when I slept alone that night. I woke up early and he made me do push-ups, jumping jacks, and squats on the wall. I also had to dig out ponds in the backyard and different manual labor.

I think my dad suffered from PTSD for a while.

Looking back, I know he spent time with me when things were easier. It was summer. He never had to wake up and take me to school. And I never felt like he was all that much invested in me as his son. We always got along as friends, but I didn't feel like what I'd expected. I can count on one hand the number of times we would talk on the phone each year. He was never very consistent. I never had an image of what a dad was supposed to be like.

My dad did show me a lot of things that stick with me—a healthy lifestyle and trying to find peace. He was a very spiritual person. He tried to educate me about things like chess and music production. A lot of the things I do today are things he introduced me to. I wanted to be connected to him, for sure. He was the closest thing to a best friend that I had growing up. But now he lives in Arizona. He moved there when I was at the end of elementary school. Time flies, I guess, and I don't keep tabs. I've only been out to see him in Arizona two or three times. I just stopped going. I saw him one Christmas, and I've been there twice for the summer. But I just stopped going. Football was a big part of why because I played over the summer. I had to train and play in the summers if I wanted to make the team.

My grandma was my strongest relationship, but I never really felt connected to anybody until Sidwell and the football team. I didn't know what a strong relationship felt like; what should I expect? Nothing else was that consistent in my life. I was always with my mom, but we never had intense conversations. She was as helpful as she could be, but I wish I had been able to spend more time with her. As I got older, I was just home a lot less. We've always been together, and my mom was the consistent figure in my life, but I don't know what being close with her was supposed to be like. How do you explain "close"?

She had a lot of boyfriends, I guess. None of them were very consistent. Two or three I liked a lot; they were pretty respectful.

Some, I could tell, were rude, or they didn't have themselves together. I would think, why is he in my space now? One boyfriend I really didn't like. He introduced me to domestic abuse. I remember big bags of his clothes. He was a big guy. He'd been to jail. My mom had a tendency to talk to guys who were incarcerated. She should have stayed away and said no to these people. This boyfriend was a very jealous person—he put oil in the bathtub. She got in, slipped, and fell, and ended up in the hospital. While she was in the hospital, I went to stay with my grandma.

Another time, my mom and this particular boyfriend got into an argument one night. While they were fighting, he took her phone and threw it against the wall. She had called my grandma, and my grandma called the cops. Eventually, the cops showed up. Watching this, I got very protective of my mom.

The last time with this boyfriend, I was maybe eleven, and I saw them arguing in her room. I came to understand that he was bipolar. He had anger issues. I went downstairs and got a big stainless steel kitchen knife, about six to eight inches, with ridges, and I walked back up the steps with the knife. I got very quiet and aggressive looking. I would have cut him if I had to. He tried to take the knife from me. I didn't let him, but I let my mom take the knife from me. Then he walked out of the room. My mom and I sat upstairs. I remember the layout of the house—living room, front door, den in the back. My mom told me to "walk down the steps," and then, "You run to the door and run across the street—try to be very quiet—and run out to the neighbors." I did, and she came out after. We pounded on their door, and the neighbors let us in. Eventually, the cops came and kicked the guy out of our house. That was a relief.

Once again, my grandma came to pick us up. We didn't stay in that place much longer. It was a rough spot—our car was bad, it was hard for my mom to get to work, we lived at the end of the block, very closed in, and neighbors across the street were wild and threw parties—we tried to get out of the area. I still remember the name of the street, Burgundy Street—I never want to go back there.

Both my mom and I understand that we have been through some things, but we don't always like to revisit them with each other. We are great friends. I kept her motivated, sane, and focused. I was her rock. I talked about some things—I'd say, This is cool, we could live here—how do you like this guy? *But there were also some things I couldn't do or couldn't talk about.*

I really wanted to chill in my own space. I wasn't the most conversational kid. I started to get defensive. The anger I felt in some of those situations—that was real anger for me. There are points where I have been so angry. But I didn't feel that way often. When I played football, coaches wanted me to get aggressive—but it was hard because I'm not mad at the guy facing me. That mindset also probably prevented me from getting into fights later on. You haven't made me that angry to want to kill you. And after a while, probably because I got so big, people stopped physically abusing me.

We moved to another apartment. Then we moved to a house in Forestville—that's the house we got evicted from. The house seemed nicer, in a better area, with more space. I was in middle school, and I started playing football in eighth grade. I lost weight and got in good shape. My football coach, Coach John, was the dad of one of my friends. He was the first dad I saw on a consistent basis—he came home from work and coached his son's football team. My friend, John Jr.—John-John—said just come out to meet him and see if you want to join the team. I also started going to John's after school—we'd do projects together, and I'd stay late at his house. It was the first friendship I had with a kid my age.

I really liked it, but it made me feel sad about my own life. I realized that when you have two people in a unit, you could afford certain clothes, a phone that worked, shoes, all kinds of cool stuff. The mom cooked dinner; she packed John-John a lunch for school. I was always eating cafeteria food, and I would ask John-John for his food.

At the same time, while I was in middle school, my mom drove me to North Carolina to visit one of her boyfriends. This guy was in prison. He was the guy who became my little brother's dad. My mom's friend's cousin matched them—I guess my mom was lonely. She started driving down there to see him. He was in prison for assault. He hit someone with a metal pipe at a bar.

I went down with her two or three times. I remember it was a long drive, and we had to stay in a hotel. We'd sit in the correctional facility waiting room. He seemed cool when I met him. He talked a nice game when he was in prison, but he was not a stand-up guy when he got out. This boyfriend never lived with us—he just came around. He worked in bars as a bouncer. I was never really respectful of him when he was out. I didn't really care what he said. My attitude was "You're not going to come into my life now and try to interrupt me." We didn't mesh well. He always seemed kind of childish.

This boyfriend had just gotten out of prison when he got my mom pregnant. He was barely around when my little brother came—I saw him at the hospital, and he came around the house a few times after that. My mom got pregnant with my little brother when I was a sophomore at Sidwell, my first year at the school.

I had gone to Largo High School for ninth grade and played football. But after my first year at Largo, things weren't going well. My grades were slipping, I started misbehaving—the music I listened to and the people I was around were not good. John-John's dad had already asked my mom if she'd be interested in sending me to Sidwell. But she had a lot of fear about it. She was afraid of me taking the Metro to school, and she knew it was a school with a lot of rich kids.

She didn't want me to see all of that. My mom thought that maybe it would be confusing or painful for me to see that. But after watching my ninth-grade year, she changed her mind.

I was pretty excited to be somewhere new. It was super shocking when I first walked on Sidwell's campus. I was a little starstruck—I remember seeing Malia Obama, the president's daughter, and thinking, "That's Malia—wow, I'm at Sidwell now. They have people in high places here. I go to school with people like this now." But despite the differences I saw in people's lives, like this guy is the nephew of the king of Kuwait, I never really felt like there was a clear hierarchy—I just knew things were different. Kids there had many different backgrounds—some kids had all these things, and some kids didn't have almost any of these things.

Football also distracted me from paying attention to the fact that I was in such a different environment. I had to go to practice. Going back to my own place in Prince George's County, it was just how it was.

I was super busy trying to balance school and football and commuting. Being at Sidwell took me away from my family. I hate to say that I was better than what I came from—but I knew that going back to my grandma's house and being more involved with the family would distract me. I didn't want to be in that environment with my family—Sidwell was a better environment. I lost contact with my grandma. I saw her less and less. And I was busy, making that trip to school every day. It took an hour or more to get to Sidwell. I had to be driven to a Metro station—Capitol Heights or Largo—and then take the train to Metro Center and change to take another train line to Tenleytown in DC. Then I either had to walk or ride the public bus to Sidwell.

It was already hard to focus. I struggled a lot of sophomore year, trying to keep up with what Sidwell was trying to teach me. When my little brother came along, that was a whole other thing. My mom had expected this latest boyfriend to be a parent. He wasn't, so I had to be. It was my job to do that! I'd need to catch my little brother on the steps when he started crawling, watch him, feed him, and basically learn how to be a dad at fifteen—my grandma passed away a few months before my little brother was born. She died in May, and he was born in July.

I don't remember doing homework at all at Sidwell—it was like a side thing. Playing football, commuting, being a parent to my little brother, plus attending one of the hardest high schools, I just didn't have time for homework.

The truth is I hate sports. Sidwell brought a lot of Black students in for the football team. I was there to play football. I was supposed to do wrestling, too—I wasn't aware of the wrestling thing when I was admitted. I said no to the team, and that started some tension—John-John's dad never really told me about wrestling. I realized early on that they were expecting me to do sports, and my position as a student didn't matter that much. The Black students on the team, we had to really try. We knew that we were brought there to play football—we were recruiting targets. They would say, "We brought you here" or "We brought you all the way here . . ."

Listening to those words, that's when I felt pressure—I'm not living up to what I'm supposed to be doing. It was so draining. The school expected me to just be a football player—but my mom and I looked at it as a stepping stone—always trying to do better no matter what situation we've been in. My mom had to put money toward Sidwell. She paid like $1,500 a year. And there was the expense of replacing the football equipment. You wear stuff out, and you've got to get new stuff. I do remember seeing that other kids had good-quality football stuff.

One of the first things I remember is winning a coupon from mom (Sandi) when she was writing the newsletter for the football team—for a free pizza. I kept that coupon in my wallet for a long time. I liked to look at it. I never used it.

Junior year, I was trying to do well in classes. I felt like Sidwell was giving me a chance to be creative with art and music, but at the same time, I got taken away from that opportunity with football and traumatic stuff.

At first, I felt very uncomfortable at anybody else's house. I felt like I was being judged. That's why I didn't make too many friends at Sidwell. I didn't feel like someone else was better than me, but I knew that I had been picked on before in school, and I knew other people pay attention to what you are wearing. And I didn't have that much. I had to get more comfortable with the idea of myself. I'm also very skeptical every time I meet somebody. I get tired of conflict.

Justin and I started hanging out more at school—we just didn't click with all the other kids. Justin and I really started to talk and get along after junior year. I actually hated Ryan during our sophomore year. I knew Sandi from the game photos, and I came over to the house one night for dinner. I remember the food. I started going to the Friday night pasta dinners—that was the best—all the food. I didn't go to the sleepovers until later—everybody else started going before me. I started coming over more senior year, trying to get more comfortable with my living situation and other people's living situations.

I love Justin—he was a really good friend to me. I really started getting close to Justin after he wasn't playing football. That coach drew him in, got close to him, took him to practice fields, and one day just turned on him, called him horrible names, and told him he'd never play tight end. He was aggressive and nasty, and he broke Justin. He just went off the rails. So, in senior year, Justin started working the camera.

Senior year, there was so much pressure. Ms. B at the school was very aggressive and very upset about me coming in late. I was tired. I was getting home late, trying to do homework, and we had the baby at the house. I knew I was building up points, and they really got on me about it. I started talking to you because you worked in the office. That was the best part of the day—we all loved coming by to talk to you—Justin's mom. You were a pleasant, reliable figure in my life; you got me lunch sometimes.

When the school told me I was about to get suspended, I was scared. I was thinking, Am I going to get kicked out? You gave me the option, the choice to try to finish strong. You made me feel safe. I remember the feeling of relief. A burden lifted. I was just shocked—whoa, someone's helping me. It's been hard for me to process help. You gave me an opportunity to do something I felt was better. I wasn't going to have to drop out. You gave me safety, confidence, freedom.

I often felt uncomfortable at first, but you really made me feel at home. I was sad, too—it was the first time I'd been away from my mom for longer periods of time in a place I didn't know—then she moved to Baltimore. I remember Ryan would come in to wake me up. It seemed like you all cared about me. I liked having somebody to wake me up. I remember all the breakfast sandwiches—arugula, tomato, scrambled eggs, ketchup, salted butter, and a smoothie. For years, I ate a lot of microwaved breakfast foods. I always understood the foods I should and should not eat, but it was hard. My mom had to pick up food on the way home from work—it was just two people every night, and she didn't make the best decisions about what I was eating, but she had a lot going on.

At Sidwell, lunches were healthy, and the foods you cooked me—you put time into taking care of me. Just like getting me to school on time. Some of the best times were in the morning, rushing to school with Justin and Ryan.

I say that I was uncomfortable, but it was also so comfortable to be in a place that was safer. Ryan was like an older brother. It was like I was getting someone else's brother who could help me out. Justin was really good to me. I really appreciated it, too, when I needed something, and Justin would speak up for me. At first, I was uncomfortable at the family dinners, but we eventually got over that hump where we started hanging out together on the weekends—after my mom moved. You all clothed me, you fed me, we went out places. I thought there was something different about the McCoys from all the other families at Sidwell.

---

twenty-one

Elijah moved in with us while I was in the throes of the college financial aid process with Ryan.

Many of the students of color at Sidwell were assigned to the same college counselor. The problem was that this counselor seemed to me to have a very limited understanding of the financial aid process and even of how to build a strong school list for students with such limited economic means. By the time I really got to know Elijah, his applications had been submitted based on the list developed by this Sidwell counselor. Some of the schools were colleges that Elijah had never heard of. There was also a lack of understanding of how big a hurdle the conception of college was to someone who would be the first person in his family to attend. "I really didn't know much about colleges," Elijah explained to me. But he understood at a gut level that the process was flawed. "I knew there wasn't much thought put into where they were trying to send me. I really wish they would pay some more attention, but they put me on the back burner." He added, "I'd hear kids say, 'I'm going to Harvard, I'm going to Yale.' I was thinking

I'm going back home after Sidwell. I didn't really understand what college was."

I looked at the list and felt a bit like Elijah, who said the counselor "just wants to get me in anywhere, and it doesn't matter where. It feels like they don't care." But out of this flawed list came one school that Elijah did want, which became his dream school, where he could pursue his interest in health and his artistic and musical side: Ithaca College in New York State.

There was just one problem: Elijah and his mother had never filed the CSS paperwork for him to receive any financial aid. When his financial aid paperwork arrived, the money he had been awarded was next to nothing. Unlike Ryan's case, Sidwell had not followed up with Elijah about his paperwork. But there was more here than administrative indifference. There was just barely a modicum of effort to counsel Elijah toward a suitable college for him. In the school's view, this issue wasn't their "problem." Almost the same as what the school had said to me about Ryan's family not paying income taxes.

Over time, in different ways, Ryan, Diamente, and Elijah each opened up to me about what is defined as impostor syndrome. They knew they were at a school to play football and nothing else. They knew they were sometimes or often treated differently. Elijah and Ryan, in particular, felt as if some teachers genuinely believed that each boy was wasting his time in the classroom simply by being there. Understanding that, I had to ensure that they could keep dreaming about the life they wanted, not the life that was somehow expected of them.

I sat down with Elijah and discussed his options, and during the conversation, I came up with the idea to do a GoFundMe to cover as much of the cost of his tuition as possible. Elijah wrote a very sanitized version of his story, and Tom and I helped him edit it. We passed the draft back and forth until we were discussing individual words. Finally, Elijah and I thought we had it right. As soon as the fundraiser was posted, the response was tremendous. But one person was very unhappy, Elijah's Sidwell college counselor, who emailed:

> Eli,
>
> This afternoon, I had an opportunity to read your letter on your gofundme [*sic*] page. I am writing to respectfully ask you to revise your letter to exclude the reference to your college counselor neglecting to inform of you [*sic*] of the necessary forms. It is an inaccurate statement. If you would like, I would be happy to share with the you [*sic*] the numerous times the college counseling office communicated with families and students that the submission of the FAFSA and CSS Profile forms are a required part of the process.
>
> I look forward to hearing from you regarding my request.

I responded that we had posted the GoFundMe, and I would be the one to handle and administer the funds for Elijah's tuition. I then explained that after receiving this note, we helped Eli edit the GoFundMe. I added, "The reason we edited it is because the point of the GoFundMe page is to enable Elijah to go to college, not to assess blame or cause discomfort. Without the assistance of many, he will be unable to attend college at all. I told you of this plan when we met after his disastrous financial aid results came in. I also told you at that time that Elijah and his mother had no knowledge of the CSS Profile requirement relative to Ithaca or any other school to which he was actually applying. We are hopeful that there will be constructive lessons learned by all of us, as there is no question that more could and should have been done for Eli in terms of ensuring that he had the support services that he needed."

I continued, "The school was doing an admirable job of emailing lots of great information and guidance, but that does not work for poor families who do not have personal computers. I am sure you did not know that neither Eli nor his mother has a personal computer. Until February, when we gave a computer to Eli, his only means of accessing information was via his phone. Many of the families who are attending school on financial aid, like Elijah's, have never attended college, and their children are navigating these waters on their own and without resources that we all assume they have. We also witnessed other financial aid students who were underserved by the school's process because of assumptions about what parent support they have. It seems clear to us that additional college and financial aid counseling processes need to be implemented in order to ensure that worthy children, who have been positioned well for college by their academic teachers and advisors, should not then be disadvantaged by the very circumstances of poverty we are all trying to help them overcome. I think we have all learned a lot this year about what these kids need." I was as restrained as possible, but inside I was frustrated and more than slightly furious.

In twenty-four hours, Eli's GoFundMe raised more than $36,000 from friends and colleagues around the country and predominantly from people within the Sidwell community. It was enough to pay for Eli's entire first year. I was pleasantly surprised, but Eli was stunned. As he told me later, "I was still much of a loner—I didn't pay attention to the fact that people knew my name and wanted to help. It was mind-blowing when I saw the money that was raised."

With enough money to make it possible to commit, Elijah and I flew up to visit Ithaca for orientation. The grounds were bright and green, the large central pond sparkled in the sunlight, and the fountain shot its artificial geysers high into the sky. We had a full schedule of events, and one of our stops was a meeting with financial aid. The woman who called him in for the meeting started with the news that because Elijah had created a GoFundMe, he would be receiving less money. My response was "You're kidding, right?" Her face told me no. She had some of the coldest eyes I had ever seen. She didn't bother to shake our hands before ushering us into her office, nor could she even be bothered to turn on a lamp or a light. Instead, she motioned for us to sit down in front of her desk and then brusquely walked around to the other side, picked up a stack of envelopes, and tossed them in front of Elijah. They were all addressed to Elijah's mother's former apartment (the one from which she was evicted before moving to Baltimore), and each one had come back stamped "return to sender."

In the most sarcastic, mean-spirited way, this woman, whom we had never met before, looked at Elijah and said, "Well, I guess you didn't complete any of those." Elijah shook his head in silence. Watching him was like watching the moment a massive tear in the fabric decimates a child's inflatable bounce house—the joyful, exuberant sounds of happy kids at play cut short as the entire structure deflates and caves in. It was as if her mission was to humiliate Eli and destroy his dream. She continued, "You've become sort of well-known, haven't you? You raised all that money with your GoFundMe, didn't you? Well, all that money needs to be reported to the government, and that's going to reduce the amount of financial aid you can receive."

Her tone was essentially "Well, you may not get to come here after all."

Right then, I decided that I was going to take control of this meeting. I looked back at her, with the same poker face that I had used to stand before countless judges, and I said in my most cutting litigator's voice, "He'll be fine. He is going to attend this school and graduate, and we, *his family*, will do everything in our power to ensure that he has that opportunity."

She sniffed. "Well, he'll have to declare that, too."

"Yes, he will," I said. And then I added, "We're done."

At that moment, it wasn't even about the money. I'm not good with money, I never have been. (When I got home, I had to tell Tom that I might have committed us to paying for the next four years of Elijah's college education.) But what I knew in that room was that Elijah needed someone to stand up for him. And I was determined to do so. Because I was the only one who could. And if there were echoes back to my appointment with the USC law school financial aid office about thirty years before, at some level, I felt those, too.

When we walked out, Elijah turned to me and, in a very quiet voice, said, "I don't know that I feel very welcome here."

I promised him, "Well, you're never going to have to see her again. If you feel welcomed by the other students and the professors, that's what you need to focus on."

And he did. He started that fall, and he loved them. And I stayed true to my promise: Eli never spoke to the woman in financial aid again.

A year later, I learned the Ithaca admissions office was actively promoting a GoFundMe page, set up to assist a student who could not afford the school's tuition.

◆

The only person who was not on board with Elijah's decision about Ithaca was his mom. I was in my car when she called. She began the conversation with "Well, I don't really want him to go to Ithaca." Her idea, as she explained it to me, was for Elijah to go to Salisbury University in Maryland. She would get an apartment near the school, and Elijah would live with her, take care of his little brother, and go to school while she worked. I pulled off the road and into a parking lot, the car idling in an empty space, with Elijah's mom's voice floating through the speakers. In the months since Elijah had to come to live with us, she and I had spent hours on the phone having long conversations about issues and choices. Usually, I was very supportive. But not this time. I did not want her choice to become Elijah's. I told her very directly that college was Elijah's time and that he needed to go out on his own to succeed. Elijah also held firm, and he went off to Ithaca. When it was parents' weekend, I made sure that I was there to visit Eli. "You are one of the first adults I can speak to about how I am feeling," he told me later. By the time he spoke those words, I was also beginning to appreciate how much effort it took for Elijah to say and feel them.

One experience drilled home for me just how deeply Elijah fears abandonment. One of the many times that Elijah was late, he was driving to Syracuse from Ithaca. He, Ryan, and I were planning an adventure that day, but were unable to do anything because, by the time Elijah arrived in Syracuse, it was too close to the time when I had to depart for the airport. I was not happy and made that clear. He was very apologetic. I suggested that we get a very late breakfast and talk about how to deal with his inability to get ready in the mornings. Our food had just arrived when I looked over at Elijah and realized that the expression I saw on his face was fear. I immediately said, "You know, Elijah, I love you unconditionally. There is literally nothing that you can do that will make me stop loving you. It's permanent. It's always going to be there. You can count on that. I may get annoyed with you, but I'll never, ever stop loving you."

Elijah stared at me. He was silent, he couldn't speak. Quietly, huge tears started rolling down his cheeks. We left our food on our plates, untouched; I dropped some cash on the table, rebooked my flight home, and then we walked to a park across the street and talked for hours—about abandonment, how it feels, how scared we both are of rejection, and how that impacts us in our lives. "I chose you, and you chose me," I told him. "I'm not going to un-choose you—ever." Eventually, we just sat side by side on that park bench in silence, knowing in our hearts that we would always have each other.

SANDI

twenty-two

UNLIKE ELIJAH, I DO HAVE the name of a father on my birth certificate: Eugene Smith. By the time I had started law school, my parents were back together. They had relocated to Searcy, Arkansas. But the change of location made no difference. They still fought all the time. I would call them on the phone—or they would call me. During one phone call, I could hear them fighting. My mother was screaming that my father had tried to run her over with a truck. I had no way of knowing if that was true, but from the sounds and the screams, it seemed as if it could be. The truck episode finally led them to start the actual divorce process. But they couldn't afford two separate attorneys, or maybe Searcy only had one attorney, so a local lawyer named "Red" helped them file and finalize the paperwork.

I spent many hours on the phone with Red, talking about how to get the two warring sides to agree to a fair settlement, which was essentially my uncle Carlie agreeing to pay my mother a sum of money to make her go away. One night when I was working late at the Finley, Kumble law office, my mother called. As I gazed out at the rows of banker's boxes stacked along my shelves, she launched into yet another round of complaints about how the process was so deeply unfair, the settlement amount was not enough, and how my father and uncle wanted her dead. I waited for her to pause to catch her breath, and I tried to explain how and why I believed the amount was the best that she was going to receive. Rather than listen, she started screaming at me, the words "bitch," "whore," and "a shit" ricocheting into my ears through the receiver. It was, I knew, the same dysfunctional pattern of my entire life.

But not what came next. Amid her venomous tirade, she threw out a sentence I had never heard before. "I don't know why you are taking his side in this," she spat. "He's not even your real father."

I felt a jolt, like a lightning strike, pass through me. I gasped, and then I became hyperalert. "Wait. What?!"

She told me angrily that my father could not have children, and she decided to have a baby to keep him at home. "I wanted a boy and got Shitty Sandi instead," she shrieked. Luckily, she explained, she was able to go back to the UCLA clinic where she had been artificially inseminated with me and was able to get pregnant again, this time with Kevin, a boy. She just wished she'd never had to "have" me to get him.

I sat at my desk in stunned silence. Somehow, I got my purse and my car keys, walked to the parking garage, and drove myself home, past the neon lights and storefronts, the TV show and movie ads pasted onto billboards, the bits of bougainvillea, and the intermittent palm trees. I remember nothing about the drive, but everything about the conversation. By the time I reached my apartment, I had convinced myself that my mother was lying. She lied a lot—this was exactly the type of thing that she would say to try to make me cut ties with my dad and be firmly on her side. But I still called Kevin. Like two detectives comparing notes after two different interrogations, we would go over and analyze all the crazy things our mother said, mostly because we knew that she was always trying to drive a wedge between us and turn one against the other. Kevin eventually called Mom. She confirmed the story to him as well, and she told him we had the same donor father.

I let two weeks slide by. Somewhere in that span, I had another conversation with my mother. This one was more restrained. In a calm, almost clinical voice, she repeated that my father was not my biological father, and then she described in great detail the process she went through at the UCLA clinic to be inseminated. She was a participant in an experimental fertility study for the procedure. There were no cryobanks and frozen sperm back then. A donor would be in one room, the woman would be in the other room, and the doctor would pass between the rooms to inseminate the woman with fresh sperm. The men who participated in the study were students at UCLA looking for some extra cash. My mother even told me that she arrived late to her appointment and saw the man who was my biological father. She described him as tall, blond, and a doctor. (About this, I would later learn that she was lying again.)

I wasn't completely convinced my mother was telling the truth, but there was too much evidence to the contrary for me to still believe that she was lying. I knew my father was coming to La Crescenta to visit Uncle Carlie, so I called my dad and asked if we could meet for lunch. We met at a restaurant in the small downtown of La Crescenta, where nearly all the houses were upscale ranch houses and split-levels, flanked by shimmering blue kidney-shaped pools.

We made a bit of small talk, ordered, and then I told my father exactly what my mother had said. The color drained from his face, he gasped, and then he started to cry. Every word my mother had said was true. He was sorry that she had told me; they had both agreed that Kevin and I were never to be told. His shoulders slumped, and he looked defeated and depressed. I found myself reassuring him that it didn't matter, but at the same time, inside, I felt relieved.

For as long as I could remember, I had felt disconnected from him and from my family. I was taller than everyone else, and I just felt uncomfortably different. Now I knew why. There was also a very real sense of relief that I did not have the genetic material of both of my parents. Ever since the beginning of high school biology, I had worried about what traits I had inherited from both my mother and my father. The possibility now that I had one "normal" parent and that I didn't have a biological connection on two sides to pathology was freeing. It was one less thing to worry about.

But if I thought that finally revealing this fact would be freeing for my mother, that it would remove a weighty secret and allow us to start a new relationship, I was wrong. The conflict never stopped; it just slightly changed forms. My mother would telephone me, send mail, or show up unannounced to visit. She did the same things to Kevin. When he went to college in Utah, she would show up at the apartment he shared with fellow students and demand to sleep on their couch, much as my father had shown up at my apartment when I was in school. Her behavior only got worse after we graduated. Without warning, Mom would literally arrive on our doorsteps and threaten to show up at our jobs. Just as she had constantly threatened to call my teachers to tell them the "truth" about me when I was younger, now she was making these threats about my employers.

One such occasion took place while I was living and working in Los Angeles as an attorney. My mother was very angry that my brother had invited our father to his wedding. She insisted that I refuse to attend the wedding if my father also attended. I, in turn, refused to do that to my brother. So she called to threaten that she would contact my law firm and let them know what a miserable person I was and how they should never have hired me. Irrationally, I was always afraid she'd show up at my office, start screaming about me, and I would end up being fired. No matter how far I rose in the legal profession, I never got over that fear. And yet, I still couldn't let go of my belief that she was a victim.

After the revelation that I had a different biological father, I pulled away from the man who was my designated father. I decided that I wanted nothing to do with him. Not even when he was diagnosed with prostate cancer. Instead, Kevin took him in. I offered to pay for a private-duty nurse, but I was working long hours on the legal partnership track. And I still blamed my father. I saw him as the monster. In the story that I told myself, there had to be a monster and a victim. I had to write a narrative of survivorship and saviorhood. Except, to Kevin, the story was different: in the story that he wrote, the monster was our mother. Kevin and I argued repeatedly over who was to blame. At first, I was having none of it, and we largely stopped speaking. Our father's approaching death seemed to do what our parents hadn't successfully accomplished in life: split us apart.

Our father didn't stay with Kevin until the end. He eventually convinced another one of his brothers to help him escape the medical facility where he had been placed. That brother drove him in a dilapidated RV across half the country until they reached a lake in Tennessee. Eugene Smith died of advanced prostate cancer in that motor home next to that Tennessee lake, in very similar circumstances to the Idaho home we had lived in decades ago. Only then did I start to reconsider, look back, and begin to understand that perhaps Kevin's interpretation was valid and even likely closer to the truth, whatever that truth ultimately was. I began to entertain the possibility that I was the one who was largely wrong. I had been brainwashed by our mother, but I had also borne the brunt of the physical violence from our father.

Kevin was always my mother's favorite and was protected by her and by me as the older sibling. So the emotional imprinting was different. But once death cut the cord in our parents' endless conflict, I could finally begin to process what had happened. It would take years for me to understand more fully.

A central question that I pondered for much of my childhood was, What's the difference between a dreamer and a liar? My dad, on his best days, was a dreamer. He came up with new business ideas and tinkered with cars to make them roar to life. But my mom started referring to him as "the liar." And overwhelmingly, that's the image he took on for me, in my mind. Now I began to revise my question: How much does the world have to crush your hopes so that you stop dreaming and start lying?

After the divorce, our mother moved in with her mother, but she still said the most horrible things about her mother, so I started to believe that my grandmother must have been horrible, too. Gradually, my mother found some stability; she managed to get a series of jobs. She trained to be a court reporter, and she even worked for a while in a VA medical office specializing in psychiatry. I think there was a subconscious desire on her part to try to understand the voices in her head—why they were there and what they were telling her. But the jobs rotated, and with distance, I saw flashes of behaviors that made me rethink my assumptions. A key moment was when Justin was little, and I observed my mom's total lack of empathy toward him.

When I was around children, especially my children, but truly all children, I felt a wellspring of passion rise from deep inside me. I would do anything to protect them. I embraced my kids, I rocked them, I smoothed their hair, I kissed their knees when they fell or their foreheads for no reason. So it was with a significant amount of shock that I watched my mother's near-complete indifference as if Justin were a zoo animal and she was a spectator on the other side of his enclosure. Suddenly, in that moment, it was as if a light had been switched on in my mind. During my childhood, I couldn't remember ever being hugged; I couldn't remember ever being comforted by my mom. The only thing that I could remember was being solicited to support her in her claims of victimhood. The missing pieces that I had not seen in reflecting on my own relationship with my mother, I found fiercely clear when I watched her interact—or fail to interact—with my son. And I immediately realized that I needed to limit her time with him. I did not want to introduce this toxicity to another generation.

But the ultimate moment of clarity came years later, when I was living in DC, and my mother was living in an apartment in Las Vegas. She must have put my name and number on a contact form because the landlord called me to say that she was destroying the apartment and screaming at the neighbors. I flew to Las Vegas, rented a car, and drove to her condominium located across from a strip mall. Her unit was almost devoid of furniture (except, as reminiscent of our homes growing up, it had a mattress on the floor). The kitchen sink had been torn out, and she was using the bathtub to wash dishes. The carpet was filthy, and the walls had obviously sustained leaks that left behind a significant amount of black mold. From the moment I walked in the door, she was in my face, screaming. It was as if I had reverted to being age six or seven. She looked like she was going to hit me, and I instinctively cowered in the corner. I was physically shaking.

I moved her to a new apartment—Kevin and I split the rent, hoping to ensure that she stayed there. But the downward spiral continued. Now it was the police who were calling. She was banging on strangers' doors, accusing them of stealing her cats. While the police had been speaking with her, she had jumped in her car and sped off. The officer on the phone apologized to me for letting her go, saying, "Ma'am, I didn't feel like I could chase an old lady."

The next call I got was from the Phoenix, Arizona, police. They had found our mother wandering around the downtown area, talking to people who were not there. The officers took her to the hospital for a psychiatric hold, and there she was diagnosed with schizophrenia. It had taken close to six decades of adulthood to get this diagnosis. The doctors put her on antipsychotics, and I had her transferred to a care facility in Mesa, where she lived for many years. The home was a good one. She had her own room with a real bed on a frame, a dresser, a TV, a desk, and a bathroom. There was a house cat at the facility that she adored. She told everyone that her "Mafia doctor" was coming to rescue her and that they would soon be living in a palatial mansion in Scottsdale. The staff humored her and allowed her to repeat what the voices in her head were telling her. But once I moved her to that facility, I could see that the drugs had done nothing to dull her hatred of me. The look on her face when I walked into her room was pure venom.

That experience finally gave me some clarity around my own life.

It's amazing what a label does to understanding, in this case, having a definitive diagnosis. Or at least what it did for me. It freed me from having to rationalize and explain what was happening in my life. It freed me from making excuses and from taking sides.

The insecurity caused by my upbringing was intense; I knew that. But now I could better understand why.

Since my earliest days as a "backup" secretary, I had always felt that I must be better than anyone else at work. Not to feel superior, but simply to feel equal to anyone around me. No matter how well I did, no matter how many accolades I received, I always felt like I was not good enough. Social events that require small talk overwhelm me because I was never taught to do that. My default reaction was often shame. When you have felt ashamed for the entirety of your childhood, when you have always been the one who was different, you don't just shed it like a snake shedding old skin. Instead, this reaction functions as a giant sieve, as the thing that everything else must filter through. If someone tells me I did a great job at something, I must filter that compliment through years of shame, then decide if I really did do a good job, and only then can I answer "Thank you" in as genuine a way as possible. Rationally, I know people often mean what they say, but emotionally, my first response to most things is to feel skepticism or shame, and my second response is to wait, with my shoulders hunched up, for the other shoe to drop, like it always did during my childhood.

Once, it was my literal shoe. I was standing inside a wood-paneled elevator at the Four Seasons Hotel in Washington, DC. I had been invited to a small dinner by a dear friend who was celebrating her birthday with a group of her closest friends. To me, a small gathering means that each person is even more on display. Hair, nails, fashion, all of it are being scrutinized. I knew some of the other women who had been invited, but by no means all. To look the part and to look like I belonged, I had worn a pair of fancy, heeled boots with narrow, pointy toes. I knew they made my feet hurt, but they were the most fashionable thing I owned. There was a valet station, and not much walking was required, but we had to stand to chat. Soon, I was shifting my weight from one side to the other, as if that would magically relieve the pressure on my cramped toes. Later, after dinner, we formed a circle and danced our hearts out. By the end of the evening, I could hardly stand up in those boots. When the party broke up, I hobbled to the elevator, stepped inside, and started wincing.

The problem was that I wasn't alone in the elevator. Another partygoer had gotten on with me: then–First Lady Michelle Obama, along with her Secret Service detail. I must have looked miserable, because the First Lady's eyes traveled from my face to my feet, and she laughed, suggesting that I take off my boots. And I almost did, except that at that very moment, I remembered the socks that I had put on earlier that evening. Unlike the rest of my outfit, they were ratty and old, with holes in the heels. But I couldn't bring myself to throw them out. Instead, paralyzed by an odd kind of deprivation and thrift, I was still wearing them. Because even though I can now go to dinner parties at the Four Seasons and navigate the table settings, I have never completely left behind the twelve-year-old girl who stuffed her clothes into black garbage bags and worried, What if this is my last pair of socks? What if I can never buy another pair again? I laughed and told the First Lady, "Well, I would, but you really don't want to see the socks I have under there." We both got a chuckle out of that. My painful boots remained on my feet.

◆

When I started to read books and articles about children raised by schizophrenics, I came to realize that I wasn't an outlier: for most of us who have been raised in this environment, the sense of being a permanent outsider is the norm. I could also begin to understand why I struggle to relate to others who are "normal." And I could better understand why almost everyone else with intense childhood trauma also struggles. Like Ryan hiding in a closet, like Diamente living amid neighborhood streets where violence could erupt at any minute, like Elijah, who just wanted peace at home.

After I learned that Eugene Smith was not my father, I never thought I would find my biological dad. But in 2007, I took a 23andMe test (when the company was just a start-up). The account sat dormant for almost a decade. Then, in 2017, I received an email from a woman through the platform. She turned out to be my biological aunt, and she connected me to the man who is my father. He had been a UCLA student, not a doctor, as my mom had said. And his hair was red, not blond. (My brother's biological father was a different UCLA student. When Kevin did 23andMe, he discovered that he had a lot of half siblings. They hold a big "sibling" party each year at their biological father's home in Palm Springs.) My biological father was a loner, and I appear to be his only child.

My biological father had donated his sperm for the money. He was still living in Los Angeles. He said that he never had any other kids, but to prove the universe has a sense of humor, he told me that he went to UCLA undergrad (like me), USC law school (also like me), and he had married a woman named Sandy.

twenty-three

Tom McCoy was the partner who interviewed me for the summer associate position at O'Melveny & Myers, when I was still a law student who was terrified by the sight of two forks and a bread plate on a dinner table and when I was still watching TV shows like *LA Law* to try to figure out how to "act" as a lawyer. After I was hired to work as an associate at the firm full-time, I saw Tom around the LA office. We were friendly but nothing more. I did not want to date anyone that I worked with. Frankly, I didn't want to date at all. I found the whole experience annoying and tedious.

Instead, I built my life around my work and the firm. There were four female litigation partners in Los Angeles; I set my sights on becoming the fifth. I was assigned a big pro bono case, revealing corruption in the LA Police Department, which attracted a significant amount of media attention because I was able to prove that the LAPD had framed an innocent man who had already served twenty-five years in prison for a crime he didn't commit. But most of my work was corporate. In the early 1990s, corporate law in California largely meant either working amid the glam of Hollywood studios or green north of Silicon Valley and the San Francisco Bay Area. I was assigned to a case involving IBM; Tom was on a case for AMD, a semiconductor company. Between the two cases, there were about seventy O'Melveny & Myers lawyers detailed to the Bay Area, and we often gathered for big group dinners during the week. On the weekends, our temporary offices emptied out and the lawyers raced to the airport because everyone else had a family back in LA and they wanted to get home. Tom and I were the only single people left. We started getting together to play board games or go out for dinner and drinks. If I had to travel to handle a deposition, he would stay at my rental house and take care of my dog and cat.

It became clear that he was interested in me, but I had no interest in dating a coworker. Everything changed the day he announced he was leaving O'Melveny to become the general counsel at AMD. I called him that day and started with the line "So, are you still interested in going out?"

I didn't stay at O'Melveny, either. I moved to another firm, Fenwick & West, which was trying to build a litigation department. By 1997, I was married, had a newborn baby, and was on track to make partner. And then one night, Tom and I were having dinner with two friends: Nancy Heinen and Dennis DeBroeck. Nancy had followed Steve Jobs when he returned to Apple after a stint at NeXT Computer. Apple, the company Jobs had cofounded, was in very bad shape. Nancy was bemoaning the mess and saying how she needed to hire a director of litigation. Then she asked me if I would consider taking the job. Apple had no money; I'd be paid mostly in stock options. It was a gamble, but I said yes to the interview process, and I was hired. The title, director of litigation, implied that there were litigators to direct. Instead, our entire department consisted of me, one junior attorney, two paralegals, and $20 million in expenditures on litigation and lawsuits. I suddenly had to manage a $20 million budget while caring for a baby who didn't sleep through the night.

Apple was being sued on multiple fronts, from appropriation of the Beatles' imagery to having the same name as an insurance company also called Apple to the Newton minicomputer. Protesters congregated in the parking lot to mourn the "loss" of the Newton, an early tablet-like computing device, whose later incarnation would be the iPad. Apple fans were incredibly fanatical. They constantly wanted updates on new product releases and would go to almost any lengths to find out what Apple would be offering next. Mac fanatics would hunt down secret information related to the timing and types of product releases and post them on the nascent internet. I routinely sent cease-and-desist letters to force them to take down the posts. In response, I would get a cascade of death threats from people who were convinced that Apple owed them this vital information. They would recite my home address in voicemails and threaten to kill everyone there. Years of dealing with my parents had inured me to these types of threats. But hearing them on my voicemail certainly did make me wonder how many more Eugene and Janice acolytes were lurking out there, feeling entitled to special treatment and ready to explode at the slightest provocation.

When Apple wasn't being sued as a defendant, it was a plaintiff suing others. Steve and Apple's chief industrial design engineer, Jony Ive, had remade the product line and created a colorful all-in-one computer, the first of its kind. Immediately, other companies began producing copies. We launched several lawsuits against the copycats, one of which was filed in the Northern District of California and another one that was filed in Tokyo in a Japanese trade court. The Tokyo lawsuit made its way through the court first.

By now, I was eight months pregnant with Elie. As with Justin, I had gained eighty-five pounds. My ankles had ballooned. I waddled rather than walked. My doctor was checking my blood pressure every day, worried about preeclampsia. And what no one had realized, least of all me, was that in this particular Japanese court, outside lawyers could not argue a case on a client's behalf; an employee for the company or the company's CEO had to appear to make the argument. That employee was me; the CEO was Steve Jobs. This Japanese legal rule was the exact opposite of how US courts operated, where it's a much better practice for in-house counsel to allow outside counsel for the company to appear in court because there is essentially no difference between in-house counsel and the client. And because the Japan lawsuit was going to be heard before the cases in the other courts, Apple needed a favorable ruling. Otherwise, our subsequent lawsuits were in jeopardy.

Steve told me I had to go. My doctor said, "No, you are not getting on a plane." The airline required a medical note, clearing me to fly.

I told Steve, "I can't go."

One of the attorneys I had hired to represent Apple in various matters, and who became a very close friend to Steve, George Riley, also argued against my flying to Japan. As he said, he didn't want "Sandi to die on the airplane." The next day, I walked into my office, a cozy space with a desk, table, and chairs for visitors and large windows overlooking the gardens at the front of Apple's Cupertino headquarters. On my chair was a letter from my doctor. I'm convinced that Steve got her to write it. To this day, I have no idea how it appeared.

I flew first class, and the entire staff of the plane seemed devoted to keeping my feet elevated and ensuring that I was comfortable. When I passed through customs and reached the taxi stand, my taxi driver was so terrified that I would go into labor that he drove no more than twenty miles per hour from Narita Airport to Tokyo, which is about fifty miles away. Cars sped past us as the taxi crawled along. On the frontage road adjacent to the highway, even rickshaws that were powered solely by people pedaling passed us.

In Japan, at the start of the twenty-first century, pregnant women did not venture out, particularly late in their pregnancies. They certainly did not litigate. I was doing both. No one wanted me to walk anywhere. The courthouse was less than a block from my hotel, and it was downhill. The staff insisted on putting me in a taxi. I insisted on walking. I tried explaining that it was more difficult for me to get in and out of a car than to just sort of throw my body down the street and let gravity carry my swollen belly and ankles toward the courthouse. It didn't matter; the hotel staff and the team of lawyers there to help me were beside themselves. The Japanese believe that women in that stage of pregnancy should be taken care of; what I was doing was borderline offensive to them. And I hadn't even set my puffy feet in the hearing room.

When I walked in, the judges were already seated—three slightly built, elderly Japanese men being approached by a two-hundred-plus-pound, five-foot-ten pregnant woman. Their jaws all but dropped to the table.

Apple's Japanese counsel had joined me to translate, and I knew that the judges spoke some English, so I started by saying, "I do not want my condition discussed at all." The legal concept of "she won because she was eight months pregnant and they wanted to send her home" was not going to sway the judges in the Northern District of California. I argued Apple's side. The judges said they would convene in private and decide. I went out to dinner with our Japanese lawyers, and in the middle of our meal of amazingly tasty fish and vegetables at a fancy restaurant near my hotel, one of the judges called the Japanese counsel's cell phone. The judge told him, "Put her on the next plane to the US, she won."

The judges' written decision was exactly what we needed, and "Apple's lead US counsel is pregnant" didn't appear anywhere in it.

Back at Apple's headquarters, everyone celebrated. Because I couldn't drink champagne, someone shook a bottle and sprayed it all over me when the cork was popped. In a quiet moment, Steve Jobs thanked me for what I had done. He had a long-standing reputation as a notoriously ungrateful person, but this time he was. So was Jony Ive, the famous industrial design engineer knighted by the Queen of England and the designer of the technology that we were trying to protect. Two years later, when he came to my goodbye party, he gave me one of the original iMac prototypes with a hole cut into the top and a vase of flowers inserted inside. He christened it my "iVase" and said he hoped I'd remember this time forever. I was leaving corporate litigation to become a stay-at-home mom.

My departure was driven by what drives so many working mothers to leave or cut back: childcare. The first episode occurred before Elie was born. Justin was twenty-six months old. He was sitting in his high chair with Tom and me at dinner one night when he said, "Nanny hit you." There was only one nanny in our house, a woman who had been working for us for nearly a year.

Two-year-olds are still learning pronouns; they often say "you" when they mean "I" or "me." Tom and I asked, "Where did Nanny hit you?"

Justin said, "Head on hard." It quickly became clear that our nanny had done something that terrified him. That night, I stayed awake, putting the pieces together. I had noticed that Justin was increasingly distant. Where he would once hurl himself into my arms the moment I walked through the door, bursting with excitement at seeing me, now, sometimes, he would run in the opposite direction. He wouldn't even let me pick him up. Tom and I had written it off as the changing whims of toddlers. But I realized we had been wrong.

I spoke to the housekeeper who worked with our cleaning service.

She only spoke Spanish, but my Spanish was good enough that I could follow her when she said that she had watched the nanny tell Justin that I hated him, that I didn't love him, and that's why I was gone all the time. When the nanny grew frustrated with Justin, she would hit him and leave him in his room.

It was a terrible flashback to my own childhood, and beyond traumatizing. We fired the nanny and took Justin away for the weekend. Tom and I both cried more than Justin did, but it was clear to me that Tom blamed me for what had happened (including saying that being pregnant with Elie caused me to fail to notice all the things that the nanny had done). It was also clear that he wanted me to quit work and stay home with Justin.

We found a therapist who helped us work with Justin and tried to address what had happened. The therapist explained that part of the way to help Justin heal was to slow down how we did everything, no rushing, no racing, not in games, not in life. It was almost a principle of no sudden movements so there would be nothing to scare Justin. I also realized that Justin had developed a fixation or even love of vacuum cleaners—probably, the therapist said, because he considered the housekeeper an ally or a safe haven. The vacuum cleaner made him feel safe. Sitting with the therapist, I could feel my knees and elbows burning, as if I were once again dragging myself over the shag carpet in the dark of night, clutching the heavy, metal vacuum cleaner parts, my mother's voice hissing in my ear that the intruders were coming, get ready.

I began to question why I was going to work, even though I loved my job. I was uncomfortable with the long hours. Did I need to stay home? Was Tom right?

After Elie was born, I tried putting both children in a day care around the corner from Apple, but when I'd drop by, I'd often find Justin sitting alone in a corner. Elie would be fine, but he wasn't. I tried another nanny and installed cameras all over the house. I would review ten hours of footage on high speed each night after Justin and Elie were asleep. This nanny had no interest in engaging with Elie. She would leave her wailing, strapped in her high chair or bouncer, while she was focused on Justin. It was a flashback to those years when Kevin was the center of attention. Everyone wanted to protect him and to have him around while ignoring me, or worse. I had vowed to myself that I would be a very different parent, that I would do it differently. Instead, the traumas of my childhood were being reenacted in my children.

Apple was poised to open its first stores and to make an exponential leap. But financially, Tom made more money than me. He had very traditional views of breadwinning, childcare, and managing the home. When Elie was sixteen months old, I broke my hip. As soon as I was discharged from the hospital, Tom had a business trip planned. His boss called me to tell me how imperative it was that Tom go. I couldn't even pick up Elie from her crib or put her down. But I told Tom, of course, go. And I hired someone to pick up and put down my toddler. From that perspective, there was almost no question that of course I would be the one to stay home.

It was hard. I imagine this must be how pro athletes feel after they retire; the constant structure of your days, the demands, the training, the preparation, the competition, your teammates, the locker room, all of it just vanishes overnight. I went from being frantically busy to sitting in the backyard rolling Play-Doh creations and watching Justin zoom around on his tricycle. But then, a couple of weeks in, I was sitting in the side yard of our house in Portola Valley, scrunched up in the low seats of a toddler-sized picnic table. I was watching Justin pedal madly on his tricycle and Elie kick herself forward with her feet on her junior trike, and a single thought overcame me: "As happy as I was at Apple, I am happier now."

THE TIES THAT BIND

twenty-four

THE AFTERNOON THAT ELIJAH AND I went to the Home Depot to look for Ryan was not a mistake.

We eventually found Ryan inside the store, coming off his break. He smiled when he saw us, a big, beaming grin that was so classically Ryan; the three of us hugged, and he was clearly very happy. We spent nearly two hours talking in a small section at the back of the store. I got Elie on my phone on FaceTime, and she talked to Ryan, shrieking in delight, and telling him how much she missed him. For almost thirty minutes, they bantered and even cried, face-to-face on the screen.

Elijah and I decided that we wanted to avoid attempting any deep conversation. Keep it light, we agreed. Our goal was simply to have all of us talking again as if no time had passed.

But time had passed.

Ryan had not been able to finish college at Syracuse. The seeds of trouble were sown almost from the moment he stepped on campus. For his first year, the university housed him with a much older student, a veteran who had served in the military. It wasn't a good fit. Ryan didn't have someone to go to dinner with or hang out with or who could sympathize and share the usual freshman angst. Nevertheless, Ryan did well in his classes. So I stopped checking on his grades—I did the same with Elijah. But for Ryan, my decision proved to be a mistake. In the second year, Ryan's academics slid. The pace of the material and the workload increased, and he lacked the academic foundation and support. By the time I discovered what had happened, it was too late to intervene and help him recover.

Instead, Tom and I helped him withdraw from the university and initially tried to help him find gap year programs, but in many ways, college was not the right fit for Ryan. The post–Washington prep school life that had been dangled before him as the perfect path was not the perfect path for Ryan. It seemed that he needed to be freed of the Sidwell expectations, and the only way he could do that was to free himself from all the trappings of Sidwell. He chose to break off contact with everyone who had been in his life before and while he attended Syracuse.

When Elijah and I saw him at Home Depot, Ryan was living on his own terms, terms that made him happy. He was thriving at Home Depot. He was operating all kinds of heavy equipment and forklifts, moving oversized items, and feeling a sense of accomplishment in completing the tasks. He was using his hands and his people skills. The store was considering him for a promotion, he said. It was very much as if he had found his place. I told him that we were all proud of him and that we supported him in whatever he chose to do. I left the door open for him to come back on whatever terms he wanted.

But when Elijah and I exited the store and stepped outside into the baking heat, we knew that the glass doors sliding closed behind us might be symbolic as well. The faint sound of their gaskets sealing was the final sound of our separation from Ryan. Of all the symmetries that ruled our lives—Elijah, Diamente, Ryan, and me—the one symmetry I had not expected was leaving. But I realize now that sometimes people leave, and they do it because it is what they need to do. It may be the only way they can heal. Whatever the cause, they have their reasons.

I still hear from Rochelle. She sends sweet messages on Mother's Day and other holidays as well. She still prays. But Ryan's absence from all our lives hurts. Elie explained his disappearance to me and to herself by saying, "I believe he suffered deeply in ways I do not think I will ever understand or know the full extent of, but that did not stop him from spreading joy to everyone around him. Ryan," she said, "was and is one of the best people I've ever known."

Justin has felt the loss acutely, too. He thought Ryan needed to heal and hoped he would, adding, "And I will be there when he returns because he will always be my brother."

The rest of my kids found their way a little more easily. Diamente played football all through college, and, in his senior year, he was honored as one of the twenty-five NCAA Division III football players named as a First Team selection for the Arthur Ashe Jr. Sports Scholar Award. Today he is a commercial construction project manager. During COVID, Tom also formally adopted Diamente as his son.

The court hearing and paper signing took place with a judge and more than fifty family and friends watching on Zoom. Before the hearing started, just the family logged in to speak and hear the lawyer review the proceedings one more time. Theressa and one of Diamente's sisters were sitting in her car, a cell phone perched in their hands. When the lawyer asked if anyone had any questions about the proceeding, Theressa spoke. "Can Sandi adopt Diamente, too?" The lawyer was more than a bit taken aback, explaining that the only way that would happen was if Theressa gave up her own parental rights. The law doesn't allow for one father and two mothers. But Theressa pushed back, saying that having me as a legal mother reflected the reality of Diamente's life. "He has two mothers," Theressa firmly explained. "Sandi is Mom Two," she said, adding, "Can't we just ask the judge about a second adoption?"

When the hearing commenced, Tom read a statement to everyone assembled:

> *When Sandi and I agreed together that I would [be] your father, I pledged not just to love you unconditionally, but to be the reliable father who raises you up, who teaches you, corrects you, forgives you, and teaches you to forgive, who speaks courage, confidence, and resilience into your heart and wisdom into your soul, who holds you accountable and walks alongside you to mentor you on who you are, who you can be, and what you can do.*
>
> *I am grateful Diamente is in many ways the rock and glue of my providential, logical family built off the base of my biological family. We all love Diamente so much, he is blood to us, and we need him for a lifetime. We have taken very good care of him for many years now, and I assure you, we always will.*

Tom's words made flesh what was already real: Diamente is forever a part of our family. Elie described it as one of the "happiest" days of her life, during which she cried a lot of happy tears. And for better, and maybe occasionally for worse, Diamente knows that he will always have Two Moms.

◆

Elijah earned a BS in communication management and design from the Park School of Communications at Ithaca College, becoming the first member of his family to receive a college degree. On campus, it seemed that he made friends with everyone. He now works in graphics design for *National Geographic* and makes a lot of music.

Justin earned his undergraduate degree from the University of California, Berkeley, and went to law school, after which he went to work in commercial litigation and will soon clerk for a federal appellate court judge. Elie followed Elijah to Ithaca and graduated summa cum laude with degrees in acting and French. When she would appear at the house during college breaks, and, in her words, "inevitably do something weird," Diamente would call out, "Elie's home," which, she says, "is much nicer than someone telling you that you are weird." She is pursuing a career in entertainment and is considering law school.

Although we are no longer gathered under one roof night after night, we are still a family. And as all my kids pair off and even, like Justin and Laixin, one of our exchange students, get married, I joke about all the grandchildren I hope to have. Or as Elijah says, "This is my family, too—when I talk to people. It takes some getting used to, but it feels right—it happened for a reason, I believe—we've all played major parts in each other's lives. I still go through things, but we are in it together, we have each other."

In Justin's words, "Home to me is not a place; people are home to me. My philosophy is: If people represent home, how could they also not be my family? I have my sister, Elie, but I also have my siblings by choice, my brothers: Ryan, Diamente, Tareq, Laixin, and Elijah. My connections with my brothers give me a true home from which I can face the world."

◀▶

For me, home today is less a single physical place than the people I have embraced. Today my place is in the Colorado mountains. I am back in the West, but on my own terms. Tom's and my marriage did not survive COVID. All those years of Tom on the road, the constant travel, the commuting across half the country, finally pulled us apart rather than together. We communicated too often by email and too transactionally. But it's not the conflict and the rupture at the end that I want to remember. I want to remember when we fought together for something, and the "for" was our children, all of them.

And wherever the place is that I call home, I am still Mom.

The night before I was scheduled to drive to Colorado to begin my new life—my car filled with my most treasured possessions, the rest of the things having been packed into one-third of a semitrailer to head west—my last night in my Washington suburban bed, as I tried to get my exhausted body to stay asleep, my phone rang. Sleepily, I grabbed it from the bedside. Theressa's name and face flashed across the screen. When I answered, she was talking a mile a minute. Theressa's main job now is as a security guard, and she often works the night shift. She was on duty at work, but had just gotten a call from a sheriff's deputy in Virginia. Diamente had been in a car crash. It was a single-vehicle accident, and his car had veered completely off the road. It was totaled. Every airbag had deployed. He was in the emergency room at a local hospital. "I'm leaving now," I told Theressa, plugging the hospital's name into my phone's GPS. The travel time showed one hour and twenty minutes.

Diamente had gone to a concert in Virginia at one of the big venues, way out along Route 66. It was late when the show finished, and as he was driving home so he could be at work the next day, he fell asleep at the wheel. His car flipped multiple times when it left the road before it finally came to rest on some low ground.

The sheriff's deputy was still with Diamente when I arrived in the emergency bay. Diamente's clothes were in tatters. They had been shredded by the force of the airbag deploying and the vehicle rolling. Standing in the emergency waiting room, he looked like a castaway stepping off an island. When he saw me, he launched himself into my arms, and we just stood there and hugged each other close.

The sheriff's deputy was a nice man who shook both our hands. There was no alcohol or any other substances involved, just a young person who was too tired, but who had thought he could gut it out and make it home. The doctor signed the discharge forms, and I put Diamente in my car, where he promptly fell asleep from stress and exhaustion.

I got him home, waited for him to shower, and then tucked him into bed, talking to him about how dangerous it is to drive tired and how, if there is a next time, he should please find a hotel and spend the night. He promised. In a few hours, he got up to leave for work, and I got up to do exactly what I had told him not to do: start driving while tired.

"I love you," I said. "Come out to Colorado and see me soon."

◀▶

I can still feel almost every mile of that drive. It is both a memory and a physical sensation. I am in my car, alone, watching the flat grasses and grains pass by, seeing occasional barns in the distance, maybe a farmhouse or two. The towns are few and far between. In maybe another ten hours, the land will start to rise, first hitting a plateau and then slowly advancing upward toward the high Colorado peaks of the Rocky Mountain range, where I know that I will find the peace and isolation that I need to heal. My packed car, not unlike the wagon trains and riders that used to follow many of these same routes, will pull and strain against gravity to make its way up the lengthening hills.

In Colorado, I began my new life by studying for the bar exam and passing it (apparently landing in the top 5 percent), and setting up a law practice with a dear friend who was once a colleague of mine at O'Melveny. It is a variation on the life I imagined for myself half a lifetime ago. Life, when I least expected it, has come almost full circle. Except that the roundness inside, what fills that circle, is more than I could have imagined. Beyond Ryan, Diamente, and Elijah, I had five other Sidwell students—Ranim, Laixin, Kennedi, Shahd, and Tareq—who came, stayed, and became, in varying measures, part of our family. Nearly all of them live in the US and visit me and call me Mama Sandi.

Even now, I still think of all those nights when I stood at the bottom of the stairs and yelled, "Dinner." The thunder of large feet would commence, the house would shake, and it was all I could do to stand out of the way as my entire family charged into the kitchen, circled the table, and sat down. All those years when I filled my car with groceries until there was almost no room left for me, or how, when I filled my fridge and cabinets, within a couple of days, everything would be gone. But nothing was ever truly gone because, in my house in those years, everything else was full.

Acknowledgments

My most heartfelt thank-you to my family:

Justin—my first son and the son whose heart brought so many others home. You are the one who built the foundation of this big, beautiful, diverse family of ours. You are a kind, generous, courageous, and genuine soul. You are the best son a mother could ever hope to have. You've been through so much and have weathered all challenges with strength and bravery. I am proud of the man you have become. I love you, my son. Thank you for being there for me always, in the best of times and the most challenging of times. You are my rock.

Elie—my sweet, intelligent, fun, and funny daughter. My soulmate. You helped so much with the writing of this book—helping me to remember small but oh-so-important moments, reading drafts, and providing such wise insight. You bring joy to my life in myriad ways, and you always make me laugh and see the positive in things. You are beautifully authentic and always by my side. I love you forever and always.

Diamente—you once said the most powerful thing to me that anyone has ever said—"I love you, Mama. The real kind of love, not the fake kind." I have that same love for you. You are such a bright and beautiful light in my life. Thank you for adopting me as your mama and for including me in your life story—because, in so many ways, this is really your story, not mine. I am proud to call you son.

Chris, you are such a light in my life, and in all our lives. You carry such joy with you all the time. You are loving, supportive, and the best wife for Justin I could ever have even imagined. You were only nineteen years old when we met, but I found myself secretly hoping that someday you and Justin would marry. And you did! I am so grateful to you for accepting our large, unconventional, and wildly exuberant family, and especially for all the support you have given me in both hard times and good times. I love you.

Ryan—I miss you so much, sweet Ryan. You are always in my heart and in my mind. We will meet again someday. I can't wait to witness the fine man that I am certain you have become. You are an overcomer, and I believe in you.

Elijah—thank you for always asking the deep questions, the important questions, and for sharing your story with me. Thank you for joining our family and adopting us as your own. We are all better for your influence in our lives. I have learned so much from you and I am so very grateful for your presence in my life.

Thank you to the members of my family who came after the time frame covered by this memoir:

Ranim, for the education in understanding the plight of the Palestinian people, for at least trying to eat my attempts at cooking ethnic food, and for the grace and dignity you always brought to our home. Laixin, for remembering to call and check in every Sunday, without fail. (Note to all the rest of you—I love this, it is a good thing, you know my number, and, yes, it is a competition!) Tareq, for giving the best hugs, loving food more than life (especially when I prepare it), and for always being present in and supportive of our ever-growing chosen family. Shahd, for taking time out of your busy schedule to remind me that family matters and that we are family. Kennedi, for being such a beautiful soul, for your contagious laugh, and the abundant love you share with all of us. I love you all the most (and that means I win!!).

Acknowledgments

Thank you to the *First,* and most important Moms, "Mom(s) One," according to the young men whose lives we have shared the privilege of shaping. You are the foundation of this family. Without you, we have nothing. You are the bravest, most generous women I have ever had the honor of knowing and loving. We are sisters in every way. We have shared hard truths and great joys. And we are bound together in life forever. Thank you for teaching me how to be a good parent and "Mom Two," for teaching me the importance of generosity and humility, and for guiding my steps at every turn. You are my heroes.

Kevin—"Broski." For helping me to remember so much of our shared history. For pointing out the differences in our experiences. For always being there for me, even while we both dealt with the influences of our childhood. You are the best brother I could have ever hoped to have. I appreciate you and love you more than words can express.

Dana—my favorite (and only!) sister-in-law. Thank you for always bringing humor to my experience—even in times when it's hard to see anything positive, you find it, you call it out, and then you make me laugh—without fail.

Mom—I can only imagine how difficult it must have been to live with the incessant, usually tortuous voices in your mind. Voices you could not turn off or send away. As difficult as it was, you taught me a lot about courage and how not to succumb to fear. I am grateful that you are now at peace.

Dad—forgiveness is never about the one to whom it is being offered. It is about the one offering it. It is about redemption and healing. So, I offer it to you here. May you rest in peace.

Thank you to the team that brought this memoir to life:

Lyric Winik—for making my words powerful, for creating the words when I could not, for listening (and listening and listening) to my story, for helping me express that story in a way that is beautiful and alive. For being patient with me when I faltered or had silly questions. You are so incredibly gifted with words and have a depth of understanding of people and a means of expression that is unrivaled.

Howard Yoon—for taking a meeting with a potential author without a proposal or the first clue about how or even whether to write a book. Thank you for seeing the potential, for guiding me through the writing, and for believing in me and in my story. It has been a journey, and through it all, you have not wavered in your support or in your efforts to see it through to conclusion.

Mindy Marqués—for seeing the potential of my story, for your vital contributions, for your patience with my complete lack of understanding of the process, for your insightfulness and guidance, and for being a true gift in my life. Thank you for your consistent and steadfast support.

To my publisher, Simon & Schuster, especially Sean Manning and Priscilla Painton, and to the many people there who worked tirelessly to bring this book to fruition, including Brittany Adames, Shannon Hennessey, Emily Farebrother, Sara Kitchen, Rob Sternitzky, and Math Monahan. Special thanks to Hana Park for her deep passion for this book and story, and her championing of the project, and to Johanna Li for her thoughtful insights and getting us over the finish line.

Thank you to my dear friends:

Katharine Weymouth—for being my stalwart and constant friend, for the long walks and talks, for the insight and the support. You are one of the few people in my life with whom I can be vulnerable and completely open. My muse and guide. You listen and steer me in the right direction when needed. You are one of the greatest blessings in my life because you push me to be my best self.

Bob Willett—for being my anchor and speaking the hard truths—even when I am reticent to hear them. For taking the Colorado bar exam with me so that we could be partners (and so that you could be sure that I'll always be okay), for worrying about whether I'll "be okay" and taking all kinds of steps to see to it that I am. You are as much a part of my family as everyone else in this book. I appreciate you and love you, partner.

Lisa Weissler—my sweet sister. Your presence in my life was all too short, but the impact you had was immense. You were so joyful, loving, encouraging, and supportive. I carry so much of your wisdom with me every minute of every day. At your funeral, I was given a small bracelet with the words "Live Like Lisa." That phrase is now my mantra, and I hope to honor you by doing just that. Your last words to me, "I love you," were not vocalized because you no longer had your physical voice, but you mouthed them slowly and intently, while at the same time locking eyes with me so that I would see and understand—you wanted me to absorb the sentiment, to carry it, to hold it, and to remember it always. I did. I am. And I will.

Lanier and Wade Whilden—you've been my rocks through so much. Your support for me and your friendship is something I treasure beyond measure. But for you, I would never have had the ability to write this book, because you carried me through hard times, loved me no matter what, and have been my most wonderful encouragers. You are family. Always. I love you and appreciate you both forever.

Kathleen Buhle—for helping me to see the need to "run away" to the mountains and just write. It is the reason this memoir exists. And it is the reason I was able to connect with myself and understand who I am and what I need in life. Thank you.

Jill Meyer and Allison Schulman—for pushing me to write this memoir. You kept after me for years, even when I consistently replied, "But who on earth would even read that?" Thank you, Jill, for just ignoring me, setting up a meeting with Howard, and encouraging me to "just go and talk to him." But for both of you, this memoir would not exist.

Joan Kristal—for the consistent day-to-day support of my ever-growing family. For the borrowed mattresses, blankets, sheets, and towels. For always allowing me to just invite myself over for much-needed breaks from the chaos. For being there when Ryan needed surgery or one of the kids was sick. For the bandages, medicine, borrowed mustard, help with pets, and, most important of all, for being a great friend and confidant.

Elsa Walsh and Bob Woodward—for always listening when Justin went through a difficult patch and for being by my side to support Elijah when we needed to ensure he made it to college. For always asking the important (and often difficult-to-answer) questions. For caring and checking in—even to this day. For meeting with Elijah before he went away to college and counseling him (and giving him signed copies of Bob's books!). I am eternally grateful for your wisdom and your support of "our kids."

And finally, to Twelve and Thor—thank you for your blind devotion, for following me everywhere, comforting me, for the long walks in the mountains, playing catch with every stick we can find, and generally just being the best dogs ever.

About the Author

SANDRA E. SMITH (Sandi) was born in California and grew up across the West. Her harrowing, nomadic childhood included living in a shack without electricity or running water. She put herself through college at UCLA and law school at USC, becoming the director of litigation for Apple Computer in 1998. She raised two biological children and, after moving to the Washington, DC, suburbs, opened her home and her heart to eight more. While in the DC area, she spent years representing domestic abuse survivors and their children, including as a guardian ad litem in the DC Superior Court. She has also been actively involved on the boards of multiple academic, public, and nonprofit institutions. Today Sandi lives in rural Colorado with her two dogs, Twelve and Thor. She is an attorney in private practice and president of her regional fire board. Her large, loving family visits her often.